Family-by-Choice

Creating Family in a World of Strangers

**Susan Ahern &
Dr. Kent G. Bailey**

Fairview Press — *Minneapolis*

Published by Fairview Press, 2450 Riverside Avenue South, Minneapolis, MN 55454.

Library of Congress Cataloging-in-Publication Data

Ahern, Susan
    Family-by-Choice : Creating family in a world of strangers / Susan Ahern & Dr. Kent G. Bailey
        p.   cm.
        ISBN 0-925190-92-6 : $19.95
        1. Family. I. Bailey, Kent G. II. Title.
HQ518.A35   1996
306.85—dc20   96–11816
                                                                                                      CIP

First Printing: July 1996

Printed in the United States of America
00 99 98 97 96   7 6 5 4 3 2 1

Jacket design: Circus Design

Publisher's Note: Fairview Press publishes books and other materials related to the subjects of social and family issues. Its publications, including *Family-by Choice,* do not necessarily reflect the philosophy of Fairview Hospital and Healthcare Services or their treatment programs.

For a free current catalog of Fairview Press titles, please call this toll-free number: 1-800-544-8207.

To: My kindest and most enduring of psychological kin, my husband Stephen, who's always supported and encouraged my growth, even when he was unsure of where that growth would take me. Jay Maynard, who helped raise me right and was the first to help me see that if I wanted a healthy, loving, extended family I had to create one. Laura Bolson, who came into my life when I needed her most, and Paula Wardell, who never let go. Joyce Lapsley, who unfailing e-mails me with encouragement and great ideas, and who accompanies me to my frequent mammograms, sweating out the results with me. That's friendship! Josie Schmidt, an inspiration because she embraces life with such spirit, who is smart, nurturing, and one of the most decent people I've ever met. To Keithley Pierce, whose friendship holds up a mirror, teaching me more than I could learn without her. Eleven-year-old Jayme Scudder, my youngest of psychological kin, who braids my hair, bakes cookies with me, and who has given me the opportunity know what it would be like to have a daughter. And finally, my two wild ponies, my sons, Spencer and Austin, who have shown me that, indeed, it is never too late to have a happy childhood! —Susan Ahern

To: My beloved parents Woody and Boohler, my brother Roger and his dear wife Barbara and their four boys, and my mother by marriage, Pat, and her husband, Willard, who is loved by all more than he knows. Sister-in-law Barbara and brother-in-law Gary, who are good friends and the most fortunate of all people for their adopted Korean daughter Mekell, whose mere presence stifles any and all conflict in the extended family. Maw maw, ninety-seven-year-old great-grandmother by choice, and her seventy-two-year-old son Jack, who have been great friends since my childhood, and who have cared for my parents with distinction while my brother and I sought our fortunes in distant places. And, most of all, Patricia, my deepest psychological kin and partner-for-life, who has been my only love since before Elvis wiggled his first hip. To her I am most indebted for our one offspring, Kendra, the light of my life. Kendra, thanks also for my great new son by marriage, Dan, and his lovely parents Jon and Vivian, and sister Andy. —Dr. Kent G. Bailey

Contents

Acknowledgments

When I was growing up, I was forever getting in trouble, from my parents and the nuns, for asking too many questions. So I want to acknowledge Mrs. Humphries and Mrs. Triplett at the Richmond Public Library for answering my millions of questions without once getting annoyed. I also want to thank Betty Booker of the *Richmond Times-Dispatch,* who published an article I wrote on chosen families, which inspired this book. I want to thank our editor at Fairview Press, Julie Odland Smith, who supported our evolving vision for *Family-by-Choice,* and Deborah Bihler, who did a fine job editing the manuscript. Finally, I wish to thank the women in my classics book group, Tina, Carol, Charlotte, and Josie, whose insightful, lively discussions perpetually rekindle the joy I find in reading and writing.   —Susan Ahern

Prologue

❦

"Dean waj my brother—not through blood, but through choice."
—Frank Sinatra, reacting to the death of
Dean Martin, Christmas 1995[1]

In my late twenties, I kept wanting to move back home, meaning where I grew up. Like legions of baby boomers, I had left home to go to college, moved farther away to attend graduate school, and finally settled where my husband and I got the best job offer. But nevertheless, I always felt a beckoning back home. Although I was working frenetically in a fast-paced public relations career, and was busy starting my own family, I still felt something missing: extended family.

I believed family love and loyalty meant looking homeward, connecting with my childhood siblings. Over the years, my three sisters had also moved; eventually we lived in four different states. There was no "back home" to go to.

I am not alone. Mobility is an entrenched part of our cultural landscape. The typical American occupies about twelve residences in the course of a lifetime, roughly twice as many as the typical person in Britain or France and four times as many as the average Irish person.[2] In addition to more frequent job relocations, other important changes over the last thirty years have produced a more mobile, less permanent, less stable society, which is no longer rooted in the nuclear family of the past. "Call 1-800-DIVORCE," the radio announcer blares. Broken marriages have become such a routine part of our collective consciousness that no one blinks an eye as lawyers crudely solicit clients over the airwaves. Thus, a high divorce rate, relatives scattered across the country, and the frenetic pace of two-career families have all exploded the now nostalgic fantasy of extended families spending holidays together, sharing the responsibilities and rewards of raising the next generation and assisting financially in rough times.

Meanwhile, three couples and two teenagers meet every Thursday evening at alternating houses in Richmond, Virginia, to share a meal. "It's a relaxed family atmosphere, where you're familiar with where the silver is and you know how to juggle the toilet handle to stop it from running," says Betty Booker, a reporter/columnist/editor at a large metropolitan newspaper. Josie, a stay-at-home mom who lives on the other side of town didn't cook a meal for six weeks when her third child was born, "because my family loves me," she says, and they wanted to help.

These people are not related by blood. They are, however, part of a new breed of families in the United States that reflect sociological changes sweeping the nation. These modern families are forming in neighborhoods like yours, in jobs and community services like yours. They are members of your support groups and your churches. These new families are the wave of the future, say anthropologists; they reflect a tremendous yearning for connectedness, as well as a growing feeling that we need to put down more roots as a nation.

"Intentional families live apart but meet regularly for meals, holidays and milestones," writes Ellen Graham in a *Wall Street Journal* article, "Craving Closer Ties, Strangers Come Together as Family." "Scores of them have arisen since the 1970s," Graham explains, and quoting Marya Weinstock, a 76-year-old psychologist in Santa Barbara, California: "There was a lot of talk back then about how families were coming apart, about so much alienation and loneliness. If families aren't working anymore, let's make new ones."[3]

Graham tells of one intentional family in Providence, Rhode Island, that has been together for 24 years and now is sustained by the second generation: Children who grew up in the group are parents now, she explains. Its members range in age from one to 91.

In her bestseller, *Necessary Losses,* author Judith Viorst distin-guishes among various types of friendships, such as historical friends, childhood buddies who "knew us when," special interest friends—characterized by the sharing of some activity, sports, opera, yoga, and so on, and crossroads friends, who shared a crucial time of our lives in the past—the neighbor whose children were the same age as ours and so we experienced the rigors of raising toddlers together. Crossroads friends can also be people we bonded with in college, or our first trip abroad.

Experts say another important kind of friendship is the intense bond that develops during a crisis—for example, the closeness that develops among soldiers in battle or the victims and families of the Oklahoma bombing. In such dramatic situations, emotional distance between strangers breaks down quickly, and a sort of "fox hole" mentality develops, uniting people as if they were family. Thousands of soldiers from World War II, who met in 1995 for their 50th reunion, shared the grief and terror of once upon a time facing life and death together. Many spoke with affection and deep love for one another.

All these friendships are important, but according to Viorst, it is intimate, long-term friends who contribute the most to our personal growth. It is intimate friends who make "the music sound sweeter, the wine taste richer, the laughter ring louder" simply because they are in our lives. It is intimate friends who "come if we call them at two in the morning," she writes. "They lend us their car, their bed, their money, their ear. Although no contracts are written, it is clear that intimate friendships involve important rights and obligations. Indeed, we will frequently turn—for reassurance, for comfort, for come-save-me help—not to our blood relations, but to friends, to intimate friends."[4]

It is not necessary to move away from home to need or create these intimate friendships, however. Indeed, geographic separations aren't the only factor keeping biological families apart. Emotional separations also create a void—a void as real for many families as thousands of miles of physical distance.

Despite scores of books that have been published over the past two decades promoting family healing, "sometimes it is not in our best emotional interest to connect with our biological families," says Marsha Abrams, an LCSW who focuses on women's and children's issues in her private practice. As children, we build sense of self by the mirroring that comes from our families, the way we are reflected back to ourselves. The mirrors are the way people treat us, the way they respond to us, whether we are made to feel special. Mirrors can be clear and accurate, and reinforce positively. Or they can be blank, distorted, or cloudy.

A troubled family is like a house of mirrors in a fun park, Abrams says. It distorts. Children emerge from a family of that kind with very distorted views of themselves, with a tremendous sense of confusion, or either a vague or shattered sense of self. Abrams asserts that continuing to go back to our troubled biological families to reinforce our sense of self is like going back to the fun house: we continue to receive these distorting, obscure reflections.

But while the past indeed shapes us, it doesn't have to trap us. With the breakdown of the traditional American family, we need not lose heart, because along with that fragmentation has come the exciting possibility for people to choose their own families.

A close-knit family is something we all yearn for, and is an integral part of a human being's sense of community. And, says Dr. Henry Simmons, a professor of religion and aging at the Presbyterian School of Christian Education in Richmond, Virginia, people isolated emotionally or geographically from blood relatives, can, "with a deliberateness, an intentionality, and with their eyes wide open, create a network of friends that function as family."

Viorst, whose childhood family is dead, whose husband's family is dead, and whose three sons are scattered around the country, agrees. In a telephone interview, she described the importance of intentional families. "What I see all around me, particularly in Washington D.C., where I've lived for thirty-five years, are people creating family out of friends, celebrating holidays with people in a very ritualistic way, year after year."

How do we form intentional families? Just as maintaining blood relationships is difficult, the making of intentional relatives is "slow work," write Sherry Ruth Anderson and Patricia Hopkins in *The Feminine Face of God*. "It takes not just caring, but the courage to tell the truth to each other and the perseverance to face misunderstanding and emotional struggles, along with whatever else needs to be worked through, in order to grow together over the long term."[5]

Because the emotional skills to work through problems and to be honest with both negative and positive feelings are not always taught in biological families, it's critical to spend time examining past relationships before jumping into a new family. By making sense of their family of origin, people can identify what was missing. They can realistically evaluate whether some group of friends can meet their needs and whether they are able to strategically build a life where they can get their needs met by the people they choose.

That choosing is the purpose of this book. It is an examination and a celebration of the chosen families we embrace as adults—of intimate friendships created to nourish and sustain us through the good and the bad. It is the story of society redefining what it means to be related.

As a society and as individuals, we've spent a lot of important years examining the past and focusing on broken family systems. But a hallmark of our growth is our willingness to go forward and embrace new relationships, says Abrams. "After we've completed the work of the past, suddenly we're open to possibilities . . . new kinds of communication, new risks with intimacy, and possibly increased trust of others."

These new relationships constitute intentional families and offer the potential for warm, alive, reality-tested connections. Professor Simmons defines these intentional families as a place where we can find affection. A community of people with whom we can take responsibility for being our own person, without living up to others' expectations, real or perceived. A place where we can make needs clear and express both positive and negative feelings. A place where we can negotiate change and operate free of guilt and fear and constricting notions of obligation. This network, whether biologically-related or not, can be a functioning family.

Our need for intentional families varies with the seasons of our lives. Yes, it is borne out of sociological trends—a mobile society and a high divorce rate—but our need also reflects life's developmental stages, such as the necessary family-like devotion teens and the elderly feel for friendship. The creation of intentional families also reflects new technology, such as the Internet, a global computer network. The 1996 edition of the World Almanac and Book of Facts estimates that twenty to thirty million computer users populate the Internet online village. Many of these users, through electronic bulletin boards, have created "cyberfamilies."

In her poignant literary short story "Between," Elizabeth Graver explores the meaning of friendship, love, and family. In the story, the central character, Annie, looks for intimacy and security in an intense, platonic relationship with a gay man. By the end of the story, Annie comes to realize the word *friend* covers "immensely complicated terrain." Thus intentional families also include support systems created by people with alternative lifestyles, such as those found in the gay and lesbian community. Historically, many gay men and lesbians have been rejected by their biological families, and by their communities at large, so they have had to forge unconventional bonds of friendship to financially support and care for one another. Their legacy is one we can all learn from. And in exploring intentional families, we also examine the richly textured, extended kinship patterns of the African-American culture—ties that in many ways replicate the natural, healthy kinship bonds of our early ancestors.

When you stop and think about it, we as a culture are already familiar with the concept of intentional families. In the acknowledgments section of his best-selling book *Men Are From Mars; Women Are from Venus,* John Gray writes, "I thank my lawyer (and adopted grandfather of my children), Jerry Riefold, for always being there."[6]

In addition to adopting honorary family members, ritual kinship has long been part of our folk culture. Australian anthropologist Derek Freeman coined the term "behavioral kinship" to describe deep emotional attachments and kin-like relations between non-kin, illustrated by Winston Churchill's lifelong attachment to his beloved nanny, Mrs. Everest.

Filmmakers Jyll Johnstone and Barbara Ettinger documented their relationship to two nannies who brought them up in the early sixties, a time when many wealthy women were busy boosting their husband's careers, and turning parenting duties over to nannies. The 1995 film is called *Martha & Ethel,* after the two nannies.

Ettinger is reported to have given a Mother's Day card to her nanny, Ethel, and was crushed at age seven to discover that she and Ethel did not share the same last name. The filmmakers described their movie as depicting a universal situation. "It's the experience of being brought up by a foster parent," Ettinger told *Vanity Fair.* "What's important is that somebody is there loving you unconditionally—that makes family."[7]

While nannies and foster, step, and adoptive parents are all obvious forms of behavioral kinship that have long been part of our historical landscape, we usually don't have much choice in choosing these surrogates. But intentional families, where the choice is intentional, have also played an important role in our history. Indeed, America itself was founded on intentional families. The early settlers arriving in the new world left much of their biological family behind, and of those they did bring, many members died. Later, when the pioneers struck out west, they also left extended family behind. And as hordes of immigrants arrived from Europe in the 1920s, most of them, too, left family behind. These explorers forged a new life and established what were then modern communities with minimal blood ties. President Bill Clinton is quoted in the book *Creating Community Anywhere,* "We are not just another country. We have always been a special kind of community, linked by a web of rights and responsibilities, and bound together not by bloodlines, but by beliefs."[8] Today, intentional families are springing up for different reasons, but the need to construct new families, establish new communities, and create new models of intimacy is just as vital now as it was for our ancestors.

Kinship is the primary organizing principle in all human relations, and much has been written about this phenomenon. Little, however, has been written about psychological kinship. Marriage, family, and kinship have formed the core of anthropological study for more than a century and are fundamental to any study in the social sciences.

Not only are law and biology part of the equation, but social customs play an equally important role in determining kinship. Consider how in the not-too-distant past, children born out of wedlock were labeled bastards and were ridiculed for being illegitimate—meaning not legally kin.

The question of kinship varies from culture to culture and can drastically change from one era to another. For example, in ancient Greece around 400 BC, women were practically domestic prisoners, while men enjoyed considerable sexual excesses.

Intercourse with slave girls and with *hetaerae* (refined paid companions or prostitutes) was common and an accepted practice. Because sexual relations between husbands and female slaves were routine, homes quite frequently contained both legitimate offspring of the wife and the children of her servants. (How many modern women would go for this loose definition of kinship?)

But children of servants did not always become slaves themselves. Slave sons could supplant legitimate children, as men were pretty much free to decide whom to raise and whom to adopt as an heir.

Ancient Greece was also known for its startling reverence for homosexual kinship ties. Amaury deRiencourt asserts, in *Sex and Power in History,* that the rampant homosexuality in Greece some three or four thousand years ago was an extreme example of society trying to eradicate female-centered kinship. In that era, according to deRiencourt, men revolted against the Great Earth Goddess and set up dominant male gods—leading to a contemptuous view of women and "even the best-endowed [*hetaerae*] had a difficult time competing with their clients' male lovers."

DeRiencourt explains that the prevalence of homosexuality was such that "it became part of the public education in Sparta and Crete; it became the essential element in Greek military formations where pairs of lovers and male beloved ones formed the basic tactical unit, fighting side by side—the Sacred Band at Thebes, presumed to be the finest fighting force in the Hellenic world, was made up entirely of homosexuals."[9]

It's also interesting to consider the question of when people actually become kin. In modern America, this question is central to the heated debate on abortion, with "pro-lifers" believing life and kinship begin at conception and pro-choice folks believing life and kinship begin at birth.

In ancient Greece, large numbers of vase paintings and literary references testify to the undoubted affection in which children were held.[10] But abortion wasn't an option and so unwanted babies were regularly "exposed"—placed in baskets and earthenware crocks to freeze or starve to death. In essence, the baby was not recognized as kin, and so in that era, the practice of exposing, which today seems horribly cruel to us, was not considered wrong or inhumane.

Women historically have designated kin—have been the "kin-keepers." They prepared and organized meals, often a major element of social events. Women organized culturally prescribed rituals, including holiday celebrations. Midwives attended to the birth of children, and women most often assumed primary responsibility for the caretaking of children and for their education, spiritual development, and discipline.

In addition, Dr. Georganne Rundblad, assistant professor of sociology at Illinois Wesleyan University, says in a telephone interview that historically women were the undertakers, preparing bodies for burial, using herbs to clean and preserve bodies and dressing the bodies with draped pieces of cloth.

Women as burial preparers continued until the Civil War, when embalming became popular. As burials became big business in the fifty years after that war, men increasingly took over these duties, says Rundblad. "Women were discouraged from getting an education because it was considered very scientific," which would require intellectual energy thought to drain a woman's reproductive energy and make her unfit for bearing children.

Nevertheless, throughout human ancestry, women have sustained kin and invested heavily in kinship ties as an inherent part of being female. History, however, shows some exceptions. In ancient Roman times, it was the father who determined kinship. A Roman father signaled his acceptance of a newborn child simply by lifting it from the floor where the midwife had placed it after birth. There would follow a period of about ten days before the child was named, in case some new reason emerged for not accepting it.[11]

The exciting news, though, is that as our patterns of human kinship continue evolving, and with the dawning of the communication age, more than ever before in history, whatever our circumstances—none of us has reason to be lonely, alienated, to feel isolated . . . to be without kin.

In preparing for this book, my coauthor, Dr. Kent Bailey, and I have relied upon extensive research. We have interviewed people who have formed intentional families in their own lives, anthropologists, family therapists and their clients. We have drawn from literature, poetry, and non-fiction works celebrating friendship. We have also drawn on our own experiences. Most of the names and many identifying characteristics of the people profiled in this book have been changed.

If you are lucky enough to have blood relatives close by—a family that warms your heart, nurtures your deepest wishes, applauds your victories, and mourns your failures—a family that bolsters your self-esteem—then treasure it! But if not, There's an old spiritual maxim that has been affirmed in my life over and over again, and it goes like this: While we may not have the people in our lives we want: the childhood families we're yearning to connect with; a lover or spouse who has defected; a much adored child who has moved across the country—while we may not have the people we initially want, if we are open and willing to embrace life's ebbing and flowing tides—the universe will provide the people we need to have a fulfilling life. The universe will provide. Our intentional families are waiting for us, but the choice to connect is ours.

1
Family Bonding

❦

"Two may walk together under the same roof for many years, yet never really meet; and two others at first speech are old friends."
— Mary Catherwood[1]

"The human heart, at whatever age, opens only to the heart that opens in return."
— Maria Edgeworth[2]

Denny's Family

"He was a perfect stranger," says Denny Gaulden, of the man who raised him. Sitting in the Florida-room of his suburban house, amidst dogs barking and the sounds of kids playing, Denny's eyes crinkle as he smiles, obviously proud of where life has taken him. Today, Denny is a deputy chief parole officer for the Virginia Department of Corrections, married, the father of a teenage daughter and an elementary-school-age son.

At ten years old in 1962, Denny lived in Indianapolis, Indiana, with his twin sister and his mother, an alcoholic, who was either absent or sick most of the time. A court injunction kept Denny's father away from the family, because he beat his wife. Denny's older sister lived with their grandmother, and an older brother had lied about his age to enlist in the Marine Corps at fifteen.

"We were right poor, lived on welfare," Denny explains. "And every Christmas the welfare department would send a volunteer to take us kids out and buy us clothes and toys, but because of some regulation, the volunteer could only take the son, me, out.

"Neill Goff was his name. He was as kind as they come. He arrived and took me to buy clothes. He felt bad that I was getting something and my sister wasn't. So he bought a few things for her. When we got home, Neill said that since we didn't get the pair of tennis shoes I needed, he would come back next week and take me out to get the shoes.

"That continued. We would forget something, on purpose, and Neill would come back. He took me and my sister to shows, movies, stuff like that. Got to the point that my mother was never there. It was us alone.

"Neill was twenty-six, had a good job as V.P. of sales for a company and made good money. He owned his own house and took care of his mother, who had never taken care of him.

"During the week, Neill would come by and make sure we had dinner. We couldn't wait until he got there, because he always brought things we'd never had. He became a fixture in the house, and we became pretty close. Neill was like a friend of the family. Mom kind of depended on him. He'd loan her money and help her with the rent.

"It got to the point where Neill started bringing us lunch every day at school. I went to a parochial school, with nuns and stuff. And if you didn't have lunch, they might give you some milk or crackers, but there was no cafeteria. We [my sister and I] were made fun of and got beat up a lot. The kids used to eat in front of us intentionally. We'd beg them for some cookies, but they would throw food in the trash can right in front of us.

"When Neill started bringing us lunch, he'd try to outdo the other parents. He brought us everything, bananas, all the fruit you needed. Every day. Same time. Same thing. We were proud to open our lunch.

"It was like a prayer come true, because every day after church, I used to go outside and pray. I wished I had a father like the rest of the kids. I wished I had the normal things, so I could be normal. Then all of a sudden, it just happened on Christmas Eve. It was divine intervention. Everything I wanted I got. Not the material things. I just wanted to be normal.

"My sister and I, we stuck together like glue, until I was twelve. My mother had to go into the hospital and the welfare department was going to put us in foster care. Neill said he would take care of me, and my grandmother said she would take care of my sister. Neill took me to his house, on a kind of a ritzy side of town. He felt comfortable about letting me live with him because his mother was there to take care of me while he worked. The three of us became a family. We went on vacations together to places I'd never been before: Chicago, New York, Washington D.C. And he took me to all these museums.

"After about a year-and-a-half, my mother asked for me back. I said, 'No, I like it here.' She knew I did. She knew I had everything, opportunities I wouldn't have if I lived with her. She hated to do it, but she let me stay. She knew I was in the best hands. She cried every Sunday when I visited her.

"My mother remarried a couple of people. They were basically jerks. I didn't like them. It would have been terrible if I lived there. Neill got me into another Catholic school. I always called him Neill. I never called him 'father,' but he played the role big time. He got me involved in athletics and never missed a single game.

"I wasn't the brightest kid in the world. They [teachers] seemed to let me go on for some reason, even though I had failing grades. In high school, I did fairly well. Neill would work with me every night. When I graduated, I didn't receive any scholarships for football. The coach didn't like me. He thought I was dumb. I'd sent off an application [to a junior college] and it was rejected. Grades too low.

"When I was growing up, I'd developed a relationship with a Catholic priest. I saw him one day when I went back to visit my old neighborhood and told him I'd applied to college in Indiana and that they'd turned me down. He said 'That's funny, I'm from [that] college.' All of a sudden, I got this huge grant to go to college. He got me accepted, where everything was paid for. I went off to college.

"Neill sent me letters every single day. Sent me care packages every week with cookies. Everything I needed—money, stuff like that.

"In my senior year of high school, my father came into the picture and tried to take an active role. He was on his feet, doing well; he was successful. He made me an offer: 'Come and live with me. You can have your own car,' basically anything I wanted. It was too late at that point. It hurt my father, but I turned him down. 'Nah, this man raised me, I'm gonna stay with him.'

"In 1971, Neill lost his job; he switched around a few jobs. The next year, after I had been in college two years, Neill called and said he'd been offered a vice president's job in Richmond, Virginia. He said he would only take the job if I came along. I had no inkling to go to Richmond, but I said, 'I'll go if it means you'll get a good job.' I couldn't deny him that after he'd taken care of me all these years.

"Neill went ahead. I finished out the school year, and then transferred to a college in Virginia. The first year was the worst. I hated it there. I was going to school, but I wasn't doing well. Basically, I flunked out.

"Finally, Neill said, 'You need to get a job. You're just sitting around the house doing nothing.' He said he saw a [want ad] in the paper, and it sounded like something I would like. It was for a corrections officer in one of the juvenile institutions. I was a young kid here, now, twenty years old. I took his advice, and I got the job. I've been with the Department of Corrections ever since.

"After I'd been married, had two kids, and been taking night courses, I'd reached the highest point I could without a degree. I got to the point where I was sick of the shift work, the hours, not being able to spend time with the kids. My wife and I decided I would go back to school. I worked full time, raised the kids full time, and went to school full time. I took eighteen, nineteen hours a semester. And I didn't get a B in one single course. They were all As. I loved it! As soon as I graduated, I started getting the promotions I'd always wanted. The degree meant everything. In the treatment side of corrections or when you work with juveniles, you have to have a degree.

"Neill didn't have a degree. In 1986, while I was in school, I encouraged him to take night classes with me. He loved it. He graduated about three years after I did.

"As for my biological father, we maintained contact on and off. My father met Neill and was always jealous of him, extremely jealous. It was guilt. And there was nothing [my father] could do about it. Although I loved them both—I had kind of two relationships going—it was kind of a friend relationship, my father and I had. In 1980, I went back to see him. He talked about why things happened; he was trying to wipe the slate clean. Then we kind of lost touch. I was raising a family, and we were so far apart. We would occasionally send Christmas cards till he died in 1990.

"My mother died a year later. I had lost total contact with her. She got so bad on the alcoholism that she stayed in the slummy areas and would only call when she wanted money. I always sent it to her. My kids met her once. I brought her back here. I wanted them to meet her so they could just know who my mother was.

"My sister, who lived with the grandmother in the old neighborhood, was pregnant at fifteen, had two kids at seventeen, and was divorced at eighteen. We're total opposites. In fact, she went to prison for drug use, and I'm in law enforcement. I'm the only high school graduate, and the only college graduate, in the entire family.

"I have no doubt. Neill made the difference. If it weren't for Neill, I would be in prison right now. Today, he lives on the other side of town and has developed such a relationship with my two kids. They don't call him 'grandpa'; they call him Neill. He takes [my son] everywhere. He's interested in these kids because they're offspring of mine. He spends all the time he has with them. Since his mother's death, he lives by himself. He spends a lot of time over here, and on major holidays, such as Christmas and Easter, he spends the night."

Neill's Turn

"I often think about the differences between *nurture* and *nature,* and I think how Denny turned out is more in his *nature* than it was in any *nurture* I provided. The very first time I saw him, I remember there was just something about him. He was such a nice, well-mannered kid. Thinking back about it, I'm glad they were out of the shoes he wanted, because if they had those tennis shoes, that probably would have been the end. But because they didn't have the shoes, I saw him the next Saturday and we went back and got them. I gave him my phone number and he called me.

"I got to looking forward to his calls. There was something, it seemed, that he and I needed, and that we provided for each other. It just worked out from there.

"He and I never talked a whole lot about how things were for him at home. Dennis always overstates how bad he was when he was a kid. I never saw the bad part of him. He was always a good kid! I never had any problems with him. He never stole, never lied, never was any trouble.

"[As a child,] I bounced around a lot. With Dennis, here was a really nice kid, who was being mistreated and maybe I could do something about it. The minute I saw him there was some kind of connection between the two of us that got deeper and stronger as we went along. It was strange. From the very start there was something unusual.

"Family, to me, is an emotional bond that is as important as a genetic relationship. A true family is one where there's an emotional affinity or emotional attachment. People take care of each other. They do things together. They are responsible for each other. And you don't have to worry about them leaving, going away. It doesn't have to be a birth family or blood relationship.

"I think I got more out of my relationship with Dennis than he did. He was my family. And Dennis and his family certainly provide a family for me now."

Reshaping the Dream

How many of us wish we could have traded in our childhood families as Denny did, trading our unhappy circumstances for a nurturing, gentle family? How much misery might we have escaped? Instead of learning mistrust, rage, and secrecy, perhaps we could have learned, as Denny did, about the crucial, affirming elements of family: constancy, kindness, reciprocity, trust, and honesty.

Of course, some of us do learn about happy families from blood relatives. Christie is one of those folks. "There are three women whom I call my sisters," she explains. "I know they would be there for me no matter what. But it just so happens that they are also related by blood. My mother, aunt, and cousin are these women.

"They have been with me through some really tough times, and I with them. We are able to disagree and move on. But what makes our group so very special is the fact that rarely do we disagree. We are one in spirit. We laugh, cry, encourage, and uplift. It feels so good to be with people who are genuinely happy when good things happen for you and genuinely sad when things go wrong. They have kept me afloat through trying times, and I love them with all my heart."

With families spread throughout the country these days, even if we have supportive relatives, connecting can be a logistical nightmare. A year-and-a-half ago Madeleine got together with her two sisters at Disney World in Florida and she says they had a fantastic time. But Madeleine, who lives in Atlanta, says she rarely sees her sisters, because one lives in Boston and the other in Cleveland. Both have three children, including an infant apiece, which makes traveling a real pain. To complicate matters, Madeleine's husband is in retail and often can't get away, so Madeleine, her husband and their two children usually spend the holidays with friends.

Geographic separations are not the only factor keeping families apart. We have to look realistically at emotional separations, say experts. Although experts say we do best if our main support system is natural kin, Dr. Nancy K. Schlossberg, professor of counseling and personnel services at the University of Maryland's College of Education, and coauthor of the book *Going To Plan B*, says a close and loving family is not a reality for many people. While our culture creates the huge expectation that we will have a family, for many it's a "non event," she says, a heartbreaking reminder of dreams, wishes, and desires that don't come true. This can be as devastating, and as much an opportunity for growth, as an overt traumatic event, such as the death of a loved one.

Even if our childhood family is not splintered by violence or divorce, but rather consists of long-distance relationships, devoid of any deep emotional connection, we will still yearn for a happy family. We still feel rage and disappointment because of the absence of sincere, heart-felt love in our lives. And the images of happy families paraded in the media are no less painful for us than for those who come from more violent or abusive homes.

Consider Michael, CPA and lawyer, father of three, who in his thirties secured a prestigious job working for a large, successful law firm. Throughout Michael's career, head hunters have lured him to new jobs and new cities with bigger salaries and higher-ranking jobs. Despite his professional success, Michael's personal relationships remain unsatisfying. He cheerlessly describes his long-distance relationship with his dad as mechanical, a relationship of predictable phone calls. "How's the car holding up? How's the weather? They keepin' ya busy at work?" his father will ask. Michael wonders, jokingly, but with a wisp of obvious resignation, what would happen if he once again tried to tell his dad the truth, if he described in detail the struggles he's having navigating corporate politics at work, or the problems he and many young people have today trying to raise a family and succeed at a career.

But after years of trying to connect with his family on an emotional level, he has given up, believing any further attempt is futile.

Michael has learned from past experience that when he mentions a personal problem, his father and brothers immediately try to analyze and solve the problem rather than express empathy and offer assistance.

The communication with his mother is even more destructive, Michael says. He describes his mother as domineering, a woman who lives vicariously through her adult children, and as a result, wants intimate details of their lives. How much did the firm offer you? would be a typical and seemingly innocent question. But Michael says she wants this information, not for caring reasons, but to be "more up on family information than anyone else"—which in Michael's family means "one up."

These days, Michael feeds her only as much information as he feels she needs, and explains that unless you emancipate yourself from that kind of web, you can stay in it for life.

Some therapists define "insanity" as doing the same thing over and over, but expecting different results.

Michael says, "I've totally given up seeking supportive input from family members. I'm tired of it. That doesn't mean I don't call or don't stop by, but I eliminate all expectations." Michael adds that he's stopped feeling guilty that he's not close to his family, because he realizes that does not reflect a flaw in him.

April, who divorced in her mid-twenties and works for the transit authority in New York City, has also limited ties to her childhood home. Communicating online, "The only blood relative I am in contact with is my father, who lives in Texas," she says. "We communicate by mail on Christmas, Thanksgiving, and Father's Day. We haven't seen or spoken to each other since 1971. I am in no contact with any other blood relative. I don't even know how to get in touch with any of them, even if I wanted to.

"I left home in 1969 to become a hippie. My mother passed away when I was twelve. I'm an only child and my father and I didn't get along. I wasn't happy at home and left. I went back twice, and left for the last time in 1971. I've never gone back and have never looked back."

Michael and April are not alone or novel in their migratory estrangement from biological families. Americans have a long history of leaving home and hearth to seek a better life.

In the United States, European dignitary Alexis de Tocqueville observed when visiting in 1835: "a man builds a house in which to spend his old age, and sells it before the roof is on." Why are Americans so mobile? One reason is the divorce rate in the U.S., which is among the highest in the world. Economic opportunity is also more dispersed geographically than it is in many countries, where the locus of economic, political, and cultural life may be a single big city. De Tocqueville speculated that the absence of rigid class distinction in America, which gave the average man greater opportunity than he would have had in Europe, also produced in him "anxiety, fear and regret," and led him perpetually to change his abode.[3]

We don't need statistics, however, to convince us that America is a nation of migration. Anecdotal evidence abounds. Look at our own lives, how many of us live near our adult siblings, parents, aunts or uncles? Not long ago, my husband and I visited our son's third-grade class on "family day." We were scheduled to talk about the things our family loves to do and what my husband and I did for a living. When my turn to talk came, I talked about writing *Family-by-Choice,* I asked the children how many of them had grandparents or aunts and uncles who didn't live close by. Out of twenty-six students present, every one of them raised their hands, excitedly calling out the different states their relatives lived in.

People move away for all sorts of reasons. Some family experts assert that geographical distance can be a covert symptom of a family's emotional estrangement. Sometimes, though, moving away is a healthy reaction to destructive blood relationships. Creating physical distance can protect us from controlling family members who are emotionally or physically abusive. Or, distance can segregate family members who share a traumatic past, and yet remain unwilling to work through or acknowledge the significance of that trauma. While superficial communication, devoid of honesty and intimacy, characterizes these families, eventually, when family members don't discuss and face unresolved events from the past, every interaction can begin to stir up emotional wounds. Connecting simply means re-injuring each other, and so moving away is one way to cope.

Other times, a geographic move is motivated mostly by economic reasons but leads to unexpected benefits. Eileen, for example, a forty-year-old, married woman with four children ages twenty-one to five, explains that moving away from her childhood family positively impacted her and her children's life, and helped her redefine what "extended family" means.

"We moved from California to Arizona five years ago," she says, speaking online. "We had both been born and raised in California, and our families are there. We're still close to our families, but we also have a strong network of friends both there and here. Many people who live here in Arizona are not natives and are in a similar position, as far as not having family geographically close. We have developed close friendships and bonds and know these people will be there for us, just as we will be there for them. We often do holidays together, or outings, or get togethers.

"Fortunately for us, our families are able to come out and visit us several times a year. But even more special to us are the visits from old friends from California who schedule vacation time to come and be with us. Family is important, but I also feel that the extended family of friends is just as vital. [Through friends] my children are exposed to different cultures, different beliefs, different ideas. By being geographically separated from our families, we are also able to limit some of our children's exposure to the biases and prejudices of one branch of the family, and that is vital to us."

While many people don't have the kind of bond with blood relatives they want, Dr. Schlossberg says what's important is our emotional reaction, which can vary from rage to envy to despair, and is a signal of how we are coping.

By facing and dealing with the physical or emotional absence of family, we can regroup and start our lives on a new path. Rather than giving up our dream, reshaping that dream is an important step toward creating a fulfilling life. For many, that means reaching out

and creating our own family—a family of close relations, not genetically linked.

If ever there was a literary figure who should have renounced
the dream of family, who deserved to feel "bleak, old, washed-up,
helpless, and alone," Lyman Ward, the protagonist in Wallace
Stegner's Pulitzer Prize winning novel *Angle of Repose,* deserved to
feel that way. Bound to a wheelchair and deserted by his wife,
Lyman feels anger at the loss of his family and at all similarly dispir-
ited families.

> In my mind I write letters to the newspapers, saying "Dear Editor,
> As a modern man and a one-legged man, I can tell you that the
> conditions are similar. We have been cut off, the past has been
> ended and the family has broken up and the present is adrift in its
> wheelchair. I had a wife who after twenty-five years of marriage
> took on the coloration of the 1960s. I have a son who, though we
> are affectionate with each other, is no more my true son than if he
> breathed through gills. That is no gap between the generations,
> that is a gulf. The elements have changed, there are whole new
> orders of magnitude and kind. . . . My wife turns out to be some-
> one I never knew, my son starts all fresh from his own premises.[4]

Despite his alienation and loneliness, Lyman nevertheless finds purpose in life by writing a biography about his dead grandparents'
adventures in the wild west. In doing so, he stumbles upon a kind of
happiness, based on solitude and purpose. Thus, Lyman Ward, like
many lonely people in our Western culture, finds happiness by losing himself in his job.

But face it—living happily ever after in the story books and in
the movies never meant having a great job. It meant having a good
marriage and a loving family. Although American society rewards
career and economic success, one of the decisive elements that kin-
dles the hearts of most people is the bond they share with family
and kin.

Indeed, Stegner's Lyman Ward eventually discovers genuine peace,
or his "angle of repose," in part by searching for life's lessons in the
lives of his dead grandparents, and by recreating a family out of paid
help. Lyman's assistants, Ada and her daughter, Shelly, who were old
friends, take on the role of surrogate kin. Lyman's description of Ada
giving him a bath reveals a family bond that is unduly intimate:

The water is so hot that it makes the cicatrized stump prickle and smart, but it must be that hot if it is to ease the aches away enough to permit sleep. Painfully she wallows down on her knees and without diffidence soaps and rinses me all over. Her crooked fingers drag across the skin stiff as twigs . . . Her doll [Lyman] sits stiffly, pointed straight ahead at the fixtures that emerge from the wall. When she is finished she bends far over and guides its arms around her neck. Then she rears upward and up it comes, naked and pink, her hairy baby, its stump bright red. Its dripping wets the front of her dress, its rigid head glares over her shoulders.

Holding it, clucking and murmuring as she works, she towels it down as far as the knees, and then she takes it around the waist and tilts it upon her great bosom and rotates until its leg, bent to miss the tub's rim, can straighten down on the mat.

Pressing it against her as intimate as [a] husband, she towels the rest of it and eases it back into the chair and wheels it to the bed.[5]

Because Lyman, like Denny, was able to reshape the dream of family, their stories powerfully illustrate that the prevailing myths of our culture—"blood is thicker than water," "family sticks together though thick and thin," and so on—are just that: myths. These examples demonstrate that we as human beings possess the capacity to transfer instinctive family love and behaviors of kinship to people who are not biologically related to us. Even if no one rescued us from an abusive childhood family, as Denny was rescued, or even if we were deserted, as Lyman Ward was deserted—we still have the ability to create a family of *choice,* rather than endlessly despairing about the troubled families many of us inherit by chance.

Battling the Myths

In *Necessary Losses,* Judith Viorst describes a woman whose family myth system, like many people's myth systems, demands "We must always count on each other and must count on no one else, because the outside world is hostile and dangerous.

" 'Our house was a cave,' my friend Geraldine says, 'and our mother was the dragon who stood guard, and unless you were related you didn't get in.' She confesses that it was not until both she and her brother had married that they learned that friends could be as trustworthy as kin, that they learned that you didn't have to be a member of the family to be trusted."[6]

April, the woman mentioned earlier, who left home to be a hippie, says her friends have become so close that they have become her family. With obvious affection in her voice, April explains that her close women friends—Lorraine, Monica, and Chloe, and her good friend Eric, who is gay—provide the only emotional contacts she has in her life.

"They are it. Without them, I have nobody. When I broke my ankle, Monica went to the bank for me, and the supermarket. She really helped me out. The day I fell down and wound up in the ER, Lorraine went to my house and fed my cat and brought me some clean clothes. I didn't have to wonder if they would help me. I knew they would."

April says her friends also helped her through a serious depression, caused in part by her lack of blood-family ties. "If I didn't have these friends, I would be the most alone person in the world. I know I can call them and be happy, or sad, or mad and they will listen. I know that we all accept each other, with our faults. Eric makes me furious sometimes. He has problems, and I don't like the way he does a lot of things. But I love him anyway. And he loves me, even when I'm a bitch. Dorothy can be an idiot sometimes, but I love her anyway. That's what makes the difference. You love both the good and the bad. Not in spite of, but along with. That is true friendship."

Many in the gay and lesbian community have had to seek out new friends and new family, when their real families turned their backs on them because of their sexual orientation.

Miriam, who is a lesbian and wishes to use her real name, lives with her "beloved" in central New Jersey, and speaking through e-mail, says that she and her lover have an "orphans celebration" on holidays. "The invitees are those who have no biological families with whom they can share the warmth of the changing seasons," she says. "Some of our adoptees are visiting in person, others from cyberspace. Many are friends and some are casual acquaintances whose welfare we care about. The bottom line is that either by choice or by necessity they don't go home, so our space becomes their home.

"This past Passover, instead of the traditional reading of the *Hagaddah* (the book which recounts the passing over of the Jewish people from slavery to the Promised Land), we suggested that perhaps more fitting and in keeping with our 'gender-challenged' [status], as one humorist put it, we told our own personal stories of passing over, whatever that meant to each individual.

"One of our friends told of her mother being murdered and raped and what that meant to her. Others told of transition, leading lives of lies, being in closets, not being okay with oneself or with society at large. And, while we told our most interesting travels on this planet, we all pigged out on home-made chicken matzoaball soup and chopped chicken liver. So many stories of tears and laughter, we forgot to make dinner (by that time, no one was hungry anyway). It was truly an unforgettable and exceptionally fitting way to revitalize and rekindle the true meaning of this ancient holiday, the storytelling of a people and their bondage.

Richard Vanaman, who lives in Las Vegas, is in his early twenties, and is a representative for Prodigy's gay and lesbian bulletin board, describes his family of choice: "I have come to define family as the people who act like it," he says. "It goes back to that unconditional-love concept. All I need from the people in my life are love and respect. They don't need to understand; they don't need to approve. They just need to love and respect me. It's really simple—if they don't love and respect me, the relationship loses its importance for me."

Family myths are ingrained in childhood, a critical, impressionable time when we frame our unconscious perceptions of the world and learn what the very concept of family is all about. These myths, or belief systems, are often unconscious. To examine and even reject them takes enormous insight, bravery, and persistence. If they prevent us from forging healthy, new kinship ties in our adult lives, we should try to get beyond them.

But why is it critical that we forge these new healthy kinship bonds when our family is emotionally or physically absent? Why is it that work, money, or hobbies cannot substitute for family? And what is this fierce drive that, in the presence of vast geographic distances, or even in the most troubled families—perpetuates our mourning of kinship ties. The drive that, when we've finally grieved enough, propels us to reach out to connect and create brand new families?

The answer may lie in our genes. Humans, it seems, inherently have a metaphysical bent. Whether this capacity for spirituality shows up in formal religious practices, or even in a spontaneous preoccupation with the meaning of life, the religious animal, say experts, is universal, and rears its head in every culture. G. Marian Kinget in *On Being Human* writes that in our culture, the common belief that spiritual concerns are more likely to arise in older people at the approach of death "does not find support in either the literature on the subject or my experiences as a clinician." Kinget explains that metaphysical concerns naturally arise either before or after the intense phase of pursuing educational or career goals—that is roughly before the late teens and after the early fifties. And traumatic events may spur a spiritual quest at any age.[7]

While family and cultural modeling of spirituality surely influences its development, the fact that even some of the most repressive governments, such as the former Soviet Union, which has outlawed the practice of religion in the past—cannot totally suppress this species characteristic attests to its stronghold in human nature.

Similarly, the drive for family bonding is so innate that we will strive to create a family when there is none physically or emotionally present. The human need for kinship appears rooted in a primate heritage of attachment and social networking. Humans and animals alike naturally mold biological families and then, in response to the environment, over time, restructure their form and operational structure.

Indeed, "around the world, in rich and poor countries alike, the structure of the family is undergoing profound changes," according to a 1995 study, released by the Population Council, an international nonprofit organization based in New York that studies reproductive health. The study, "Families in Focus," which analyzed data from a dozen countries, concluded: "The idea that the family is a stable and cohesive unit is a myth. The reality is that trends like unwed motherhood, rising divorce rates, smaller households, and the feminization of poverty are not unique to America, but are occurring worldwide."[8]

Yet, consider what author Helen Fisher has to say in her controversial, bestseller *Anatomy of Love*. She asserts that divorce, single parents, remarriage and blended families are as old as the human animal, creations of a distant prehistoric age, when people were not biologically designed to mate for the length of our modern lives.

What is different, Fisher states, is our modern habit of generating what might be a truly modern family type: the association.

> Associations, anthropologists say, are composed of unrelated friends. Members talk to one another regularly and share their triumphs and their troubles. They assemble for minor holidays like birthdays and Labor Days, and they help care for one another when one is sick. These people have a network of friends that they consider family. This network often breaks down, however, during major festivals like Christmas when people join their genetic relatives. No wonder holidays can be so stressful. Displaced from their daily family world, people find themselves out of touch, out of place.
>
> So for the first time in human history some Americans and other industrialized peoples have begun to pick their relatives—forging a brand-new web of kin based on friendship instead of blood. These associations may eventually spawn new kinship terms, new types of insurance policies, new paragraphs in health plans, new rent agreements, new types of housing developments, and many other legal and social plans.[9]

Indeed, with the growing phenomenon of people selling their life insurance benefits before they die, no longer is the traditional transmission of wealth always occurring in families—from generation to generation, from blood to blood.

As if confirmation that the American family is indeed evolving, the corporate bastion of family values—The Walt Disney Company—in 1995 decided to offer health insurance to live-in partners of its homosexual employees. Disney representatives say that the decision brought health benefits in line with the company's other non-discrimination policies. Indeed, if Disney hadn't brought its policies into the twentieth century, the company stood to lose many important members of its creative staff. Large universities and other institutions around the world are also redefining their definition of family, by extending health and retirement benefits to both heterosexual and homosexual partners of their employees. In addition, rent-control programs in large cities such as New York are frequently being challenged to include many different definitions of family, embracing both live-in heterosexual lovers, and gay and lesbian couples.

Marketing Family

Billions of dollars are spent each year at advertising aimed straight at our hearts, at family bonding. Take, for example, the AT&T series of famous commercials urging viewers to "reach out and touch someone." Those clever, heartfelt commercials poised AT&T as the vital medium through which family love survives. Yes, kinship is indeed marketable!

Hallmark Cards, Inc.—another corporate fortress of family values—has not missed the opportunity to create products for this new market of intentional families. "Friends are the family we choose ourselves," has been selling on the cover of one of its "Saturdays" line of cards.

If warm, loving, altruistic family love is at one end of the family marketing continuum, then the opposite end might very well be phone solicitors and high-pressure sales people, or the organizers of those notorious marketing pyramids. These people capitalize on human nature: Most of us prefer doing business with people we like and to people with whom we feel close. Companies know this and spend millions of dollars each year training salespeople to create a feeling of kinship with their customers.

Indeed, many companies train their salespeople to inquire about customers' families and to clue into feelings and moods strategically, by imitating the concern of a relative or close friend. Many firms hire professional sales motivators to train their force to be constantly on the hunt.

About a year ago, my husband and I got a surprise visit from our home-owners insurance agent. We hadn't seen in him years, and had faithfully been paying our premiums to the large, national insurance company our agent worked for. He told us the visit was routine, that he liked to get out every so often and see the homes he insures and visit the people he covers. A month or so later, my husband and I got a statement from our insurance company informing us that our premiums were going up substantially. Nice, friendly visit, right! Meanwhile, my son had gotten a post card greeting from my insurance agent: "Happy Birthday from all your neighbors at [the insurance company.]" My agent has no relationship with my son, and the greeting and the signature were obviously mass printed. I suppose our insurance agent thought this kinship behavior would soften the blow of higher premiums. It didn't.

Ever notice how waiters and waitresses now introduce themselves, using their first names, when they approach your table? They strategically emphasize familiarity, and the best of them ceremoniously simulate care and concern, attuned to your every need. Twenty years ago, the practice of servers introducing themselves wasn't standard in a typical restaurant. But industry executives have realized that when employees mimic kinship behaviors, customers are more likely to buy higher-priced dinner or lunch specials recommended by the server, order more drinks and deserts, all of which rack up bigger bills and higher tips.

And we've all had the following experience, or something like it. We're sitting in Arby's, relaxing as we eat, when our child's soccer coach comes up, sits down, chats politely for a few minutes, before he springs for the kill. "Do you know the magic word?" our would-be friend asks, with a smile that hangs on just a hair too long. An expression of ignorance provides the invitation to pounce, to recruit us into some new marketing scheme.

True, the economic strain of maintaining a middle-class lifestyle, or even to survive, drives people to pretend kinship and put high-pressure sales tactics on friends and acquaintances. And also true, many salespeople are capable of turning off their sales persona and valuing companionship and kindness over the next sale. Unfortunately, however, for some salespeople the concept of true friendship is lost. Every dinner party, every trip to the mall, every church service, every backyard barbecue is fertile sales ground.

Many times, such economic cannibalism is practiced on families. Take the insurance salesperson who convinces grandpa to roll over his lump-sum retirement distribution into investments, where the insurance broker gets a hefty cut up front. Or take the insurance agent who sells his twenty-eight-year-old stepson "whole-life" insurance, when buying term and investing the rest, say in no-load mutual funds, on his own, without the insurance agent, would have been a far better move.

And how about the car salesperson who sells cousin Jamie the great car lease with amazing low monthly payments? Cousin Jamie isn't too good with money, so she questions neither the whopping 25 percent interest rate, nor the fact that three years later when the lease runs out the car will be taken away unless she pays an exorbitant amount to purchase the car she's been leasing all along. The salesperson realizes all this, but do you think it gets spelled out for cousin Jamie?

Savvy home-shopping networks and religious broadcasters also appeal to viewers' sense of family. Some viewers see right through the effusive compliments, terms of endearment, and exaggerated interest in the lives of little old ladies. But evidenced by the large sales on such networks, and the millions of dollars raised by religious broadcasters, many watchers don't realize their emotions are being manipulated, and they are paying the price—literally.

Reciprocal exchanges or materially based business that typically occur between acquaintances or strangers, employ kinship-like behavior—often deceptively. For many folks in commerce, the ends pretty much justify the means. According to sociobiologists, unrelated individuals tend to help each other in the context of reciprocal altruism. Such reciprocity, however, draws less from naturally rewarding, kin-attachment structures in the brain than from a more general desire to acquire material rewards or social status. Warm, pleasant interactions with kin are inherently enjoyable, nourishing and fruitful, whereas reciprocity between non-kin is governed by economic rules, i.e. laws, and bolstered through guilt and social ostracism.

Psychological Family

People aren't into creating new-age models of family, experts say; people aren't ready for California-style, free and easy, communal living. But in today's dog-eat-dog world of impersonal business transactions and relentless marketing, filled with hectic schedules and overtime hours, with family scattered across the country, people are looking to recreate through friends a familiar, comforting feeling of extended family, says Leith Mullings of the Department of Anthropology at City University of New York's Graduate Center.

Therapists today observe a natural yearning in their clients for closeness between the generations. For many people, their grandparents lived down the street when they were growing up. They were part of daily life. Now, these same people want their children to have a similar experience. But if grandparents are geographically distant, or some conflict prevents them from being close to parents—people often will pull someone else in to fill that role of the wise elder.

As one therapist told me, "I see families in therapy where the mom comes in and says, 'Don't be surprised if Johnnie talks about gram and grandpop.' But they're not really his grandmother and grandfather, and he sort of knows that they're the nice people who live across the street who have taken an interest in us and we've taken an interest in them."

A Personal Story of Psychological Kinship

I, too, have reached out and cultivated psychological grandparents for my two young sons.

I was one of those people who for years thought that the main reason I moved away from my family was to attend college and pursue a good job. But I see now that moving was an instinctive geographic cure for coping with my childhood family. A friend, joking, once said, "Your family would have made a good talk show!" Unfortunately, she was right. My childhood was rife with turmoil that would disturb even the most Oprah-weary, or tabloid-hardened mind. But my three sisters and I survived. Indeed, our distressed background created exceedingly strong women. Because we all coped in drastically different ways, however, communicating with each other is quite painful to this day, because it stirs up old, unresolved issues. Perhaps it won't be forever; but it is for now.

Delia, the protagonist in Anne Tyler's award-winning novel, *Ladder of Years,* shares a poignant moment with her sister that sums up the dilemma in my own family. "Once Delia had asked [her sister] Eliza why she and Linda [another sister] weren't close and Eliza had said, 'Oh, people who've shared an unhappy childhood rarely are close, I've found.'"[10]

One of the things I have learned is that triumphing over a difficult past does not simply require healing, working through the requisite stages of grief. A critical companion to healing is taking the next step: learning entirely new, healthy ways to take care of yourself. And then doing it.

In my own life, a move away from my family provided the environmental stimulus, and recurring conflict over the past cemented my reasons for creating a family of choice.

Almost a decade ago, when I was pregnant with my oldest son, an elderly neighbor who lived across the street—Edna—took an intense interest in my pregnancy. After my son was born, although I didn't know it at the time, she was insulted because three weeks passed and I hadn't taken my baby over to visit. She had gotten my son a gift and couldn't wait to give it to him. Deprived of contact in the early weeks, she seemed determined to make up for it by creating an intense bond later on.

Hundreds of miles from any blood kin, my husband and I had an unusual situation in that Edna wanted to care for our son, leaving my husband and me free to go out for a mid-week dinner after work, or spend lazy Sunday afternoons snuggling and reading together. After I went back to work, when I ran into daycare problems, Edna would keep my son for a few weeks until I could slowly transition him into a new place.

In Russian culture the *babushka* is a ranking elder authorized by the culture to correct and guide young couples in their parenting, a roving grandmother. Like a good Russian babushka, Edna loved to give advice, the kind given by extended family since, I'm sure, time immemorial. Because of my own troubled childhood I was inclined to spoil my son. Edna, however, would frequently remind me, "Children are like horses; if you don't raise them right, they won't be a pleasure to you." And Edna would know: She owned several beloved horses out in the country and went every day, in sleet or suffocating humidity, to visit, feed, clean, and ride them. One horse, Sassy, Edna has had for over thirty years. Both Sassy and Edna's show horses have been an enormous source of comfort. They have given Edna a zest for living that I have seen in few seventy-plus-year-old women. So yes, using her horses as a reference, Edna would offer lots of advice. Some I found handy, some was not to my liking. I took what advice I liked and ignored the rest.

When my oldest child was two years old, and we'd just had our second son, we moved across town into a bigger house in the suburbs, mostly to be near some church friends and because the county had a better school system. My husband and I quickly learned how spoiled we'd been, because Edna had provided us many needed breaks from the physically and emotionally challenging job of parenthood. (The type of breaks people often got when they lived close to family.)

We missed her dearly. But we still called regularly and visited Edna, whose husband had fallen as much in love with our children as she had. On Friday nights, my husband and I would drop the kids off and go out to dinner and a movie. If we took a parenting class or couples' workshop in the city, Edna would watch the boys. She was the first to notice my oldest son's intense love for balls.

By now Edna would not take money for watching the kids, but we would return the favor by bringing food. Edna frequently said her cooking years were over. She cooked mostly frozen meals or reheated fast foods in the microwave. So, I would bring pizza or cooked chicken or meatballs and sauce for a meal. I frequently called to hear all about her care-taking of "Mamma," Edna's ninety-plus-year-old mother who lived down the street from her.

Our family bond was firmly cemented when one afternoon, with tears in her eyes, Edna shared a story that is never talked about in her family: the death of her toddler son, thirty-eight years before, when Edna lived out in the country. She talked softly, trembling, about how she held her son (whom, even in her denial, she knew was dead) in her arms for almost forty-five minutes until the ambulance came. Her oldest son had been traumatized by the whole ordeal and had never married or had children. It was easy to see why Edna played the role of grandmother to my children. We needed her as much as she needed us.

Judging by the myriad of photos atop every surface, a stranger entering Edna's house would automatically assume that my boys are Edna's grandchildren. Over the past ten years, we've visited on holidays. Every year on Edna's birthday and her husband's birthday, my husband, kids, and I take over dinner and a gift. This past Mother's Day, Edna called to tell us that of all her family, we are the best to her.

I miss my sisters, spread across this country, and am hopeful that we will one day get past our traumatic transference—that is, blaming each other for the pain our childhood stamped upon each of us. But I now believe that when natural kinship is not available, we can create kinship that is as intimate and rewarding as that found among family. There will be disagreements and misunderstandings, just as in all families, but that doesn't have to stop us from finding family and, most importantly, finding love.

2

The Psychology of Kinship

*"All history is the history of reproduction and succession;
in other words, of kinship."*
—Robin Fox[1]

"We have two families: the family we are born into and the family that we choose," says Debra, responding online to a public bulletin board notice about adopted families. "I've been far from home for years now, and I have been incredibly blessed by good friends who have become my family. It may well be that they're almost better than family, because these relationships lack the history and subsequent feuds and idiosyncrasies that traditional families are notoriously riddled with."

Everywhere we look, we see people like Debra, creating family out of friends.

My coauthor, Kent Bailey, a professor of psychology at Virginia Commonwealth University, has spent much of his career theorizing about the emergence of newly manufactured kin, which is actually the creation of psychological kinship—defined as "feeling and behaving toward another 'as family,' regardless of whether you share family genetic material." While technically it's a way of extending kinship and a sense of familiness beyond biological boundaries, emotionally, psychological kinship is an ancient human strategy for adapting to a world of continuously changing family structures.

When you think about it, all kinship relationships are psychological, since the recognition and classification of kin basically occur at the psychological levels of perception, emotion, motivation, and cognition. We classify others in terms of what we see, hear, feel, and think about them. Once we classify another as psychological kin, we begin to feel that very special emotion which we associate with kin: love.

Love is the distinctive emotional and motivational component of kinship. While having kin-like feelings toward others not classified as kin may include admiration, infatuation, liking, respect and fondness, these feelings do not involve love in the deeper sense of family love.

Traditional biological and evolutionary approaches to kinship do not seem to grasp its full essence. Perhaps that essence is to be found at the psychological level of experience. Psychological kinship represents a middle ground between the historic, blood-kin family relations sociobiologists speak of and the more neutral, but increasingly common, interactions between strangers. Psychological kinship represents a flexible category where non-kin can be used to extend the biological family, or to substitute for the biological family when the need exists.

The old focus of psychoanalysis was to help the immature, traumatized child inside to grow up, to mature. Today, many therapists believe a much quicker way of healing is to teach the older, wiser, more mature parts of a person to comfort the frightened, sad child within.

Reaching out and creating new psychological kinships can help provide that comfort. Indeed, social research has frequently reported that voluntary interpersonal attachments, such as friendships and group affiliations, are linked to a positive quality of life. In a study of friendship that was published in the *Journal of Marriage and Family*, sociologist Christopher G. Ellison contrasts the voluntary aspect of friendship with the obligatory nature of blood kinship. "Friendships are based upon shared values and activities, affection, and expectations of mutual pleasure or benefit. They are initiated and conducted with relatively little societal regulation, and they can be ended without substantial social penalty," he writes. "On average, people with more friends, more frequent interactions with friends, and close friendships in which intimate communication is present are likely to express higher levels of personal happiness than others."[2]

When something is voluntary it is based on choice. When we develop a new psychological kinship, we are essentially choosing to classify that person as a member of our extended family. This is a very important process of classification, for when we accept someone into our family there are new obligations, responsibilities, and challenges. We expect our new family member to stand by us in times of distress, and he or she expects the same from us.

The person who has a support network is likely to be more healthy physically and psychologically than the person who goes it alone. Research shows that feelings of security, desirability, and kinship nourish people's sense of self-identity, improve their self-concept, and encourage self-expression, which lessen their vulnerability to inevitable stresses and strains of life.

It is our nature as human beings to thrive in warm, satisfying social relationships, and to shrivel when relationships go sour or when we feel rejected, unloved, and unwanted. If fate has not provided us with loving biological families, we must choose our own. Just as a delicate flower must have fertile soil to bring out its beauty, each human being must have family if he or she is to thrive. There is simply no way out of this problem—human beings must have family, one way or another.

In their ground-breaking book, *The Courage to Heal,* about turning the severe, long-term effects of trauma into self-nurturing strengths and capabilities, authors Ellen Bass and Laura Davis suggest creative kinship as a way to cope with broken family ties.

> If your original family is not a source of enrichment in your life, put your energy into cultivating what you want from sources that can actually yield. Although you may have only one mother, one father, one sister, or one Aunt Bea, you can create an alternative

family of your own choosing in the present. Look to your friends, the members of your [support] groups, your partner, or your children. Although they will not replace what you have lost, they can offer abundant opportunities for nurturing, closeness, and comfort. This is what makes a healthy family.[3]

The Evolution of Natural Kinship

Human beings are both mammals and primates, but we are distinctly human as well. Our humanness evolved over the span of six million years, beginning with the common ancestor to apes and humans and leading to the present human line—*Homo sapiens*—around 200,000 years ago. Our evolutionary ancestors went through several stages on the journey to modern humans, but we can be pretty sure that kinship and social behavior were fundamental at every stage. In fact, many scientists believe that social behavior was so important in the everyday life of our ancestors that, for all practical purposes, the evolution of the modern human brain was social more than anything else.

What was life like on the African savannas of human evolution? Of course, we have no living witnesses to interview, but the evidence suggests three things: human beings are very social by nature, our ancestors were hunters and gatherers throughout much of our history, and they tended to live in small, intimate groups. These three things go straight to the heart of human nature.

During the early phases of evolution, our ancestors lived in small bands of perhaps twenty-five to fifty people. In general, these early humans encountered very few strangers, mostly during hunting ventures or invasions from rival bands. Most of their encounters were with people familiar to them. They classified these folks as kin because they usually were related by blood.

In *Making Silent Stones Speak*, anthropologists Kathy Schick and Nicholas Toth describe how these creatures might have looked:

A new group emerges from under the flat-topped acacia trees. Even from a great distance there is no mistaking these animals: vertical figures in a predominantly horizontal, quadrupedal world. These slowly approaching figures betray their lineage by their distinctive bipedal gait and graceful, swinging arms. Their dark skin and hair are still glistening from the rain. There are about twenty of them, and the adult males are somewhat larger than the females, several of whom are carrying infants. Two of the juveniles are chasing each other and occasionally wrestling as the group moves through the grasslands.[4]

Between 500,000 and 150,000 years ago, *Homo erectus* was giving way to archaic *Homo sapiens,* and the final threshold to modern humanity was crossed sometime in the last 200,000 years. In a mere four million years, the human line had gone from a small, ape-like creature with simple social skills and no stone technology to the tall, mega-brained, artist, politician, and science-minded populator of today's world. During this trek, our ancestors increasingly moved from the original small, intimate, tribal clans, ever onward toward sprawling nation states and global economies. No one has written more eloquently on the transition from clans to nation states than has Roger Masters, Dartmouth biopolitician and author of *The Nature of Politics* and numerous journal articles on the topic. At a professional convention in Toronto in 1993, he explained to coauthor Kent Bailey how absolutely vital this transition has been for the individual and group psychology of modern humans.

Today, the mammoth global village is upon us. With these changes, the classification of kinship grew and evolved as well. It seems both natural and adaptive that kinship has extended beyond genetic boundaries, with an ever increasing exposure to non-kin strangers, and an exploding population and move toward urbanization. Today, we live in a veritable world of strangers. In one trip to the mall, we probably see more people than our early ancestors encountered in their whole lives.

According to Pierre van den Berghe, author of *Human Family Systems: An Evolutionary View,* if human kinship is the most basic, universal, successful, and ancient basis of social behavior in all animals, and if the selection and need for kin continues to be a powerful force in even the most complex human societies, we can expect that the idiom of kinship will be extended to organizations larger than the family. Such extensions include fictive kin, honorary family members, and ritual kinships, such as with godparents, indicating that psychological kinship has historical roots in both our evolutionary history and in our culture.

The benefits of psychological kinship are obvious for those who have no biological family ties or a weak family structure. Intense, mutually beneficial relations with new kin may be the only resort for persons faced with death of loved ones, abandonment, natural disasters, war, kidnapping, and the like, and may be the difference between survival and death. Under such circumstances, depending upon strangers or weak biological kin would be far less likely to guarantee survival.

Given that evolution is extremely stingy—it is a process that expends as little energy as possible to reap the largest rewards—and given that evolution favors expanding old systems over erecting new, one can argue that the creation of psychological kinship today involves basically the same emotional and cognitive wiring as that used by our ancestors to create and serve blood kinships. These mechanisms involve classifying relationships and assessing benefits and obligations. They allow us to get close, share resources, touch and comfort one another, as kin have done since the dawn of humanity.

Psychological Kinship

Psychological kinship is a means for expressing kinship feeling and behavior in the absence of any actual genetic bond. In particularly strong psychological kinships—namely, marriage and close in-law relations—classification as kin may appear as secure as that among blood relatives. However, research needs to be conducted over time to determine more specifically the similarities and differences between psychological and biological kinships. For example, in what instances do biological and psychological kinship look almost the same (for example, sibling relations and very close friendships)? And when do they diverge (for instance, sibling relations and lovers)? In what cases might psychological kinships be even stronger than biological kinships?

A Psychological Model of Kinship

About fourteen years ago, a clinical psychologist in Virginia Beach referred a young, white woman named Jennie to my coauthor. She had just been released from Riverside Psychiatric Hospital in Hampton, Virginia. Jennie was a challenge from the first day. She was abusive, argumentative, appeared to be high on drugs or alcohol, and expressed complete disdain for the counseling process. Nevertheless, at hour's end, she agreed to come back next week, "just for the hell of it."

During her twenty-three years, Jennie had a history of substance abuse and minor brushes with the law. One psychiatrist had even diagnosed her as schizophrenic. She was of medium height, a bit overweight, and had a chip on her shoulder. She came from the backroads of Alabama. Her mother had cast her off to relatives as an infant, which initiated a childhood of physical and sexual abuse, including being thrown into the river by a drunken uncle. Eventually, she was passed to a kindly aunt and uncle. They cared for her needs, but were extremely rigid, demanding, and affectionless in their parenting approach.

When she was in her teens, Jennie ran away to Norfolk and was informally adopted by a loving, but mentally ill, woman, Wanda. Despite being near death from cancer and suffering from manic-depressive psychosis, Wanda became her true mother and continues in that capacity today.

In the early stages of treatment, it was obvious that Jennie was really a loving and intelligent person beneath a tough exterior, and the therapist's job was to bring that person to the surface.

He saw her once a week for a six-month period, and the results were remarkable. Once a kinship had formed, she became very compliant and her charming and zesty inner self emerged. She dressed differently, spoke differently, expressed a positive, upbeat attitude toward life, and was, for all practical purposes, a different person.

The kinship relationship served primarily as the *medium* within which therapy took place, but to a degree it was a form of treatment itself. Treatment was loud, boisterous, and painful, as Jennie was forced to confront deep hurts, resentment and anger, and a lifelong pattern of self-destructiveness. The bond of kinship sustained during these tough times.

It was Jennie who, more than anyone else, inspired the kinship model of psychotherapy. Her own biological family was a miserable failure, and her unrequited, lifelong quest was to find family replacements. She never found that many—her current family of choice consists of only four or five people—but those few people are literally the difference between life and death for her. She often considers suicide, but does not want to hurt the people who love her.

For years, psychotherapists have discussed the importance of the bond between client and therapist, but kinship has never been mentioned. But kinship is so prevalent in human relationships, the very roots of human social behavior, it is actually difficult to imagine how feelings of kinship could be avoided in such intimate interaction.

Because therapists often become parent surrogates, respecting sexual boundaries is absolutely critical to maintaining trust in any kind of therapy. When therapists cross sexual boundaries, they become participants in the patient's illness, and they wipe out all chance for the patient to examine objectively what thought and behavioral patterns are causing his or her life to derail. This point is made forcefully by Carolyn Bates and Annette Brodsky in their insightful book, *Sex in the Therapy Hour: A Case of Professional Incest.* But, as in family relationships, love has a place in the client-therapist relationship. The esteemed psychiatrist, Dr, Karl Menninger wrote in his book, *The Vital Balance:*

> Psychoanalysis has shown us with great vividness how much the interference with the giving and receiving of love disrupts and demoralizes the integrative patterns of life, and makes us feel ill and act in opposition to our desire. It has shown also how important it is that someone, such as the physician, serve as a temporary or transitional love object—and hate object as well—for patients struggling to reattach or further attach themselves to their human environment constructively . . . It is this intangible thing, love, love in many forms, which enters into every therapeutic relationship. And it is an element which binds and heals, which comforts and restores, which works what we have to call—for now—miracles.[5]

Research in Psychological and Biological Kinship

Gustavo Nava, a doctoral student supervised by coauthor Kent Bailey, studied the kinship behavior of college students. His research suggested that modern extended families have proportionally less biological kin and more psychological kin than probably existed in the original, ancestral families. Early humans probably considered all members of their small band as biological kin, and only a very few were classified as psychological kin.

Nava's subjects, undergraduate psychology students, were asked to list in a five-minute period the blood relatives they could depend on in times of trouble. Subjects were then asked to take another five minutes and list people they were not related to, but who would also help them in times of trouble. The data revealed that subjects listed five or six people for each category.

Thus, researchers concluded that psychological kinship plays a very important role today. Students were, no doubt, more dependent financially on biological kin than psychological kin, but researchers found both categories to be equally important sources of perceived social and emotional support.

The results of the Nava study may not come as a surprise. We all know psychological kinship exists, but until now, researchers have neither studied or attempted to quantify it. Similarly, anthropologists and sociologists around the world are only now beginning to take seriously the phenomenon of extending kinship beyond blood relations.

The Nava study was the first in a series using Dr. Bailey's twenty-item Kinship Scale. Data indicate that the scale primarily measures degree of family love, or K-love. Moreover, family love is strongly correlated with independent measures of interpersonal closeness, such as romantic love, liking, affiliation, and social support. And the Kinship Scale is very sensitive to who is being rated—mother, closest parent, closest friend, acquaintance, and so forth.

As expected, family love tends to be rated higher in reference to biological or psychological kin (a close parent or friend) and lower in reference to more distant relationships (acquaintance, job supervisor, or stranger). Biological kin are generally rated slightly higher than psychological kin, but some instances were found where, for example, a boyfriend or girlfriend is rated higher than closest parent.

In the Nava study, the subjects seemed to be in transition from primary family affiliation, biological kinship, to romantic love, which is a variation of psychological kinship. Further, this was more true of males than of females. The young men seemed to be highly attached to and emotionally dependent upon their girlfriends, rather than their closest parent, whereas the young women seemed intermediate between old family commitments and new romantic ones.

Dr. Bailey's research program took a major step forward when Helen Wood, another graduate student in clinical psychology, joined the kinship team. Her focus has been on the role of classification in kinship relations, and benefits and obligations associated with kinship. Her findings support the notion that kinship is composed of two major properties—classification and love. Once we classify someone as kin, it is likely, although not inevitable, that we will love him or her as well.

The crux of psychological kinship is this: natural biological kinship can be extended to non-relatives so that they become psychological kin, or genuine members of the family. Choosing family is becoming increasingly important in the nineties, as divorce, ever expanding populations, dwindling resources, increased mobility, television, perpetual technological revolution, and a host of other factors continue to diminish intimate human contact. Many of us in today's society must choose new family structures in order to survive. If blood families are not nearby, geographically or emotionally, we can re-create supportive families. And indeed, we who are stretching kinship bonds beyond their biological confines and extending them to a world of strangers—which grows larger with each passing day—are pioneers, poised on a new ledge of human evolution.

3

Ancient Roots of Kinship, Love, and Community

"Ancient mammalian traits lie at the root of the profound and special emotional intimacy between the average human mother and her baby today—honored in folk wisdom as mother love."

—Sydney L. W. Mellen[1]

"When I was growing up, there were two separate sets of people who were very important and who were both like family to me," says Dr. Leslie Butterfield, a mom and a professor of psychology, who is planning to move to the Pacific Northwest. She asked that we use her real name.

"In one was my godmother, whom my parents had known since they were eighteen. Someone with whom I had dinner every week from seventh grade until I graduated from high school. Someone who gave me birthday parties. Her son was really like a brother to me; he stayed at my home when she went out of town. She was very different from my parents but an integral part of my life. I didn't have to have her because I had my parents. But the fact that I did have her made an enormous difference in my ability to have a flexible outlook on things and to know about a different way of life than what my parents had. And she was someone who would have taken care of me if something had happened to my parents. [Having her] was a secure feeling. She wasn't someone I would have been shipped off to if my parents had been killed or something. She would have been someone I knew very, very well.

"And so for our son we [my husband and I] have designated godparents who have children his age, and whom we see on a regular basis. [Godparents] are a nice way of having an intentional family for your children, because it's people you know, you trust. If something would happen to you, and they end up in the guardianship role, they would be able to tell your children about you—who you were and what you were like, and really allow your child to still have their parents in some way. I think that's really important.

"I had another intentional family that was not picked by my parents, but was picked by me," Leslie continues. "My family moved almost every year of my life until I was fourteen. My father worked for a company that was an adjunct of the military, and when the military moved, he moved.

"I'm an only child. Every year when we moved, I would pick a friend who was from a large family. I don't know how I did this; I certainly didn't plan it. But it happened so that in the last place we moved, I ended up being friends with a girl my age who had two sisters, two half-sisters, two brothers and her mom. All of their relatives lived in town. I became a member of that family. Even up until last year, my husband and I went on vacation with them. My children know their children. I've spent either Christmas or Thanksgiving with them almost every year, and I've spent summer vacation with them since I was fourteen. I'm now thirty-eight.

"Being an only child, I was lonely a lot, and it felt good to be in the heart of a large family that was different from mine. Their family was much more casual; they had to be, with that many kids running around. One of the things I want for my son is to have my friends spend time with him. That way, when my friends have children, he will have some kind of built-in closeness.

"As my son gets older, I hope to have the graciousness to allow him the freedom to choose other families he wants to spend time with; allow him the freedom to have some ways of living different from what we have. It was difficult for my mother that I spent as much time as I did with this other family, especially the other mother. I had a different, more freeing, more equal kind of intimacy with her. She gave me the freedom to air out ideas and try things my family was nervous about me trying. When I was younger, she was the better listener. But as I got older, we listened to each other. To my mother's good credit, she did allow [the relationship], and it was good for me."

Leslie's story reminds us that the warm, satisfying feelings of belonging we share with family and friends are among our deepest human experiences. These warm feelings flow from the wellsprings of our mammalian and primate natures that reach far back into evolutionary time. More than 99 percent of our human DNA is shared with our closest evolutionary ancestor, the chimpanzee; we can call a mere 1 percent our own. As Jared Diamond explains in his book *The Third Chimpanzee,* humans are basically chimpanzees with a very large brain, and the capacity for language and complex behavior.

Love is one of our strongest feelings. Loving our own and fearing strangers is not a human invention; it is far older than the human race. In his book, *The Lemur's Legacy,* biologist Robert J. Russell argues that the basics of human social feelings go back to the lemurs fifty million years ago. Lemurs are the oldest creatures in the primate order, and the first ones, mouse lemurs, were tiny and delicate with large eyes, and hands instead of claws. They were easy prey and only ventured out at night. Females were socially dominant, they did all of the parenting, and mothers and daughters were extremely close. Males received some mothering early on, but they quickly moved into bachelor groups. Mature males did no parenting and only interacted with females at mating time.

The lemur legacy is obvious in much of human social behavior-great mothering and poor fathering, female social togetherness and mother-daughter kinship, male promiscuity, male aggression, male same-sex bonding, and antipathy toward strangers. Starting with the apes around 20 million years ago, there was a shift from female to male social dominance, but, otherwise, modern humans are uncannily like their ancient lemur ancestors socially.

Human beings share the basics of sex, love, and power with the lemurs, but we share much with the apes as well. The ape and human lines split off from a common ancestor around six to eight million years ago. According to Richard Wrangham, professor of anthropology at Harvard, the common ancestor's basic characteristics may be inferred by studying the shared features of living apes. Thus, it was probably an ape-like creature that walked on all fours. It lived in small, closed social networks where warm relations occurred among kin, but outsiders were feared and perhaps even attacked on occasion. Unlike lemurs, females probably formed few alliances among themselves, and they tended to mate out of their group. Males were now dominant and much larger than females, and, like lemurs, aggression, poor parenting, and promiscuity were features of their daily life.

Today, the social relationships of modern human beings fall roughly into four basic categories: those we know well and like; those we know well and do not like; those we do not know well; and those we do not know at all. In these four basic social interactions, we are not that much different from our common ancestor, but our possibilities for intimacy today are far more complicated. We humans were designed to live in small bands of kin, only encountering strangers occasionally.

The apes branched off from the Common Ancestor (CA) in one direction and prehumans in another. Our earliest ancestors were basically apes socially and mentally, but apes that walked upright. Males and females interacted more than did their lemur ancestors or the CA, but males continued to be aggressive and poor fathers. Members of a particular band kept on the move and typically consisted of twenty-five to fifty individuals bound together by blood and mating ties. Some groups might have been larger—perhaps a hundred or more—but the smaller ones offered easier mobility. Such bands likely consisted of several families comprised of biological kin (parents, offspring, grandparents, uncles, aunts, and cousins) and a few psychological kin (mates, in-laws, distant blood kin classified as close emotional kin).

Aside from the exchange of women, kinship and bartering between bands were probably infrequent, though hostility and inter-band warfare were probably quite common. In ancestral times, a person could not exist for any length of time alone. Thus, kinship strategies originated primarily through a kind of Darwinian selection for preferring kin over non-kin, sharing food and shelter, protecting community offspring, avoiding incest, and other nepotistic social arrangements. According to the attachment theorist Mark Erickson, these evolutionary strategies produced a sense of familial attraction and family bonding that promoted these adaptive kin-directed behaviors.

Kin-selected behaviors all contributed to the evolutionary fitness of each individual—that is, the total number of family genes that survived for future generations. Our siblings carry fifty percent of our genes, so by helping our siblings' offspring to survive we are contributing to the survival of our own and our family's genes through future generations. As evolutionary strategies, then, kinship behaviors helped our ancestors adapt and survive. They increased the likelihood of the individual's genes—and those of close relatives—being represented in future generations.

Natural Kinship in Humans

The first human-like creature to evolve from our common ancestor, was *Australopithecus afarensis*. They lived in Africa about four million years ago as our forebears descended from the trees, moving into the open savannas to carve out a precarious living. Anthropologist Donald Johanson and his colleagues found the bones of one of these first branches of the human line and affectionately named her Lucy. Hairy but human-like, Lucy was small, perhaps three-and-a-half feet tall, and looked more apish than human. Although she walked upright, she could easily be mistaken for a chimpanzee at a distance.

About a year after discovering Lucy, researchers returned to Ethiopia and uncovered an even more exciting treasure. In his book, *Lucy's Child*, authored with James Shreeve, Johanson described a collection of bones, representing at least thirteen separate individuals, that came to be known as "The First Family." These individuals may or may not have been actual family members, but they were certainly members of the same species. Also, the two hundred or so bones suggested that the thirteen individuals varied considerably among themselves. They probably looked perceptibly different to each other and had their own distinctive personalities. This substantial variation among individuals so early in human evolution implies two things: natural selection was exerting strong effects and the first family was probably capable of kinship recognition and rudimentary systems of classification.

Because of their small stature, Lucy and her kin were vulnerable to large predators; thus staying close together was the band's best defense. But they also had to stay on the move to gather new food sources, including berries, roots, fruits, and seeds. Males provided some protein to augment the plant diet by scavenging the open savanna for carcasses and sometimes killing small animals.

Within the band, life was a kind of biblical Eden of togetherness for Lucy and her kind, but it was also a brutal time where death by disease or violence could come at any moment. In *Darwinian Medicine,* Nesse and Williams shatter any romantic myths we might have of an earlier natural paradise. They remind us of the enormous hardships of ancestral times. Water and air were pure and the sun warm, but dangers, in the form of wild animals and savage neighboring bands, lurked at every turn. Many children failed to reach maturity, food was often toxic and difficult to chew, venomous snakes and predators abounded, and a variety of worm, protozoa, and viral agents could bring agonizing death at any time.

Always standing firm against these brutal threats was kinship and the joy and relief of a shared quest for survival. In fact, the stress of survival and a common threat can intensify togetherness, kinship, and love. The father of attachment theory, John Bowlby, says that attachment behavior "is most obvious whenever a person is frightened, fatigued, or sick, and is assuaged by comforting and caregiving."[2] Like a puppy in a thunderstorm, we gravitate to loved ones in time of trouble.

In ancestral environments, people were frightened, fatigued, or sick much of the time, and the need for tender loving care from family and kin was very strong. It is natural to want to be with loved ones, especially when times are tough. We suggest that this need was wired into our brains over millions of years, and, further, that kinship and the phenomenon of intensely bonding to kin when we are under stress are adaptations that historically promoted individual survival. Ancestral lines that lacked the emotional mechanisms to form bonds of kinship probably became extinct.

These mammalian and primate roots of love and togetherness

gradually developed into increasingly complex systems of kinship. As society became increasingly complex, the human maturation process extended further. Dr. Helen Fisher, in her compelling book, *Anatomy of Love,* suggests that as the human brain expanded and women began to bear helpless young with a long teenage period, the need for kinship intensified.

> When our ancestors began to produce helpless young that took almost twenty years to mature, these new pressures must have hastened the evolution of one of humankind's greatest social inventions: formal relatives with specific roles—the glue of traditional human life.

> One might argue that with the origin of dependent teenagers, parents became obliged to remain together longer in order to provide for their adolescent young. But [divorces around the world historically] tend to cluster around the fourth year of marriage—about the duration of human infancy. Nowhere in the world do people characteristically remain together to raise their young through the teenage years, then systematically depart at that point.

> Since our ancestors did not adopt the reproductive strategy of extending their partnerships to rear their adolescents, nature took a creative tack: human kinship evolved. What an ingenious twist, a web of related and *unrelated* individuals locked in a formal network of ties and obligations, an eternal unbreakable alliance dedicated to nurturing their mutual offspring, their shared DNA.[3]

From the time of Lucy to the first *Homo sapiens* around 200,000 years ago, our ancestors became larger, smarter, better talkers, better toolmakers and more skilled socially and politically. They developed language and art, but they never lost the sense of obligation, attachment, and love that characterized the kinship dynamics of the band.

The Evolution of Love

We are indebted to our animal ancestors for many things, but perhaps their greatest gift to us is love. All animals like to be with their own kind, and love goes with kinship. Once an animal or person classifies another as kin the relationship changes from one of distance and wariness to one of closeness, sharing, and love. The sight of the infant chimp clinging to its mother's chest, and her tender expressions of affection and devotion, illustrate both the intensity and the innate characteristics of family bonding. We humans are creatures of love; we spring from an ancient ancestry of love.

Love is everywhere, but, historically, it has not been defined all that well. Even the masterful Sigmund Freud couldn't accurately define it. He referred to love as "aim-inhibited sexuality": in other words, he believed love was sex, but sex that you don't carry out in actual behavior.

There is, however, a clear distinction between sex and two different kinds of love—mother love and romantic love. Mother love is the most ancient and purest form of love, erected over millions of years of evolution. The mother-infant bond is the primary and most powerful form of kinship; we view the love that goes with this bond as the official kinship emotion. Following the attachment theory of John Bowlby, we believe that any and all types of kinship love draw their energy from this original fount.

"We come from a mammalian line in which for many millions of years, mothers have nourished and loved their young," writes anthropologist Sydney L. W. Mellen in his book *The Evolution of Love*.[4]

Most definitely, as we grow and mature, our culture, media, and school systems teach us about kinship. But all of us—regardless of our racial, ethnic, or cultural backgrounds—learn about kinship love primarily from our mother. She is our first model for family bonding. In the primal bond between and mother and infant, we see the fundamental importance of mechanisms of "recognition, classification, categorization, valuing." And we also see what Canadian evolutionary psychologists Martin Daly and Margo Wilson call "child-specific parental love."[5]

A kinship approach to love is based on three fundamental assumptions. First, mammalian and human love are most fully realized in the mother's powerful, positive feelings toward her child immediately following birth. Second, a mother's love for her offspring, irrespective of the mother's age, is typically more powerful a love than any other kinship configurations, for example, father-daughter, sister-sister, mother-father, psychological, and other kinships. Third, mother love is characterized by maximal valuing and minimal evaluation. Through a mother's love for her child, the process of kin classification is, for all practical purposes, suspended.

Once a mother is satisfied that her infant is not obviously defective in some way, it is then her baby. Re-classification would occur under only the most extreme circumstances. Indeed, mother love approaches the suspension of conditions of inherent worth that philosophers and humanists speak of, meaning the mother uses few outside, societal influences in valuing her baby, and loves the infant simply for being her offspring. Indeed, when a child is truly wanted, other love relationships pale by comparison.

The mother forms a kinship with the infant far before the infant forms one with her. She is aware of the biological link between her and the infant, and she then chooses to classify the infant as kin. Initially, the infant attaches to the mother in an instinctive way. It may be well past six months before an infant can classify the mother as kin. As the well-respected bonding theorist Mark Erickson tells us, it is these earliest expressions of family bonding that occur between infant and mother (or mother surrogate), that later promotes adaptive kin-directed behaviors, such as kin preference and incest avoidance.

The human fetus becomes conditioned to the mother's heartbeat and general biochemical environment in utero. The newborn quickly comes to recognize the mother's distinctive odors, body contours and patterns of vocalization; and by the sixth month, the human infant (especially females) exhibits clear patterns of differential smiling and fear of strangers.

As the infant develops, well-defined patterns of attachment to the mother emerge, supported by specific behaviors, including eye-contact, cooing, and proximity-seeking behavior. Other attachment behaviors include protests in the form of shouting and screaming when mother is absent.

Eventually, the mother comes to represent a secure base to the infant, from which he or she may explore, play alone, or otherwise be apart from the mother without fear of abandonment. It is during this period that the infant's kin-recognition mechanism is activated, and it is able to distinguish between itself and the mother.

Gradually, the infant is able to make more refined social distinctions, including that between mother and other biological kin, between kin and non-kin, and between the in-group and out-group. Indeed, the distinction between "us" and "them" develops very early. And the greatest of all "us" relationships is the first one, the relationship between mother and child.

The other form of love is romantic love, which fuses mother love and sex into one of the truly great inventions of nature. Romantic love has shaken the ramparts of history, inspired the world's greatest literature, consumed the will of many a soul, and imparted more than its share of joy and ecstasy. When the popular crooner intones, "Baby, baby, I love you," the maternal and sexual roots of romantic love stand out in bold relief. In our deepest infatuations, we love like babies and copulate like adults.

Prior to mother love, man and woman must come together, bond, and begin to establish a family. Sex plays a major role in this bonding process. In *The Sex Contract,* Helen Fisher suggests that sex has historically been the glue that, in ancestral environments, bonded man and woman; even family bonding was the result of amorous exploits or highly orgasmic "female sexual athletes." Fisher says that ancestral female's continuous sexual receptivity (versus an "in-heat" period you see in some animals), not only kept the male nearby, but eventually induced him to be a better provider, parent, and soul mate. Fisher expanded this line of reasoning, in her book *Anatomy of Love,* where she asserts that evolved sexual prerogatives (priorities) that guide human behavior are tangible and knowable, because they lie in the roots of our ancient biology. These prerogatives, she believes, underlie much human misery: family breakdown, loneliness, adultery, divorce, poor parenting and child neglect and abuse.

What exactly are these human prerogatives? Among them are female orgasm, which can direct the intensity of women's bonding; serial monogamy, male jealousy and obsession with paternity; flirting, clandestine adultery, struggles over sexual equality, and perhaps even an inborn tendency to abandon our mates under certain conditions. While Dr. Fisher believes that extended-family kin networks eventually evolved to hold families together—because individual mateships typically did not survive—she asserts that these sexual variables, for better or worse, have helped shape the human family we know today.

Whether romantic bonds lasted forever or not, sex and romantic love in ancestral bands likely arose within a clan context and were basically egalitarian. Sexual bonds were monogamous while in effect, although when lovers and spouses grew tired of each other, or stressors pulled them apart, they sought love on the side or abandoned the relationship entirely.

Speculation about ancestral environments suggests that rather than women and men competing with each other, there was a clear division of labor and a "sexual contract," where males and females bonded with one another for sexual and reproductive purposes. Men and women needed each other, they respected each other, and they enjoyed each other's company within the bond.

Not until the 1970s did scientists attempt to seriously study and define love, and Freud's definition did not fare well. There is now ample evidence that love and sex are mediated by different parts of the brain, and are influenced by different hormonal supports. Yet in romantic love, these separate systems merge with explosive and dramatic effects.

Hormonal Kinship

In a recent issue of *Natural History*, there was a special section on motherhood with contributions by noted experts in the field, led by Sarah Blaffer Hrdy, an anthropologist at the University of California at Davis and recognized expert in mother-infant relations and infanticide. In an article "Hormonal Cocktails for Two," Dr. Hrdy and C. Sue Carter, a professor of zoology at the University of Maryland, discuss some of the important hormones involved in milk production, infant recognition, nursing, and parenting. Prolactin, for example, is an ancient molecule whose original function was to maintain salt and water balance in early vertebrates, but the hormone has evolved to mediate many newer functions including infant caretaking behavior. Prolactin is thus a major ingredient in the maternal cocktail that prepares mothers for that little gift from heaven.

But perhaps the quintessential mammalian hormone is oxytocin. As the main ingredient of the cocktail, it is present when the mother first greets her new bundle, and it continues to be released whenever she is nursing. But oxytocin is not just a mediator of birthing and nursing reflexes. It exerts powerful psychological effects on the mother, and promotes calming and mother-infant bonding.

Oxytocin appears to be one of the most basic kinship hormones. Produced by the brain, it sensitizes nerves and stimulates muscle contraction. In women, oxytocin helps uterine contractions during and after childbirth, and seems to inspire mothers to nuzzle their infants. Oxytocin may even encourage similar cuddling between adult women and men and may help promote group bonding by making these activities highly pleasurable.

Oxytocin may affect the primitive, maternal-like aspects of falling in love. Many other brain chemicals are involved as well. In a 1993 *Time* cover story on the chemistry of love, scientists assert that the sheer euphoria of falling in love is the result of chemical cousins of amphetamines swimming in the brain, including dopamine, norepinephrine and especially phenylethylamine (PEA). But this thrilling, passionate high doesn't last forever. As with any amphetamine, the body builds up a tolerance to PEA, and it takes more of the substance to fuel the rush of romance. After two or three years, our bodies simply can't crank up the needed amount of PEA, thus fizzling chemicals spell the end of delirious passion.[6]

Still, many love affairs continue long after passions simmer. Scientists believe that's because another set of chemicals, the kinship chemicals, replace the PEA hormones. "Unlike the fizzy amphetamines, these endorphins are soothing substances. Natural pain-killers, they give lovers a sense of security, peace, and calm."[7]

People marry for many reasons: cultural imperatives, peer and parental pressure, desire for children, and so on. But many experts believe that successful marriages begin with infatuation and romance—a kind of reservoir of passion couples can draw on throughout their marriage to keep it exciting and alive. But, as most of us know, the vast majority of marriages are not constantly dominated by fireworks and ardor. Ideally, enduring, long-term relationships include a more trustworthy element—the kinship bond. The "cuddle chemical," oxytocin, and the calming, attachment endorphins may indeed promote this bond.

These attachment hormones may help explain why the unfaithfulness of a lover is so devastating. Our biochemistry ties us to our mate, and if we feel the threat of losing our loved one, we experience withdrawal symptoms as terrifying and disorienting as if we were withdrawing from a narcotic. In long-standing relationships, an affair shatters much more than a romantic union; it shatters the kinship bond—loyalty, trust, dependability, attachment—all the things we typically associate with family.

Dr. Frank Pittman, author of *Private Lies,* explains that humans tend toward monogamy, but it's nature's way that if our mate dies, we can bond again. So if we sleep with someone other than our mate, instinct tells us our mate is dead and the bond is broken.

Love and sex do overlap with one another in erotic love—that terribly brief, yet aching, desire for mystical union with another. But long-term kinship love differs from thrilling eros. Originating with a mother's love for a child and branching out to extended family—ultimately including the psychological kinship of marriage—kinship love is vital to our human species.

Alice S. Rossi, Professor of Sociology at the University of Massachusetts at Amherst, in an article in *Psychology Today*, defines this kinship love for us:

> I find it helpful to distinguish among lust, eros (romantic love and infatuation), and caritas (loving, kindness and attachment); once sexually mature, lust clearly exists (that hot, moist fire in the belly and genitals that it takes maturity to control and channel), though cultures vary in the specific ways in which sexual attraction shows itself. Eros is a heady experience, when we yearn to merge with the desired one, but alas, it is of short duration. It is caritas we hope follows eros, a steady bathing of our being with calm and security, like that a mother provides to an infant, or if we are fortunate, that holds a marriage together for decades. Lust and eros assure that coming together of male and female through coupling and procreation; caritas takes over to assure loving care of human children.[8]

Indeed, the role of the parent/child relationship is the source for all human bonding. "K-Love," as one student of psychology called it, is simply the love people who are related to one another have for members of their family.

K-love is a very special kind of love that comes with the activation of the kinship mechanism. When this mechanism is activated, there's a desire to get close to another person, to share resources, to touch. Touch is important in animal groups as well as in human societies. Elephants constantly touch each other to express feelings of friendship and protectiveness. Baboons spend a lot of time grooming each other's fur.

Being both mammals and primates, human infants are born with a powerful desire to be touched and with deep needs for attachment.

Attachment is one of the deepest forms of human relationship; and love is the emotion that goes with kinship. In *The Evolution of Love*, Sydney Mellen echoes Sociologist Rossi mentioned above in asserting that mother love for her infant is the prototype for all other forms of love within a group.

Although deeply rooted in our natures, kinship love is not something we humans should take for granted. Granted, some forms of wild dogs, such as coyotes and dingoes, stick with their mates all year long or form small family groups. But many male animals, such as with cougars, stick around only long enough to mate. They then go back to defending their territory and living alone. Observing relationships in higher primates, such as orangutans, the males spend almost all their time alone, too. Like the lemurs mentioned previously, the predominant kinship bond in these animal families is between mother and child, not between mates or extended blood families. How lucky for our species that, although nature endowed us with the capacity to feel jealousy and hostility for family members, the overriding emotional wiring is for us to feel love and attachment for kin.

Fewer Kinship Bonds Today

Anthropologists tell us, and our own experience confirms, that we are simply not emotionally wired or physically able to develop intimate bonds with the almost six billion people inhabiting our Earth. Indeed, despite a ballooning population, despite our ever increasing exposure to strangers—whether through work, neighborhood, or church—we humans, like our primitive ancestors, still tend to form loving bonds with about twenty-five to fifty people; and, like our ancestors, deeper intimacy is usually limited to around seven or eight family members or surrogate kin.

As we've become more transient and as our technology has enhanced communication, this basic network of twenty-five to fifty people has increasingly become a mobile tribe—a distant nexus of a few blood relatives (parents, siblings, or children), a few childhood friends, and perhaps a best friend or two from college, the military, or our first pivotal job. Exchanging cards at holidays, sending e-mail over computers, and calling periodically to catch up on old news, we feel a sense of connectedness and belonging. It is not, though, the kind of support system we can usually rely on to battle the daily challenges of our increasingly complex, frenetic, two-career families.

Tribal Mentality

In the earliest stages of human evolution, family and tribe were not all that different, since perhaps the total group numbered no more than fifty. But as the group grew in size, to perhaps two hundred and larger, the family became a proportionately smaller component. Our dearest biological and psychological kin make up our families, but members of the tribe are family in the wider, metaphorical sense.

We all love belonging to a tribe. Our kinship chemicals may be secreted and our kinship mechanisms activated in the tribe just as they are in the family. Perhaps with less force, but activated nevertheless. Family and tribe make up our "in group," the group that we belong to, the group that defines what and who we are. Unfortunately, all others are part of the "out group"; they are outsiders. Our reservoirs of love are not unlimited; our human nature sees that our physical and emotional resources go to the right place: to family and those who can benefit us in matters of exchange and mutual support.

But that innate human wiring to reach out and connect with family can be expanded. The enterprising Disney Corporation routinely profits by creating and spectacularly marketing heartwarming, hopeful, ethnic tales about unfriendly tribes who reach across cultural and racial barriers to create a psychological kinship. While the individual plots in each screenplay vary, the classic formula remains the same in such marvelous films as *Beauty and the Beast, The Little Mermaid, Aladdin,* and *Pocahontas;* hostile strangers mistrust each other because they are different. But as one brave representative from each tribe crosses barriers and falls in love with an outsider, both clans are taught a lesson about finding unity and harmony with fellow human beings, despite vast differences.

In *Pocahontas,* Native Americans are at war with the English in the 1600s. But Chief Powhatan's daughter, Pocahontas, and her lover, Captain John Smith, extend the olive branch. By the end of the movie, Pocahontas's father calls John his "brother." And the beautiful dark-skinned Pocahontas tells the pale John Smith that, even though she won't be going back to England, she "will always be with him" in her heart—a sentiment we humans usually reserve for kin.

The children's film *Mary Poppins,* is a classic tale of psychological kinship, in that she, a stranger, understands her charges better than their own parents. Another example is the stirring stage musical *Les Misérables,* about a father's jealous rivalry with his adopted daughter's lover. In an inspiring metamorphosis, the father comes to love his rival as the son he'd never had. And Steven Spielberg's, *ET,* a heartwarming story of love that blossoms between a young boy and a visitor from a different planet, is an epic story of psychological kinship—but one that forms across species.

Indeed, once we are attuned to this popular theme, we begin to see it everywhere, in books, movies, sit coms, talk shows, and in real life all around us.

An incident in my childhood taught me an early, vivid lesson about the power of psychological kinships and taught me that mighty divisions, even if just for a few moments, *can* be transcended.

In 1968, I witnessed the black civil rights movement from my bedroom window. I watched young men protesting the assassination of Martin Luther King (as they were doing in neighborhoods like mine throughout the country). Although it certainly wasn't my cause—a white, gray-eyed, eleven-year-old with strawberry-blonde hair—I was energized by the black pride and militant might exploding around me.

One Saturday morning, a riot broke out a block from our house. Just days before, arsonists had secreted firebombs in pipes under an entire block of stores. The ensuing fire raged out of control, and the charred smell of burned wood and singed cement hovered in the humid air for days. Television and radio reports warned of snipers hiding on rooftops in the projects across the highway from our house. Our phones had gone dead. Being one of the few white families in our blue-collar, black neighborhood, we were prisoners in our own home.

Hearing the crowds heckling near our row house, my younger sister, afraid, began crying. I, on the other hand, feeling mostly intrigue, and mirroring the frenetic energy outside, paced curiously around our house, stopping at windows to stare. My father, fearing our house might be fire-bombed if I was seen, kept yelling "Get away from the windows!"

When I was a kid, my mom nicknamed me "Bernadette Devlin of 27th Street," mostly because, like the Irish revolutionary, I had reddish hair, ornery ways, and a quick temper. So it was not uncharacteristic that I snuck out our cellar door to witness the riot up close. Racing to the four-lane highway at the end of our street, I saw hordes of angry black folks balling their fists and chanting civil rights anthems, including "We shall overcome." I'd grown up with the young men who were shouting so, not surprisingly, not one of them vented their long-repressed rage on me. See, I wasn't some anonymous white oppressor. I was the neighborhood kid who loved to play kickball and dragged all the teenagers into street games. Intuitively, I had learned early to navigate between the diverse cultures of my black neighborhood and my white Catholic grade school. So I don't remember feeling fear as I stood, the lone Caucasian, witnessing a race war.

Instead, I stood mesmerized as these muscular black men, caught up in a primitive frenzy, snatched a white man from the car and ferociously attacked him. All great philosophical battles eventually come down to individuals fighting, don't they? Soon, though, I couldn't see the fighting very well, because the cheering spectators blocked my view. Suddenly, many youths from other neighborhoods joined the band. When they turned their attention to another car occupied by white folks, I remember finally feeling uneasy. I could trust my angry black neighbors, but even at that young age, I knew I was not safe with strangers. Realizing I'd pushed my rebelliousness far enough, I ran home.

Indeed, at our very essence, we are tribal people who instinctively seek community and kinship. We are made to love our own and to fear and sometimes hate the stranger. Although today most of us are educated in a mass public school system, designed to purge our inherent clan behavior (and many would argue individual creativity as well), we still tend to form groups who luxuriate in being with our own kind, and who fear and hate outsiders.

For example, the emphasis on affirmative action since the sixties (implemented to stop the rioting and designed to help minorities gain lost economic ground) and the more modern focus of multi-culturalism (a tolerance for ethnic and cultural diversity) are both currently lightning rods for racial tension. According to *Newsweek's* April 1995 article, "Race and Rage":

The most profound fight—the one tapping deepest into the emotions of everyday American life—is over affirmative action. It's setting the lights blinking on studio consoles, igniting angry rhetoric in state legislatures and focusing new attention on the word "fairness." When does fairness become "reverse discrimination"? When is it fair to discriminate on the basis of race or gender? Louder than before, Americans seem to be saying, "Never."[9]

But examining history carefully, it is easy to observe the repeated emergence of dominating majorities in race, gender, and religion. The first wave of court challenges against affirmative action began in the early 1970s. So, by now, Americans may be weary of quota and set-aside programs. And Gerald Early, in an essay in *Civilization* magazine, writes, "the greatest psychic burden of the African American is that he must not only think constantly about being different but about what his difference means." Affirmative action, he writes, "which promotes group identification and group difference, tends to intensify black self-consciousness. And black people, through no fault of their own, are afflicted with a debilitating sense of self-consciousness when around whites."[10]

But the other side of that reality is until our society achieves racial and gender equality, or until new balancing programs are designed, affirmative action is critical to overcoming our inborn, divisive tribal mentality. Tribes or groups—where religious, racial, or political majorities instinctively empower themselves to reap most of society's material rewards—tend to create inequalities and imbalances in the distribution of cultural rewards of prestige and power.

Take the case of Oliver Lee, profiled by Rochelle Sharpe in a December 27, 1995, article in the *Wall Street Journal*, "Oliver's Twist: Affirmative Action Lifted Mr. Lee, and He Has Never Forgotten." Lee is the son of an illiterate garbage man with a third-grade education, who was plucked from an all-black junior high school in Savannah, Georgia, in 1965, and then transferred to Cheshire Academy, a Connecticut prep school. This was done under the auspices of A Better Chance (ABC), a program designed to give low income youth the opportunity to attend elite private schools. Lee's rags-to-riches story is an inspiring one, and he is now a successful lawyer and mover and shaker in Georgia politics. What chance would he have had to attend Dartmouth College or

Vanderbilt Law School, had the playing field not been leveled early on? Indeed, a major point of the article is that Lee's journey out of the ghetto has been replicated by many of the 8,000 other students who went through the ABC affirmative action program, and studies show that the percentage of ABC graduates who attended college, including prestigious ones, was significantly higher than similarly talented students from impoverished backgrounds who went to public schools.[11]

Thousands of years after primitive people walked the grasslands, we see the tribal theme everywhere. Nationalism, which is good in the sense that it builds solidarity within a country, is exclusionary by its very nature, and historically has led to horrifying bloodshed. Even religion, a wonderful source of spiritual nurturance and inspiration for many, is a tribal mechanism often used to exclude others, and a mechanism far too often used to justify killing men, women, and children. As the late sixties rock musician/philosopher Frank Zappa once said, "Given that all religions preach brotherhood, love of your fellow man, and tolerance for all people without exception, why is it that the world's different religions have never been able to achieve unity?"[12]

When we pre-judge and are hostile to others because they are a different race, because they are of different economic means, or because they have a sexual preference we don't approve of, we are again giving in to our primal inclination to form tribal bands and attack outsiders. Nowhere has this mentality been more evident than in the landmark trial of O. J. Simpson. "Throughout the trial, the vastly different views about Simpson's guilt among blacks and whites led many people to conclude that the United States is really two nations divided by biases that warp perception. The divisions are so deep and so seemingly irreconcilable."[13]

Hope exists for humankind. There are many ways to extend family and tribal groups beyond their natural but narrow confines. Our evolutionary history built into us a deep love for own kind or kin, as well as fear and suspicion of outsiders. The good news is that the very same hormonal and kinship mechanisms that originally developed to cement family and tribal bonds can be extended into the netherworld of strangers. From the most unlikely sources— friends, loved ones, mates, in-laws—a mega-extended family of adopted relatives may be created. We believe it is even possible to love the human race in total, if we allow ourselves to overcome our egocentrism, ethnocentrism, and narrow tribality. Indeed, this is the central theme of most of the great religions of the world, and as we increasingly become teleconnected with a global village, it is an idea whose time has come.

4

Fish in Little Water
Solutions to the Modern Mismatch Dilemma

🔥

"The genes sing a prehistoric song that must often be resisted,
but cannot be ignored."
—Thomas J. Bouchard, Jr., and others[1]

As we've seen, humans yearn to be close to kin. Yet divorce, death, geographically scattered families, frenetic dual-career couples, and strained family relationships leave many of us feeling isolated, lost, and out of touch with these natural feelings of kinship.

Severed bonds, domestic upheaval, and utter isolation are rife in our society, say evolutionary psychologists, and this is not the way we humans evolved to live. Thus, say these experts, following a new line of thinking called "Modern Mismatch Theory," we have, rooted in our genes, a desperate craving for warm, caring bonds with other people. This is the essence of mismatch theory: we are genetically mismatched with our modern, fast-paced, lonely Western society.

53

My coauthor, Kent Bailey, outlined the five basic principles of mismatch theory at the international Human Behavior and Evolution Society conference in June, 1995: (1) Our human nature originally evolved in specific time periods called EEAs (environments of evolutionary adaptation), (2) The human species ceased to evolve, to any great degree, beyond late *Homo sapiens* 40,000 years ago, (3) Yet, massive cultural and environmental changes have occurred in the past 40,000 years, (4) Thus, current human beings often find their naturally evolved selves mismatched, or at odds with their current physical, social, and cultural environments, and (5) The frequency and magnitude of mismatch is related to diseases of both body and mind.

The science writer Robert Wright discussed mismatch issues in his August, 1995, *Time* article, "20th Century Blues." He explains that the roots of numerous contemporary maladies—stress, anxiety, depression—lie in our genes. These maladies result from the contrast between the modern environment and the ancestral environment, the one we evolved in and were designed for.

There is certainly no shortage of mismatch maladies to study. In some industrial countries, rates of depression have roughly doubled every ten years. Suicide is the third most common cause of death among young adults in North America, after car wrecks and homicides. Fifteen percent of Americans have had a clinical anxiety disorder. Moreover, pathological, even murderous alienation from others is a defining feature of our time. Somewhere along the evolutionary way, the Age of Kin became the Age of Strangers, with K-love slipping into the background, displaced by fear, competitiveness, and even hatred.

Vanishing Kinkeepers

Today, a middle-class lifestyle costs about $70,000 a year, not including costs for extras, like private schools, or even significant savings for retirement. Increasingly, just to afford the middle-class lifestyle many baby boomers grew up with—the average suburban home, decent transportation, and a week's summer vacation at the beach—it takes two wage earners in a family. That's a big reason why, according to studies, 72 percent of school-age children today have working mothers.

But our parents' generation could often afford to raise children on one income, why can't we? Despite the epic trend of corporate downsizing, doubling, even tripling some people's workloads, and despite the fact that even as important sectors of our economy are rebounding, as evidenced by a robust stock market (not just fueled by baby boomers investing)—we workers are not seeing a corresponding raise in wages. In fact, real wages, adjusted for inflation, have fallen 35–40 percent, say economists, since 1970. So while women initially joined the job force twenty years ago to supplement their husband's income, today wives' earnings are a requirement just to make ends meet.

Indeed, women working away from the family is yet another evolutionary mismatch issue that deserves our full attention. There is a serious time famine in our culture, according to a 1995 survey by the Families and Work Institute, the Whirlpool Foundation, and Louis Harris and Associates. The study showed that nine in ten women said they had serious time pressures and many said that families did not spend enough time together.

Work increasingly eats up family time: More often these days, parents are unavailable to take their kids to baseball practice, piano lessons, ballet, swim meets, and so on, evidenced by the proliferation of kid shuttle services in the market place. And have you noticed the proliferation of holiday and summer day camps offered by local daycare and YMCA centers? With no extended family around to watch the kids, parents need a place to park them when school's not in session. In a *Knight-Ridder Newspaper* article, Lori Lineberger quotes a food consultant who observes that more and more people aren't cooking these days, but rather are stopping at the local grocery store to pick up an already cooked meal. According to the food consultant, "We are so stressed out in today's life style. We have become 24-hour workers between e-mail and voice mail and faxes and online, that clearly we have a lot less time than ever before."[2]

We can see evidence of the vanishing kinkeeper everywhere we look. For example, flyers posted at my son's school suggest kids turn to PhoneFriend for help when they are alone after school: "Kids! You're alone at home after school and you can't reach Mom or Dad—maybe you're lonely or scared, maybe you feel like talking to a friend. . . ."

In reality, these lifestyle trends are neither right nor wrong; they are simply cultural adaptations to the modern phenomenon of women leaving home to work. But they will most likely have consequences. What poses a problem, the dilemma, is that in many households today, there is no adult family member at home. No one is available for the children. Not all time spent with kids needs to be interactive, or quality time, but when at least one parent is around after school, he or she can keep an eye on things—the nuances of their child's lives—with the attention only a parent would give.

This parental presence is not just important for young children. Many people mistakenly think that as teens are vocally pulling away from the family, it's appropriate for them to be left at home alone for long stretches of time, especially after school. But this isn't always a sound decision. A *Wall Street Journal* article, "Working Parents' Torment: Teens after School," reports, "new research shows that a teenager's initial experience with sexual intercourse now occurs most often at home after school."[3] In addition, when teens get in trouble, the stakes are so much higher than when they were elementary-school age. Furthermore, knowing a parent is around often gives kids a sense of security, even when they begin to separate from the family.

This modern time crunch falls particularly hard on women, who historically have been the nurturers and caretakers of the family— keepers of kin. No doubt we've all read in the newspaper legions of headlines about working women who still do most of child rearing, house cleaning, cooking, and grocery shopping.

In *Redbook's* "8 ways to Get Your Husband to Help," Elizabeth Rapoport writes that working women still "drag themselves home from the office to perform two-thirds of the household chores."[4] But it's not just housekeeping women are responsible for.

How many modern men in dual career families take the lead in choosing and interviewing day care providers? How many men find substitute care when their kids are sick, or when school lets out early, or when teachers have conferences? How many men schedule doctor's appointments for their kids, inform teachers of planned absences, shuttle kids to the appointments, and then take them back to school? How many men keep the calendar of anniversaries and birthdays in the extended family and, with no reminders or coaching, choose appropriate gifts and cards and either deliver them or get them in the mail? And how many guys make up grocery lists and head off to the store for the week's food?

Most women can easily rattle off a list of male relatives and friends who come over for a meal, yet fail to make the slightest effort to get food on the table or to clean up afterwards. These guys don't intend to be rude, certainly. Many men simply do not see it as their job. A recurring theme in mega-successful author John Gray's book, *Men Are from Mars, Women Are from Venus,* and in his earlier book, *Men, Women and Relationships,* is that men typically focus all their energies into "one big thing" in their lives, and that's usually work—the business of earning money. Relationship building and house duties tend to fade into the background. It's not that a man doesn't love his wife, asserts Gray, but focusing on those things are simply not part of a man's "instinctive tendencies."[5]

At one time in ancient human history, women may have been formally recognized as the kin-keepers. In *Women's Evolution,* Evelyn Reed argues that the earliest human groups were organized into clans and tribes based on maternal kinship; only much later did patriarchal families and male cultural supremacy emerge. The ideas of primitive matriliny kinship (descent through females) and matriarchy (rule by women) have a long history, yet their existence and perceived importance continue to be controversial.

While scholarly arguments over female lines of descent and kinship have not been settled, there is little doubt that the earliest human societies were "feminocentric," in the sense that social life in the camp centered on food gathering and feeding activities, birthing, and the rearing of young—with special emphasis on social etiquette along kinship lines. Adult women controlled these activities, for any band or tribe that assigned these critical responsibilities to males, juveniles, or the very elderly would have been on the path to quick extinction.

With legions of women working outside the home, joining men in a modern version of the primitive hunt, the contemporary division of labor in most families does not match our ancestral environment, obviously.

Mismatch theory tells us that we didn't evolve to live in a world where there is no kin-keeper available to bond families together and to nurture the fragile and impressionable children who will lead us all into the future. In a book in progress, *Human Paleopsychopath-*

ology, my coauthor, Kent Bailey, argues that both women and men must finds ways to solve the mismatch problem by balancing ancient prerogatives with current challenges. Clearly, the balancing act for women is one of gargantuan proportions.

An additional dilemma faced by working women today is finding time for friendships. Listen to Melissa, online, "I work in a small company where there's no such thing as socializing after work, like in my pre-kids life. So I really don't have work friends. On the other hand, I don't have the time like stay-at-home moms to hang out and get to know other moms or anyone else, because I usually want to spend time with my kids (and maybe even my husband.) My only real friends are people I've known for years, and even then I don't get to see them very often. There should be a better way." Having close friendships helps women balance the rigors of family and work life, and can help women feel connected to that important, familiar, ancestral sense of community.

Dr. Margaret Gibbs, director of training programs for Fairleigh Dickinson University in New Jersey, and a clinical psychologist who specializes in women's issues, says loneliness is a major problem for her clients, and the problem is central to our western culture. Much of our communication today is either electronic or a one-way connection through the media, she says. And this impersonal communication is very different from the one-on-one, physical human contact that we women crave and evolved to need.

Research shows that women's friendships are very different, according to Gibbs. They're stronger, and they involve warmth, altruistic caring, the sharing of feelings, and, unlike men, more urgent, conscious feelings of wanting to be with their companions, which leads women to actually reach out more. While men's friendships are equally companionable, they often lack the emotional intensity or empathy that characterized women's relationships.

This isn't all bad, explains Linda Sapadin, a therapist in private practice in Long Island, New York, during a telephone interview. Also a writer and instructor at Hofstra University, Sapadin explains that male friendships have many positives. Women who have male friends often appreciate how full of laughter and easygoing these friendships can be, she says.

The difference between female and male friendships is often likened to the difference between face-to-face friendships and side-to-side friendships, Sapadin explains. "In face-to-face relationships," she says, "women will tend to meet over coffee, or for lunch, and talk. Talking is the main activity. While for guys, it's not 'Let's get together and talk,' it's, instead, 'Let's get together and play some ball.'"

Side-to-side friendships revolve around an activity that both or several men are relating to, Sapadin says. "It's almost like a third party: You, me, and the game; you, me, and the work project; you, me and cards.' It's a different kind of intimacy."

Women generally introduce the emotional connections, and clearly, one down side to men having less intimate relationships is that they are more likely to expect their wives and children to be everything to them emotionally, says one therapist in private practice. This can put a lot of stress on a marriage, because the emotional exclusivity of modern traditional marriages is not natural.

G. Marian Kinget, in *On Being Human,* asserts that relationships that hold promise of better and longer wear are "based upon greater mutual acquaintance, more equality, and better and fuller communication than the traditional conjugal bond. The partner's interests and attention are socially more open-ended, less exclusively focused on each other, and less susceptible to the side effects [of break up]." In these kinds of healthy relationships, according to Kinget, the "highs are something less than ecstatic, but the lows are considerably less than agonizing. In sum, it is a relationship, cemented by sex, that may result in a formula for marriage that qualifies for the ancient's characterization of erotic friendship: the last gift of the gods."[6]

Woman: the Gatherer

In ancestral environments, the process of classifying kin and the organizing of daily social interactions were mainly controlled by women. But surely, we cannot go back to a time period when women stayed home, simply because they were female. We've learned that without networks and relationships outside the home, women become isolated and depressed. And while there are a growing number of support groups and kids playgroups to help stay-at-home moms connect, this is not enough. Even with these new kinds of support, many women feel frustrated because full-time childrearing leaves them little time to nurture skills and outside interests, or use an education that often took decades to acquire. Today's reality of divorce places the stay-at-home mom in an economically dependent, vulnerable position.

But is there a middle ground somewhere? Is it possible for the ancient prerogatives of home to be reconciled with the modern demands of work? My coauthor, Dr. Kent Bailey, argues that this mismatch dilemma cannot be solved by either returning to the Stone Age or, conversely, sacrificing ourselves to the modern demands of the job, which leaves little time for kinkeeping. Somehow, we must balance or reconcile our ancient, home-loving natures, with the pressure-cooker demands of the twenty-first century workplace. Essentially, human beings cannot be happy and fully actualized unless their lives are satisfying both at home and at work.

For women, successful reconciliation often involves increased emphasis on the work side, whereas, for men, there is increased emphasis on the home. Indeed, the biggest surprise in the 1995 study of working women and the time famine in our culture was how many men wanted to spend more time caregiving. If money were no object, 21 percent of the surveyed men would opt for the caretaking role. Even more surprising is this *American Demographics* statistic: "since 1990, there has been a 26 percent increase in the number of men leaving the work force because they were keeping house."[7]

According to the U.S. census bureau, there are now over two million at-home dads nationwide. Tim is one of them. He enjoys playing guitar, cooking, volunteering for a national political party, and owns his own baseball-card trading business. It happened that the lease on his retail store was up, and the rent was going up, just about the time that he and his wife, Lois, decided to start a family. He had wanted to get out of retail, so he closed the store and moved his business home where he could also take care of his son, Teddy, who is now eight months old. Tim's wife, Lois, is a high-school librarian.

"I'm kind of a domestic guy anyway," Tim says. "I always did all the cooking, 'cause I like to cook. And I can do some cleaning. It's fun. I'm enjoying staying home with him."

Men choosing to participate in the role of kin-keeper, is just one solution to the social dilemma of women working outside the home. Women are in the work force for good, and both men and women are in working and care-giving roles, according to Margot Adler, reporting in a segment on National Public Radio's "All Things Considered."

What is surprising, she reported, is how many *men,* as well as women, would opt to work part-time. "Thus employees need new models for less than full-time work, with decent pay and prorated benefits," she added. Indeed, part-time work is another important aspect of reconciling the modern mismatch issue of women joining men in the workplace.

Feminist Betty Friedan, author of the 1963 book, *The Feminine Mystique* agrees. "The first stage of the women's movement was a simple demand for equality. We haven't achieved that completely, but we've made enormous strides," she said, during her well-publicized trip to the 1995 Women's Conference in China. "We have to move with a new vision of community," she said, suggesting "shorter work weeks and higher minimum wages as a means of sharing jobs and incomes more equitably among both men and women."

But as men adapt to society's changing roles by assuming more kin-keeper duties, women must relinquish their hold on this role they've performed for millions of years. Take Diana's story, for example.

"I got to a point at around forty, when I realized I was always somebody's teacher, somebody's spouse, somebody's mom, or somebody's housekeeper. I was never *me,* the myself I was in college." Diana adds, responding online: "Now I do things on the spur of the moment . . . like the bear going over the mountain just to see what she could see: I talked two co-workers into going skiing, after not having skied for ten years. I am planning to take a class on the local Native Americans next week. And I joined a karate class with my daughter."

I, too, have found a creative way to combine work and family life. My husband and I have always shared cooking on the weekends. About seven years ago, I proposed, that in exchange for my cooking meals during the week, he could do the grocery shopping. Since we both work, it made sense that we both participated in the tedious process of gathering and preparing the food we needed to survive.

After surveying the store for several months, my husband compiled a computerized grocery list, organized in the same order as his route through the store. (He's a CPA, so organization comes natural-ly to him.)

Every Saturday morning, he prints out a new list, and I check off what we need for the upcoming week's menus. And since it's my husband's job to make school lunches for our children, he's better able to judge what he needs to buy. Neither of us are "food" people, so we buy pretty much the same stuff each week; we vary the meals by season, which keeps the list manageable. My sons take turns going with him each week. My husband and I agree that teaching our boys about the cost of various foods, how to get a good deal, and how to provide healthy meals for a family is important.

A good friend of mine, whom I met at a writer's group, hooked me up with Jean, a wife, mother, and owner of a computer-training business, who has developed an ingenious way of balancing her work and kin-keeper roles. For almost five years, Jean has partici-pated in a cooking co-op with two of her friends, Lynne and Susan, who live close by in the same neighborhood.

Gone are the hours spent chopping and cooking food during a busy work week. Jean cooks one night during the week, on Monday, for all three families, which she says isn't hard. When pulling out pots and pans and going to the trouble to prepare a home-cooked meal, she says, tripling the recipe is not that big of a deal.

Her friend, Lynne, a lawyer, cooks on Tuesdays; Susan, an audi-ologist, cooks on Wednesdays. Thursdays the families have leftovers from their co-op dinners, and Fridays are eat-out or pizza nights. Families cook their own meals on the weekends.

Jean says her older kids don't think anything of the fact that every Tuesday and Wednesday nights dinner is delivered hot and ready to serve—it's been going on since they were infants, she explains.

As a result of the cooking co-op, Jean says she doesn't go to the grocery store as often, and she has more time with her kids—three sons, one of whom is an infant.

"Last night, I came home with the kids. We knew dinner was coming at six, so the two older boys and I made cookies. And we did it right up until six o'clock. I could never have done that if I had to put dinner on the table. The dinner hour is the most frantic for us, when we have to prepare our own meal. With it coming, it's so much more relaxing for everybody. The element of stress is gone."

The women have known each other for nine years, and they socialize together. Every other month the women sit down and plan the recipes, being brutally honest about what meals they liked and didn't like. This social aspect of the co-op is fun for Jean, whose in-laws and biological family live in different states. "Sometimes, my kids help me deliver and they play with the children of the other two families . . . as much as we can," she says, adding that she likes the guaranteed contact with other adults. "In the wintertime, it gets dark early and you just never see anybody. Sometimes you get so wrapped up, you know, you get up in the morning, put the kids on the bus . . . the whole routine. It [the co-op] is a nice break in the routine. You feel like part of the neighborhood when you see your neighbors."

Since a local news story about her cooking group ran, three or four other cooking co-ops have already gotten started in her neighborhood.

A World of Strangers

Unlike our ancestors, we work outside kinship groups, depending upon virtual strangers for survival. Many of us live far from biological kin, unable to count on them for any physical, let alone emotional, support. It is a fact of modern-day life: strangers control our economy, they police our streets, they make the movies we see, and they wrench away most of our salaries every April. If we are to succeed in the modern world, we must confront the strangers with whom we are forced to interact daily. And, unfortunately, Mother Nature, which equipped us to deal with strangers in mostly hostile ways, gives us precious little help.

In addition to our struggle to survive amidst strangers, we must also deal with overcrowding. Today, walking down a crowded urban sidewalk, we see not one familiar face, we often avoid eye contact, and smile at no one. This estrangement, indeed this strange way of relating to our fellow humans feels unnatural and uncomfortable to most of us; that's because our ancestors knew most of the people they encountered throughout their lives. Evolutionary psychologists contend that we aren't genetically wired to live in a world swarming with people, and we pay a huge price.

Whereas kinship relations are characterized by love and reciprocal relationships are characterized by cool neutrality, relations with strangers are often characterized by hostility, discomfort, and stress, and appear to have a wide range of negative health implications. People frequently exposed to strangers under crowded conditions; those victimized by hostile strangers during war, military occupation, or especially concentration camp confinement; victims of stranger-on-stranger crime, as in stranger rape, kidnapping, assault, burglary, and mugging; and children molested or abused by strangers—all are at high risk for a variety of physical and psychological disorders. The horror and, especially, uncontrollability of these stranger-induced stressors are important factors in stress disorders. Of course, tension and violence are found among intimate relationships too; in fact, parent-initiated sexual abuse may be more devastating than stranger-initiated abuse. Nevertheless, fear of victimization by strangers is one of the major stresses encountered today.

In the spring of 1996, Richmond residents were bombarded with terrifying stories of murderous violence against elderly women in the west end of town. All evidence indicated a serial killer loose in the city, whose apparent approach was to gain the trust of kind, senior women, enter their homes on some pretense, then beat, strangle, and kill the victim. From 1990 to April 1996, fifteen women ranging in age from fifty-five to eighty-nine were slain. With the city in near-hysteria, the FBI was called in to assist local authorities in what became known as Operation Golden Years.

Betty Booker, in a *Richmond Times-Dispatch* article on the killings, urged older women to do something that is unnatural for them as kinkeepers and generally nice people: be rude to strangers. The article pointed out the era of politeness is gone when a stranger might be invited in for a drink of water or to use the phone. Stranger violence has robbed us of politeness, niceness, and the extension of kinlike feelings and behaviors to needy strangers. As Betty Booker says, be wary of kind words (that is, "kin" words), for they may be used to deceive with deadly consequences.

Welcome to the Great Indoors

Also contributing to internal tensions is the disappearance of our familiar, natural landscapes. Yet another mismatch issue.

Barry Lopez, in his book *Arctic Dreams: Imagination and Desire in a Northern Landscape,* explains how the Eskimos in the Arctic still possess a sacred relationship to the land. We southerners seem to have lost the value of our physical surroundings. Our lives are spent on impersonal freeways, frequently in search of better jobs. We abandon houses, and even cities, almost as readily as we change our wardrobes each season.

The Eskimos, on the other hand, treasure the land by attaching sacred memories to it. They strive to preserve it. These memories include stories of travel and special events that happened in certain places: "This was the place my daughter was born"; or "this is where by brother-in-law killed two caribou the winter a bear killed all my dogs."

According to Lopez, because we humans can circumvent evolutionary law, it is incumbent upon us to develop another law to abide by if we wish to survive. We must learn restraint. We must derive some other, wiser way of behaving toward the land. He writes:

> A Yup'ik hunter on Saint Lawrence Island once told me that what traditional Eskimos fear most about us [southerners] is the extent of our power to alter the land, the scale of that power, and the fact that we can easily effect some of the changes electronically, from a distant city. Eskimos, who sometimes see themselves as still not quite separate from the animal world, regard us as a kind of people whose separation [from the land] may have become too complete. They call us, with a mixture of incredulity and apprehension, "the people who change nature."

> Lying there in the tent, I knew, as does everyone I think who spends some time hunting with the Eskimos, that they are not idyllic people, errorless in the eyes of God. But they are a people . . . still close to the earth, maintaining the rudiments of an ancient philosophy of accommodation with it that we have abandoned. Our first wisdom as a species, that unique metaphorical knowledge that distinguishes us, grew out of such intimacy with the earth.　　• • •

> This is a timeless wisdom that survives failed human economies. It survives wars. It survives definition. It is a nameless wisdom esteemed by all people. It is understanding how to live a decent life, how to behave properly toward other people and toward the land. . . . It is, further, a wisdom not owned by anyone, nor about which one culture is more insightful or articulate.[8]

Today, the physical mismatches in our industrialized nation are self-evident. Our evolutionary environment, of which the Arctic tundra reminds us, had no cars, no eighteen wheelers bearing down on us on at a moment's notice, no airplanes noisily whirling overhead, no ear-splitting drills blasting outside our work areas. It was, quite simply, natural people in their natural environment. Our new, alien world creates subtle stress that we learn to tune out. But these stressors are always present, chipping steadily away at us.

What is ironic is that we consumers spend billions of dollars a year on interior decorating: wallpaper, furniture, paint, art work, and so on—all to beautify our indoors. The tradeoff for this enormous outlay is the destruction of our environment, the erasure of outdoor beauty. Trees are slashed and other natural resources are squandered to create consumer goods. Roads are paved to deliver consumer goods. Monstrous, frighteningly ugly power lines dominate the roadways, in large part, to fuel the making of future goods, and, among other things, to light up our homes so we can enjoy our material gadgets in the dark—at night, when we humans used to sleep.

We live in a fabricated world, a world created and domesticated by human beings. Ethologist Desmond Morris aptly described our increasingly unnatural world in his book, *The Human Zoo,* written more than twenty years ago. ("Ethology" is specific brand of European biology and zoology that emphasizes inborn patterns of behavior in animals and humans.) Morris was perhaps the first of the mismatch theorists, and he likened modern humans to zoo animals, trapped in a relentless upward spiral of cultural progress, technological complexity, and compulsive materialism. With each new complexity, he says, we move farther from our natural state and fall deeper into the bored, indulgent, domesticated role of the zoo animal.

What is the best natural match for humans? The answer lies within. A wooded area, open farm country or a mountain fragrant with flowers—nature creates peace. It makes us breathe a little deeper, a little slower. We relax. It's really not surprising, since we evolved in similarly natural settings. Overcrowding, ever present strangers, noise pollution, air pollution, mountains of cement, and blacktop stretching for miles—all were all absent in our ancient environments.

"We see beauty in nature," says one Unitarian Universalist minister. "I was taught that being aware of beauty around us was a way of being spiritual. It was a window to illuminate the soul." As we march into the twenty-first century, that window to the soul is getting dirtier and dirtier. Whether we are conscious of it or not, we are feeling the grime on our souls. That is the essence of the mismatch theory.

Fish in Little Water

What evolutionary psychologists are discovering is that the quantity of mismatch, at a physical or psychological level, produces stress (although not always apparent), in human beings. Stress is produced when an organism is thrown out of kilter or out of its natural balance. If you take a fish out of water, for example, it will experience stress and attempt to cope. Coping attempts are almost always directed toward returning to a natural state of homeostatic balance. The most common way to do that is to return to the natural environment: for the fish, to water.

If you keep that fish out of water for too long, however, it will die—quickly. In many ways, humans beings living in the twentieth century are fish out of water. Actually, the harried, stressed-out, white-collar worker, whose career is mostly sedentary, and who downs three gin-and-tonics after work to relax is, metaphorically speaking, a "fish out of water." And according to authors Boyd Eaton, Marjorie Shostak, and Melvin Konner in *The Paleolithic Prescription,* modern people who, like our ancestors, vigorously exercise on a regular basis, eat a natural diet of fruits, grains, and vegetables, and who seek out nature to relax, are fish in "little water." Surely, little water is better than no water, however.

Whatever the case—being a fish out of water, or a fish in very little water—today's environment causes stress for most human beings. And, like other living creatures, when we are faced with extreme stress, when we are isolated from our support system, when our survival is endangered, we react with aggression. We evolved to live close to our kin. For those millions of people who are without family, who live far from relatives, or who have no real emotional bond with kin, severe "mismatch stress" is the result. While it is often turned inward, manifesting itself as depression and loneliness, sometimes this stress is turned outward, in raw aggression and violence.

My coauthor, Kent Bailey, in his book, *Human Paleopsychology*, discusses a scientific term used to describe a situation where culture is pretty much turned off and ancient feelings emerge in raw animal form. That term is *phylogenetic regression, phylo* meaning "species characteristics" and *regression* "to go back." We see this phylogenetic, stone-age regression occurring in many aspects of our modern, violent human society.

Take the disgruntled postal worker who believes his livelihood has been snatched unfairly, and then retaliates by attacking former bosses or co-workers. Or the infamous Unabomber. Over a seventeen year span, according to an article in *The Wall Street Journal*, the Unabomber—so called because he first targeted universities and airlines—has planted or mailed fifteen bombs, killing three people and injuring twenty three. The last two bombs killed a lobbyist from Sacramento, California, and an advertising executive from New York.[9]

A reclusive former math professor, Theodore John Kaczynski, fifty-three, was arrested April 4, 1996, in his small shack near Lincoln, Montana; police suspected he was the mysterious Unabomber. He was charged with possessing illegal bomb components and a partially assembled pipe bomb. Through a steady flow of leaks from enforcement officials and saturated media coverage, the story of an "ecovillain" emerged: Kaczynski graduated from Harvard at age twenty, later got his Ph.D. at the University of Michigan, and then taught mathematics at Berkeley for a time. But he dropped out of sight two years later and began a solitary life in the wilderness, shunning modern conveniences, and growing food by using his own waste to fertilize his gardens. He became obsessed with the alienating power of modern technology and rebelled against a world where competition, materialism, and individualism have conquered the human spirit, a spirit that evolved in bountiful, unfettered, sacred nature.

In Kaczynski's shack, FBI agents found weapons, a list of corporate executives, maps of San Francisco, several typewriters, and numerous documents and notes. Kaczynski fits the FBI profile for the Unabomber, and incriminating evidence continues to mount, although it may take years before a jury renders its verdict. One thing for sure, Kaczynski is one of a dangerous breed of "mismatch revolutionaries" whose hatred of technological progress is so great that it fuels murder. Once can hardly think of a worse solution to the already dehumanizing mismatch dilemma.

When you think about it, Kaczynski was himself out of touch, out of sync with the humanity he supposedly revered so much. True, our psyches were shaped in ancestral environments characterized by coexistence with nature. But an even greater piece of our human evolutionary history was our inborn drive for participation and cooperation within a community, a tribe, a family. Interdependence among people, not isolation from people, was a powerful mediator of homicidal tendencies. Whether or not he is the Unabomber, Kaczynski's bombs were obviously meant to cause injury to others. And if Kaczynski is the Unabomber, his estrangement from his fellow humans may well be a major reason he could carry out such chilling, calculated madness. A human embedded in kinship love, apart from an unbridled crime of passion, would be prevented from hurting others because he would feel, at the soul level, the horror he was perpetrating onto others. Because of his own love for family and friends he would, indeed, understand, in excruciating emotional detail, the pain of loss.

So the Unabomber, in rebelling against a society that reduces humans to income-producing widgets on the mass assembly line of life, himself becomes such an alienating, inhuman widget of destruction.

Warrior Without Portfolio

We also see mismatch dynamics played out in the indigent inner-city male, who daily, desperately, and often violently ekes out his existence within a human jungle. For poverty, according to the experts, is a great predictor of pathological kinship and stranger-on-stranger violence.

The engine of our western industrialized world is capitalism, our proverbial "water" is money. Indeed, three-fourths of our economy is dependent upon consumer spending. We live in a culture that promotes, even demands, spending at every turn. Otherwise, our economy would collapse. So to survive in this society, unlike that of our ancestors, we need money. The maturation process to adulthood culminates in self-sufficiency, which in our society translates into paying others so we can stay alive.

Think about it: going to the bathroom, taking a shower, washing your hair—it all costs money today, if you factor in sewer bills, utility bills to heat the water, and shampoo. It even costs money for a woman to have her period in our modern society—about $5 a month for tampons or sanitary napkins. For a woman making minimum wage, it takes more than an hour of net pay just to menstruate—the most natural and essential process to the evolution of our species. Now imagine that same woman, as a single mother making minimum wage, forking over another hour of pay to buy a box of cereal to feed her children. Bare sustenance is an expensive proposition.

The documentary film *Hoop Dreams,* which premiered at the New York Film Festival in 1994, is about two talented young men who dreamed of playing basketball in the NBA. But the movie is also a poignant chronicle of two poor families struggling to live in inner-city housing projects. The mother of Agee, one of the basketball players in the film, is up against the wall, metaphorically speaking: her husband of twenty years is unemployed, into drugs, and absent on and off throughout the film; the welfare department has cut off payments for Agee, who is eighteen but still in high school; and a back injury prevents her from working. With three kids to feed, clothe, and shelter, she is trying to live on the $300 a month she gets from welfare.

She asks the viewers of *Hoop Dreams* to wonder how her children will survive, adding desperately, "it's enough to make people want to lash out and hurt someone!" Though a talented and sensitive boy, Agee demonstrates that when someone is living in such deprivation, right and wrong seem somehow irrelevant. He embodies the fish in little water. From this perspective, it's easy to imagine how people living at lower socioeconomic levels feel futile and are often fueled with hair-trigger rage.

True, a rural person living off the land in pre-industrialized China has the cyclical stress of crop survival and natural disasters. But for those living in our capitalistic system with little access to the very passport for survival—money—that stress is chronic. Hunting and gathering skills, finding shelter, the ability to make a fire to keep warm or cook—these don't spell survival anymore. Cash does. Lack of money equals extinction. This is surely one of the greatest, most anxiety-producing issues of mismatch that modern families face.

In his 1969 book, *Understanding Poverty,* Senator Daniel P. Moynihan, from New York, poignantly described the link between deprivation and human savagery. It is a link that still rings true today:

> From the wild Irish slums of the 19th Century Eastern Seaboard to the black riot-torn suburbs of Los Angeles, there is one unmistakable lesson in American history: A community that allows a large number of young men to grow up in broken families, dominated by women, never acquiring any stable relationship to male authority, never acquiring any set of rational expectations about the future—that community asks for and gets chaos. Crime, violence, unrest, unrestrained lashing out at the whole social structure—that is not only to be expected; it is very near to inevitable.[10]

Across this country, particularly in our inner cities, broken families and overcrowded conditions abound. There's not enough food, an absence of medical care, and thus, tribal warfare, shootings, and so on. These hot beds of humanity yield brutality, physical and mental disease, and social upheaval.

History has shown that educationally and financially advantaged people can adapt to the highly mismatched conditions of the city, and even prosper there. But, there is little evidence that the poor and educationally disadvantaged have ever prospered in the cities. More often, their role is a servile one. The poor and disadvantaged are left to rely on their natural wisdom and kinship skills, but the city is likely to take even these away. We hear much today about the breakdown of the family, but we seldom recognize the mismatch implications of this phenomenon.

The urban black male is one of the greatest mismatch victims in all of modern American society. Only a few centuries ago he was perhaps a proud African warrior in the tradition of Shaka Zulu, a tribal leader, and a protector of his family. But today's American black man sees himself as "unnecessary," African-American columnist William Raspberry commented after the famous Million Man March on Washington in 1995. The American black male does not suffer a different kind of mismatch from the rest of us, he just suffers it more poignantly, more agonizingly.

Relatively few people are rich, powerful, and renowned in our capitalistic society. But whereas the middle classes and blue-collar working classes feel the sting of unrequited dreams, harboring a wistful, inner sense of failure, or at least a mild sadness at what could have been in our great land of opportunity, the American black man sips a daily, deadly poison that kills his soul. For what greater poison is there than to be "unnecessary" in a world that worships fame, success, and wealth?

From the time most Africans came to America in slave ships, civil rights, educational opportunities, and a place at the social table were denied them. Denied even the most basic opportunities, black males were able to survive by calling upon the ancient African wisdom of family, kinship, and racial unity. When the doors of opportunity were nudged open a mere thirty years ago, the African American male was not prepared to compete with far more privileged competitors. These events set the stage for the social malaise, the sense of "unnecessariness," that plagues the black male today.

Recent surveys indicate that one in three young black males has been involved in the criminal justice system. Some of these young men are so alienated from our economic system (and its inherent values) they will kill a human being for five dollars, or even a pair of fancy sneakers. Many of these young men have given up on a system that sees them as a problem to be solved. In their own way, they are desperately seeking to achieve cultural success, rising to the top of their own natural hierarchies (gangs). Yet, they remain clearly outside of mainstream society. These "warriors without portfolio" are "becoming more numerous, more violent, more addicted to substances that exacerbate their aggressive traits, and becoming increasingly alienated from family, community, cultural tradition, educational opportunities, and other constraining influences," writes Kent Bailey.[11]

These African-American males are "walking zombies," says Dawn Lewis, who is writing her doctoral dissertation on psychological kinship in the African-American culture. Statistics show that a significant number of black males, as compared to white males, never make it to their eighteenth birthday. With those odds, Lewis asserts, it is not surprising that many don't bother making long-range plans for a secure financial future. There are faster, easier, more reliable ways to obtain money—for example, running drugs—

than planning for a college degree they may never live to obtain. Morals aside, a pretty normal reaction to an abnormal situation.

Indeed, why would a poor, inner-city African American feel an allegiance to middle-class morals of education and hard work, anyway? When you travel to almost any inner-city across this country, blacks are disproportionately pooled in rickety housing; attend substandard schools; work predominantly in menial, low-paying service jobs, living on the edge. How moral is this?

While the antisocial behavior of the black male is clearly an adaptive strategy aimed at solving his mismatch dilemma, it ultimately will not solve his problems and only serves to make matters worse for himself, his family, and community. The rest of us are burdened by the mismatch problem of modern times and we hope for a personal solution. But the black man must find a solution or suffer annihilation at his own hands.

Economic segregation, which we will discuss in more depth later, is the modern face of racism. And until this inequity is addressed, more studies on violence, more police overtime, abolishing parole, or even building a thousand more prisons will be no match for the interminable bloodlettings. This racial violence is actually a modern civil war. And while violence is mostly confined to a specific race and certain core geographic rings—in 1994, 94 percent of black homicide victims were murdered by other black people—the violence is steadily seeping outward.

My city, Richmond, is Exhibit A, because it illustrates this phenomenon so accurately. Richmond is burdened by a legacy of astounding and almost primitive economic segregation that still defines the city today. Quite predictably, the violence in Richmond is spiraling out of control. Most of the crime involves burglary and drug money, sure-fire revenue raisers of the economically segregated. But the tragic part is that while the city is ranked seventy-sixth in terms of population out of the top one hundred U.S. cities— Richmond is also ranked third per capita in terms of its murder rate.

When you examine the cities ranked highest in per capita murder, they are predominately in the South, cities—such as Atlanta and New Orleans—with an enduring history of economic segregation. The exceptions are Washington, D.C., St. Louis, and Detroit, all of which have high murder rates, but also have high populations of

African Americans, and again, entrenched economic segregation in the inner cities, where most of the crime occurs.

So, today, when we pull up to a fast-food restaurant and see a disproportionate number of black people in low-paying, dead-end jobs, when we drive through dilapidated inner-city neighborhoods and see mostly blacks, or when we stand next to a black person cashing food stamps, we should remember that their loss, their mismatched economic segregation, is our peril, too.

Aberrant Crimes and Serial Murder Another Mismatch Issue

Mismatch theory and phylogenetic regression are evident in some of the most famous, horrifying murder cases in history. Jealous, territorial murders of the kind O. J. Simpson was *accused* of committing could be construed as a form of phylogenetic regression. People don't *learn* to kill that way—something is released from deep in the brain that even the killer does not understand. Somehow, for a deadly moment, the killer rematches with those ancient evolutionary environments when our ancestors stalked and killed their weaker prey, and tore them to pieces. Indeed, the type of violence used to kill Nicole Brown Simpson and Ron Goldman is a macabre reminder of the depth of our inhumanity—a depth some experts believe lies at the bottom of all humans beings' brains.

An evolutionary theory of the brain, developed by eminent neurologist Paul MacLean, of the National Institute of Health in Maryland, suggests that the human brain is actually three brains in one—each evolving in vastly different time periods, all trying now to get along. MacLean calls this multi-layered mind the "triune brain." (MacLean's father was a Presbyterian minister, and it is not a stretch to imagine that the Christian concept of a trinity inspired this three-brain theory.)

According to MacLean, the outer gray matter, the neocortex, is the largest part, and the thinking part of the brain. This philosophical, moral, spiritual brain is responsible for understanding dichotomies and solving complex problems, and is capable of controlling violent impulses. It's the latest of the three brains to evolve. The next oldest part is the paleomammalian brain, which houses basic emotions—love, hate, jealously, and a host of other deep feelings that promote survival and reproduction. MacLean named this brain the "limbic system" more than four decades ago.

Deep in the brain stem lies what MacLean calls the "reptilian" brain, which houses "primitive biological intelligence." This automatic, vital, intuitive processor is where our instincts lie: feeding, nesting, homing, courtship, dominance, aggression, territorial impulses, and many other species routines. MacLean also includes primitive deception (for example, extending feathers to appear larger), ritualistic behavior (for example, greeting routines in monkeys), and imitation in the reptilian category.

In 1983, Kent Bailey wrote Paul MacLean and asked whether the idea of phylogenetic regression-progression was consistent with his triune brain theory. Can a person regress down or progress up the triune brain hierarchy? In his kind and gentlemanly way, MacLean replied that it is up to the critics to prove such a common-sensical idea wrong. Thus, there is good reason to believe, for example, that a person may be very human (neocortical) one minute and quite inhuman (reptilian) the next.

Serial murders represent dramatic and violent examples of phylogenetic regression to the level of the reptilian brain. Take Jeffrey Dahmer, who killed, mutilated, and ate his victims. And the instant when Susan Smith let go of the brake, allowing her two small sons to plunge into that lake, she was most likely in a state of phylogenetic regression. When brutal murderers say they "weren't themselves" at the time of the act, they don't know how right they are.

In an era of mass murders, serial and torture killings, the textbook case of Ted Bundy, a brilliant law student who sexually violated and mutilated at least thirty-three women throughout the 1970s, is one of the most notable cases of the reptilian brain taking over a human being. Yet, on the surface, Bundy seemed as far above the reptilian brain as is possible for a human.

As Ann Rule writes in *The Stranger Beside Me,* "Ted has been described as the perfect son, the perfect student, the Boy Scout grown to adulthood, a genius, as handsome as a movie idol, a bright light in the Republican Party, a sensitive psychiatric social worker, a budding lawyer, a trusted friend, a young man for whom the future could hold only success.

"He was all these things and none of those.

"Ted Bundy fits no pattern at all; you could not look at this record and say: 'See, it was inevitable that he would turn out like this.'

"In fact, it was incomprehensible."[12]

Indeed, Bundy's psychopathic pattern of brutal, grizzly murder was incomprehensible. Although the details varied from case to case, the basic pattern was the same. Beautiful young women were sought out, then either forcibly abducted or tricked into entering Bundy's battered old Volkswagen, after which they were usually bludgeoned about the head with a crowbar or other blunt instrument, sexually brutalized, and often mutilated.

Bundy seemed to relish the thrill of the hunt. He was convicted on forensic evidence: the teeth marks in the buttocks of one of the victims matched Bundy's teeth. With a blood lust, he had bludgeoned her to death with a piece of wood. All strong indicators of phylogenetic regression.

In the wake of these horrors, we must ask why. Rage, hate, animalistic mutilation—the polar opposite of loving, altruistic, kinship behavior.

Feeling enraged, wronged, and betrayed, many of us have committed murder in our minds, in our fantasies. So Ted Bundy is not remarkable for the tendencies and predispositions carried deep within his brain, but he is remarkable in that these tendencies were released in such grotesque fashion. It is not that Bundy learned to rip and tear at this victim like a predatory animal, but that all of the acquired social and moral inhibitions, positive social modeling, and ample reward for being a "perfect" man failed to prevent pathological release.

His upbringing is not the answer. Bundy's early life was not typical in every respect, but it was not a hotbed of pathology either.

Theodore Robert Cowell was born in a home for unwed mothers in Burlington, Vermont, in 1946. His mother was a "good girl" from a deeply religious family in Philadelphia, and his father, whom he never saw, was a traveling salesman, a graduate of Pennsylvania State University, and an Air Force veteran.

Although the Cowell family was disappointed by the illegitimate birth, the mother, Louise, was taken back into their middle-class home in Philadelphia. There began a charade in which the grandparents became the "parents" and Louise assumed the role of "sister" to Ted. Ted adored his father (his grandfather) but to keep the secret intact, Louise moved to Tacoma, Washington, when Ted was four and changed his name to Theodore Robert Nelson. Soon after, at a Methodist Church function, Louise met Johnnie Culpepper Bundy, a small, mild-mannered cook. They were married in 1951. Ted always considered himself a Cowell, however, and never really identified with the diminutive Johnnie. Yet, Johnnie accepted Ted as his son and made a strong effort to be a good father. Eventually, four half-siblings came along, two girls and two boys. But the bright, attractive Ted remained the favorite in his mother's heart.

While there is clearly a difference between the natures of animals and humans, the new, controversial field of *human paleopsychology* examines the possibility that much of our complex human behavior today comes from our archaic, biological roots. *Paleo* is simply a Greek word meaning "old." Thus, paleopsychology is the study of ancient feelings and behaviors expressed in today's world, says Kent Bailey, in his 1987 book, *Human Paleopsychology: Aggression and Pathological Processes.* Why we love, reason, and reach for the stars—and yes, some of the reasons why people like Bundy hate and kill—also stem from this ancient genetic legacy.

In view of Bundy's Jekyll-and-Hyde behavior, the question begs to be asked: In what setting do the most moral, phylogenetically advanced humans occur—in a setting where the beast is released from its cage and petted into submission, or one where the cage is reliably secured by moral and religious pressures? Both history and the chaos of our modern age tell us that self-control is a tenuous thing, even when nurtured and supported by social customs, laws, and religious morality. Thus, experts do not really know for sure which exact mechanisms break down, allowing a human being to commit the kind of brutality Bundy committed.

Indeed, when asked themselves why they commit such murders, many killers, including Ted Bundy and Susan Smith, say they don't know, adding that it was as if some monster lay within. It does, say paleopsychologists, and that monster is the reptilian brain. Genetically based impulses and corresponding fantasies may over-stimulate lower brain centers, these experts suggest, creating powerful urges the psychopathic Bundys of the world cannot quell. How else can we explain the inexplicable?

Behavioral geneticists today distinguish between sociopaths and psychopaths, as David Lykken says in his book, *The Antisocial Personalities*. Inner-city criminal males, as described above, coping with the stress of surviving in a human jungle, sometimes become sociopaths. Their brain chemistry is normal, but they react to the strains of their environments with violence. In a different setting, the sociopath might not exhibit aberrant behavior. Anyone can behave sociopathically if survival stress passes a certain point.

On the other hand, Bundy, Dahmer, and other sadistic, serial killers are, in all probability, psychopaths. A particular genetic vulnerability may incite fearlessness, dominance, and bizarrely aggressive behavior. Psychopaths are also most often highly sexually active. Although healthy and ultimately life sustaining, as opposed to life threatening, sexual behavior, with its primal humping, grunting, and moaning is itself a phylogenetic regression. But when sexual impulses commingle with violent impulses, you have the makings of the most savage kind of killer. Unlike the sociopath, the psychopath will exhibit some deviant violence in almost any environment. And the greater the environmental stress, the greater the deviance.

Overpowering instinctive urges do not solely determine murderous behavior, however. Human conduct is shaped by a complex web of social and biological influences, such as hormones, for example, and learned variables we simply do not yet know anything about.

Some experts say the growing violence of the last several decades may be a reaction to our increasingly stressful modern society. Mismatch theory incarnate: Increased alienation, overcrowding, distant or shattered kinship bonds, the loss of natural landscapes, and high-tech gadgets that reduce human communications to distant modal operations.

In addition, studies show that, unlike our ancestors, by the time the typical child has reached school age, he or she has already seen thousands murders on TV or in the movies. Exposure to violence primes a child for aggression, although the causal linkages are extremely obscure and difficult to quantify. But, add mismatch stress to an individual's particular biochemistry, predisposed toward violence, and these factors may very well induce the phylogenetic regression seen in Bundy. Such regressions would have been less frequent in a less stressful society a hundred years ago, prior to today's urban malaise and provocative entertainment.

The Power of Kinship Disruption

Today experts believe that many physical illnesses and psychiatric maladies are caused, in some form or another, by stress. Many of these stressors involve antagonisms, deprivations and disruptions in interpersonal relationships. Mismatch theory asserts that if kinship and social relationships deviate too much from, or are insufficiently matched with, ancestral social arrangements, then social tension, alienation, and individual and group pathologies are likely.

Whether these kinship disruptions be immediate—breaks in the family circle, sexual relationships, classroom, or boardroom—or global—pollution, famine, terrorism, war, social disorganization—their roots are predominantly social in some way. In addition, the stress of being mismatched with our environment is also linked to ever increasing rates of kinship disruptions at home and at work.

Throughout most of human history, our joy and satisfaction came primarily from our biological and psychological kin—that is, family. Today, extended families have been annihilated and the nuclear family is often under too much pressure to be a major source of nurturance for most people. So, a large measure of cultural success in our Westernized society is based upon how well we survive these kinship disruptions and how well we accommodate and profit from the vast numbers of non-kin we encounter—how well we negotiate a world of strangers.

Severe kinship disturbances, such as early childhood separations from primary caregivers, can be extremely traumatic for human beings. As best-selling author Judith Viorst describes in *Necessary Losses*:

> We survive our mothers' brief absences but they teach us a fear that may set its mark on life. And if in early childhood, most especially in the first six years, we are too deprived of the mother we need for and long for, we may sustain an injury emotionally equivalent to being doused with oil and set on fire. Indeed, such deprivation in the first few years of life has been compared to a massive burn or wound. The pain is unimaginable. The healing is hard and slow. The damage, although not fatal, is permanent.[13]

Considering Bundy's case history in this light: the estrangement from his father, and his early confusion about his parentage, combined with his excitable temperament and the psychopathic flood of impulses—all may have conspired to push him over the edge. The absence of one or more of these factors might have altered history. Perhaps we never would have heard of the Bundy beast who dominated the media and shocked humanity.

Jeffrey Dahmer, the serial killer who ate his victims, lived through the bitter divorce of his parents and was traumatized by domestic upheaval. Susan Smith was sexually molested by her stepfather, and abandoned by her mother, who refused to leave her husband when the offense came to light. It is likely that critical disturbances in attachments to caregivers is always involved in the reptilian regressions of the Bundys, Dahmers, and Smiths of the world. Most insecure and troubled attachments do not lead to violence, however; they more typically lead to psychological agony, self-doubt, and depression.

Unless you've experienced firsthand the trauma of sexual abuse by a trusted caregiver, you cannot fathom how drastically it can distort someone's notions of security, trust, responsibility, and love. Like "behind the looking glass" in Lewis Carroll's *Alice in Wonderland,* good can begin to look like evil, and evil like goodness. You also cannot imagine the frightening abandonment terror, overwhelming rage, and confusing illusions that are later transferred onto spouses and children. Such betrayal creates dissociative states in its victims, used to blot out the pain, and sometimes even the memories. But sometimes that horrifying pain creeps back in. Susan Smith had to be in terrible pain to do what she did to her two small sons. Ellen Bass and Laura Davis, in *The Courage to Heal,* describe such dissociative splits from reality:

> One of the common ways children deal with the unbearable experience of being sexually abused is to flee from the experience, to split. Most survivors have experienced this to some degree. In its milder form, you live exclusively on a mental level, in your thoughts, and aren't fully present. You cannot feel, because it was once too dangerous to feel. At its most extreme, you literally leave your body [or split into other personalities]. This feat, which some yogis work for decades to achieve, comes naturally to children during severe trauma. They cannot physically run away, so they leave their bodies.[14]

In such shattered states, it's not hard to imagine the reptilian brain taking hold. Sometimes the trauma leaves the moral and spiritual brain so broken, there is little energy left to halt the raging monster within.

Of course, not all abused children grow up to be gratuitously violent themselves, but experts believe it is a priming condition. We need to make one thing clear, though: neither the evolutionary theory of the reptilian brain, nor the theory that kinship disruptions increase the risk for depression, anxiety, and even murderous aggression, are excuses for killing anyone. In fact, only a tiny minority of people primed for psychopathology and violence actually kill; the Dahmers, the Bundys, and the Smiths represent an even smaller minority.

For whatever reason, precious lives were lost—lives that can never be brought back, no matter how accurately we theorize about why they were taken. At some point, all human beings are responsible for recognizing when they need help: when they're losing a grip on their impulses, when they're slipping down into the reptilian brain, into a phylogenetic regression. That recognition is made possible because of the neocortex that helps keep the inner beasts at bay. We humans have little control over our ancient instincts—what we feel, what drives us—but we have much choice in our behavior.

It seems we are forever frustrated in seeking human causes for inhuman actions. But the reality is, human murders begin in the human mind. By trying to understand the multitude of factors in the epidemic of violence in our society, perhaps lives can be saved in the future.

Some experts believe we can never force the sociopaths of the inner cities, or the murderous psychopaths led astray by aberrant brain chemistry, to stop hating, to stop exploiting human nature. So instead, another tact might be to teach them to love, to teach them how to take care of other people. And teach them long before it's too late: when they are children, showing the first signs of antisocial behavior.

The concept of teaching love may explain why two children in a troubled family turn out drastically different—one successful and the other depressed and suicidal. Or why one child raised in a drug-infested ghetto goes on to college while another ends up a criminal on the streets.

In *Resilient Adults: Overcoming a Cruel Past,* Dr. Gina O'Connell Higgins, a licensed psychologist in private practice and an instructor at Harvard Medical School, explains the "bricks and mortar" of how humans overcome tragedy. Her book focuses on the effects of "surrogates," who were able to teach love to children at risk.

Higgins found that children who forged a relationship with surrogate parents grew up to be strong, self-reliant, optimistic, resilient people. These surrogates made the critical difference in the troubled children's lives, providing a kind of emotional inoculation against the damaging effects of a stressful environment. These resilient children often had "an unusual ability to see possibility, light and goodness," Higgins adds, "and to be grateful for it." They were able to absorb these surrogate figures into their psyches. While other siblings may have had similar access to the surrogate, for some reason, they weren't able to forge the same healing bond.

Higgins's study, which formed the basis of her book, consisted of forty case histories. All the people in her study grew up in dysfunctional families and were either physically or sexually abused. Higgins says that one half of the people in her study came from impoverished backgrounds, and most had at least one parent diagnosed with a serious mental disorder. Thirty-six of the resilient adults she studied had bonded to surrogates, which she calls "locuses of hope."

Where did these surrogates come from?

"You name it," Higgins says in a telephone interview. "They were neighbors, aunts, teachers. Almost anyone available for recruitment. Surrogates are everywhere. Someone cited her fifth-grade teacher, someone else cited the enormous impact a sixteen-year-old girl had on him from birth to age four. One guy was psychologically adopted in adolescence by people who worked in a grocery store. Because grocery stores are open long hours, he basically lived there and was more or less [raised] by the people who ran the store, in particular, the manager in the stock room."

While Higgins says that none of her subjects were in therapy as kids, some had bus drivers that became a surrogate parent by talking to the child and being emotionally available. You see, some children have parents who are physically present, and have all their physical needs met, but they lack the emotional bonds with their parents that are necessary for the normal development of human kinship bonds.

Although these surrogates were sometimes present in the child's life for a short time, they had a powerful, humanizing impact. The surrogates provided a model, an internal image, of whom they could become. These surrogates became a well from which the child could draw values and positive human qualities.

Higgins adds that what is startling in her study is the clarity of recall about surrogates. They were so important that the child kept feasting on the memory of these special people, kept on being illuminated by those experiences and were inspired throughout their lives. Coauthor Kent Bailey tells of a neighborhood child (a friend of his daughter), who volunteered to help him with a medical regimen following a serious accident. This simple encounter inspired her to pursue a career in nursing, and she graduated this spring. To this day, she loves to recount stories of her recalcitrant patient.

To grow up in a troubled family is alienating and painful. But just growing up in the modern city or vast urban sprawl can lead to feelings of alienation, anonymity, loneliness, and anxiety about strangers. Paradoxically, however, in the stranger lies our salvation. Friends, ministers, physicians, psychotherapists, an orthodontist, and even a hairdresser, can glide into our lives, offering relief, objectivity, patience and interest that our closest family members cannot provide. When the family is broken or unavailable, the city's benevolent strangers may be our only refuge. For it is from the ranks of benevolent strangers that most of our enduring psychological kinships are formed.

Healthy Role of Strangers

It is tempting to conclude, based on our ancestral heritage, that strong biological and psychological kinships are all that we need to achieve good health and emotional well-being. But if we are to solve our evolutionary mismatch dilemma of increasing strangers, we must begin to see strangers through a new lens, a kinder, more tender one. We must teach our children to see the *humanity* in other people.

The logic of mismatch theory quickly points to the central role that non-kin play in crowded urban and suburban life. No doubt kinship, social support, and tribal acceptance did go a long way toward good health in ancient environments, and these, along with ability to get along with one's enemies, also appear crucial to success in the modern world. Walt Whitman's prophetic poem entitled "I Dream'd in a Dream," published well over a century ago, foreshadows the growing importance of strangers in human life:

> I Dream'd in a dream I saw a city invincible to the attacks of the
>   whole rest of the earth,
> I dream'd that was the new city of Friends.
> Nothing was greater there than the quality of robust love, it led
>   the rest,
> It was seen every hour in the actions of the men of that city,
> And in all their looks and words.[15]

A sensitive, reflective man, Whitman explored this theme of alienation of the soul and the importance of embracing the stranger in many of his poems. Also consider "To a Stranger."

> Passing stranger! you do not know how longingly I look upon
>   you,
> You must be he I was seeking, or she I was seeking (It comes to me
>   as of a dream)
> I have somewhere surely lived a life of joy with you,
> All is recall'd as we flit by each other, fluid, affectionate, chaste,
>   matured,
> You grew up with me, were a boy with me or a girl with me
> I ate with you and slept with you, your body has become not yours
>   only nor left my body, mine only,
> You give me the pleasure of your eyes, face, flesh, as we pass, you
>   take my beard, breast, hands, in return
> I am not to speak to you, I am to think of you when I sit alone or
>   wake at night alone,
> I am to wait, I do not doubt I am to meet you again,
> I am to see to it that I do not lose you.[16]

Examining the archetypal stranger in our lives is far more critical to cultural and economic success today than it was in Whitman's era, because today, access to many social rewards and most material prizes in our industrialized society are controlled by strangers. Given the modern importance of material acquisition, money, and the desire for status and prestige, it seems reasonable to conclude that skills in mastering relationships with non-kin, acquaintances, and even enemies may be fundamental to survival and prosperity in our modern society.

Despite the overwhelming mismatch issues and kinship disruptions of today, it is not desirable to go back to loincloths, cooking by open fire, beating a drum to communicate, and hunting and gathering in small bands. But by creating kin-like bonds with acquaintances and strangers, we are drawing on the wisdom of our ancestors and restoring some of the balance lost in our hectic world. By re-creating these bonds we are throwing the proverbial "mismatched fish" back into water.

5

Alienation of Family

❦

"This family must take care of itself; it has no mother or father; there is no shelter, nor resource, nor any love, interest, sustaining strength or comfort, so near, nor can anything happy or sorrowful that comes to anyone in this family possibly mean to those outside it what it means to those within it; but it is, as I have told, inconceivably lonely, drawn upon itself as tramps are drawn round a fire in the cruelest weather; and thus and in such loneliness it exists among other families, each of which is no less lonely, nor any less without help or comfort, and is likewise drawn in upon itself. . . ."

—James Agee and Walker Evans[1]

Competition, says Christopher, and lack of emotional bonds, is what created the emotional separation and distance in his nuclear family. His poignant, heart-felt tale of a family gone awry holds lessons for us all.

A tall, fair-haired engineer in his early-thirties, Christopher grew up in Atlanta and describes the atmosphere when his relatives came to visit. "It was show time," he says, likening it to his teenage experience as a waiter at a local dinner theater. "When we had popular musicals, the manager made us go out in front of the big crowd in the lobby and yell: Ladies and gentleman, the show is about to begin! Like you were at a three-ring circus or something. Everybody would turn around. All the good-looking girls would laugh. You know, you had this goofy-looking bow tie on and an outdated fifties outfit, and here it was in the late seventies! You felt stupid. It was the last thing you wanted to do, but you had to do it to keep your job.

"That's exactly what it was like at [our house] with relatives: Go out and do this. Say this; act like this. You were totally coached. My mom had this image that you had to live up to."

Speaking in a rapid, annoyed tone, Christopher described holiday celebrations. "Obviously, we got to open our Christmas gifts like everyone else. But when the relatives came to visit, between Christmas morning all the way till New Year's Eve, you couldn't play with your toys. If [the presents] were clothes, you couldn't bring them upstairs. You couldn't move things around, you had to put them all back in the boxes, because when the relatives came you had to show all your gifts: 'This is what Santa gave me; this is what Uncle Marvin gave me; this is what Mom gave me.'

"And then I'd get the obligatory gift from my aunt, who was my Godmother. It was forever this ugly, outdated, odd-colored, nerdy shirt—to which I always, always, always had to reply, 'Wow, this is great. Thanks. Just what I needed.' It was stupid. I can't imagine she thought it was a sincere compliment. But it was something we always had to say.

"Those times stick in my mind because they're very typical of the way our family lived. The image was important, the show. In reality, it was crap. No one would say the truth. Over the years, it became uncomfortable to have my cousins and aunts and uncles around. I became accustomed, as a kid outside my house, to living somewhat of a truthful life.But I got sick of having to say and do the right thing [in my family].

"We all lived outside ourselves. My mother lived outside of herself for her job. As for my father, God knows where he was. Somewhere. But not there. There was no relationship. And I had no relationship with my sisters and brothers. There was nothing real, truthful, in that family. These 'Christmasy' experiences were a show, a rehearsal. They became arduous, at best; at worst, excruciating.

"You dreaded the notorious bell being rung by Aunt Julia, who always showed up, unannounced, just as we were about to sit down and eat [Christmas] dinner. After ten years, why didn't someone just say, 'Aunt Julia, we're eating between six-thirty and eight. Please don't come then.' Because that would be *truthful*. That would be honest. You don't want honesty, you want show. It was work. It was absolutely no fun. When I think about being with my relatives now, I don't have endearing memories.

"My mom told me several years ago that the competition between my aunts and uncles started when the kids came. According to my mom, they were [once] very close. But now, money, success meant everything. Family was nothing. Family was there to be stepped on; family was there to allow you to elevate yourself, to give you a place to parade your status. I remember one year, we got this expensive car. Within a year, every one of our aunts and uncles upgraded their cars for one like ours. Some of them really had to stretch to do it. Family gatherings existed so you could show your latest bauble, your latest mink, your new furniture. That was where you paraded your kids doing great in school or having a great job. It didn't matter about being happy. What mattered was that you were succeeding and they were failing, that second part being most important.

"For example, my Aunt Julia didn't give up until she talked to [a relative] one day and finally, finally found out that my 35-year-old sister did nails for a salon in the Pacific Northwest. For years, my aunt kept asking, 'How's Lisa doing?' hoping that one day she would find out what my mother's code words for my sister's job— 'the cosmetics industry'—really meant. It meant my sister manicured nails for a living. Now [my aunt] knows; now she doesn't have to ask anymore. Now my aunt can go on with her life and can scoff at my sister. There's no concern: 'Lisa is a bright, college-educated kid; You'd have thought she would have done a little more with her life. It's kind of a shame. Gosh, maybe I'll call. Maybe I'll say, Is there anything we can do, Lisa? Can we help?' You never got that. My relatives didn't want to help. They weren't there to help. They were there to criticize.

"You ask how I feel about getting together with my cousins or my sister and two brothers. Well, can I go through electric shock instead? The minute I sit down with them, there's gonna be the briefings, and debriefings: 'Oh Christopher, how's your job? How are your kids?' You just want to say, 'I'm making $600,000 a year. I'm driving a Mercedes. and you know what? I'm so-o-o-o unhappy,

I can't stand it. How about you?' Oh, god, it so painful I don't want to get together with them. I'm tired of it; these are not real relationships. I happen to be in this family genetically, which I have absolutely no say over. I wouldn't be on a deserted island with these people.

"I love my parents, but they were so traumatized by the [Great] Depression that status and security were paramount. My mother couldn't accept that we'd attained a certain status, and that she could relax, that she could enjoy her children and their childhood. There wasn't enjoyment. Enjoyment is not a word that's in my parent's vocabulary. Security is there, dependability, reliability, economic security. But love, trust, friendships, emotions—none of those things are in my parent's vocabulary."

Because of the lack of true family bonding in his childhood family, Christopher has done what many of us from unhealthy families do: we build a new family with our children, and work very hard to change the unhealthy, painful patterns of the past.

"Tonight is a good example," Christopher says. [My daughter] is playing Operation. I'll go down and spend twenty, thirty minutes playing with her. My son, before he went to sleep, I laid in bed with him for a second and talked. I told him, I said, 'Kyle, put your hand on your heart. You feel how hard that heart is beating? That's the love your mommy and daddy and [your sister] have for you. Think about that right before you go to sleep.' You have to make a choice to have these kinds of things in your life. They don't just come naturally. It's not a movie set. It's not a director going, 'Cue, roll'em. Okay cue line, let's hear the bells ringing.' You gotta find time. You gotta make time."

Family, with all of its familiar images of coziness, comfort, and intimacy is a wonderful, wonderful concept. Unfortunately, as Christopher's story shows us, that kind of family is not a reality for a whole lot of folks.

Many people are bound to their blood families: A sense of duty keeps them putting family first. It's quite natural, even though their families, through physical distance or friction, offer little nurturing, positive love, or esteem building. Indeed, geographic separations are not the only factor keeping today's families apart. You also have to look realistically at emotional separations, says Judith Viorst, best-selling author of *Necessary Losses* and *Redbook* columnist.

She used to feel that under no circumstances do you ever sever a relationship with blood relatives, she said in a telephone interview. "I have changed on that tune. Some people I have talked to have tried over and over again to repair relationships. Sometimes it's so bruising, so agonizing, to maintain a relationship, you have to walk away from it, always with the stipulation of leaving the door open a little bit in case a reconciliation is possible at some point later."

Families frequently get angry when members turn their back on relatives, but when you think about the natural affinity children have for their parents and families, you realize that it takes much trauma—emotional or physical—for children to pull totally away. The distance, though, say experts, usually correlates to the amount of pain inflicted upon those who leave.

Often, those who distance themselves from family feel guilt. Part of what drives this, say therapists, is not common sense or reality-tested experience, but the hyped-up media images of close-knit families, especially around the holidays. "Yet we've all had the experience of having some very bad times at [family] gatherings, says one expert, and we've sworn to ourselves, 'Never again!' "

In Cynthia Grant's young adult novel *Kumquat May, I'll Always Love You,* she aptly describes such a moment between family members. The heroine, fifteen-year-old Livvy, is living alone. Her mother has disappeared two years ago. Livvy is desperate to keep it a secret. "I was determined that no one would discover Mother's absence, picturing the twilight world of foster homes, or worse, the Twilight Zone of mother's brother, my Uncle Sargent."

But her uncle and his family show up on Thanksgiving. "Although I barely touched my food, I doubted that I would ever eat again. This was no dream; it was hideously real. I was marooned with a mob of relative strangers, hunched around a big dead bird; its skin shorn, its leg bones bared, its thick flesh clogging my throat."[2]

Indeed, families become warring tribes for a variety of reasons: competition, an inability to express emotions and love, jealousy, and issues over money and inheritance. "Scapegoating" is another common divider. Many of us have seen it happen in our own clan—just as sharks will instinctively turn on a wounded member of its school and eat it, humans will often emotionally, verbally, and sometimes even physically assault the hurting members of their family, emotionally spurning the wounded one from its midst.

This often happens in families where there is trauma—emotional, physical, or sexual. Trauma is a kind of stored psychic energy, and, say experts, to heal means to release that energy through grieving. Talking can release the pain. Crying can release it. And any kind of art form that *consciously* connects a person to unresolved grief—can release the bottled-up energy of trauma. When families minimize or can't face certain truths, they attack the messenger, sayer of the truth.

Despite perpetual conflicts in our families, however, many of us yearn for a kind of primal love from our families, described as "the instincts of the lioness for her cubs" by Ellen Bass and Laura Davis.

> This fierce, clear love isn't available to many survivors from their families. Instead, you may be offered love that is smothering, manipulative, controlling, or desperate. Love that doesn't take into account your needs is not really worthwhile. And love that requires you to compromise your integrity, your values, or your healing isn't ultimately love.
>
> Yet it can be terrifying to say no to any kind of love. You want it. The need for kinship and closeness is a basic human need. Even the songs tell you, All you need is love. If the love your family has to offer is the only kind of love you've ever known, it can be hard to trust that something better will take its place. When there is some real caring mixed in with the distorted need, it can be even more difficult to turn their love down. But when you start saying no to the kind of love that drains you, you open yourself to recognizing and receiving nourishing love.[3]

Although the recovery movement of the past twenty years offered hope that our toxic families would be cured—appealing to the hopeful child in all of us that wants to believe all fractured relationships can be repaired—for some, connecting with family is neither healthy or in their best interest.

Separations

"Separations from family can be part of developing healthier relationships," write Bass and Davis in *The Courage to Heal*. "A period of separation can help you sort out the good from the bad and determine exactly what, if anything is salvageable. It can also help you replace the child's longing with the realistic vision of the adult.

"If you decide to make a separation for the sake of your own healing, you will have to let go, grieve, and move on. If you want to reconcile at some point in the future, you can try from your own willingness, knowing there are no guarantees. And if you decide that a permanent separation allows you to live a saner life, that's a responsible decision."[4]

But how do we let go of our non-functioning biological families in a healthy, non-punitive way and prepare ourselves to succeed in forming close friendships? Here, the experts are in agreement: mourning. According to the authors, Bass and Davis, by grieving— purging the sadness, anger, fear, and the guilt that typically accompanies your family not being what you wanted it to be—you free up tremendous amounts of energy and make room for new emotional connections. Despite our differences and no matter how far away we move, we still love our biological families deeply. Our shared history can never be replaced. Nevertheless, breaking free from the family fold to form deep adult bonds is a natural maturation process, even in healthy families.

The Teen Years

For many of us, the process of re-creating family is an unconscious part of a series of natural developmental stages in our lives. The boundary between adolescence and young adulthood is marked by leaving the family to make our way in the world. So, to prepare us for that leavetaking, starting in our early teens, we begin seriously and systematically to transfer our feelings toward family, by forging the intense, all-consuming friendships that are a hallmark of adolescence. We begin to form our first intentional families.

Anthropologist Dr. Helen Fisher, in *Anatomy of Love,* asserts that it is to a teenager's adaptive advantage to make alliances with peers. The teen years are literally a time of "hanging out" of the family, but not too far, because this vulnerable age is also fraught with ambivalence. "I have the role of pushing out of my family," explains fifteen-year-old Heather. "My [younger] sister sucks up to my parents. I have to break the ice for everything." In the next breath, Heather adds, "When I don't feel well at school, though, I usually call my mother, because I need to hear the sound of her voice. My friends are like that with their mothers, too."

"Friends assume an overweening importance at this stage for an expedient reason: they make it feel safe to break away from the parental fold and forge a separate identity—the central developmental task of adolescence," Ellen Graham writes in a *Wall Street Journal* article, "Going from child to adult, you go over a bridge of your peers." Friends naturally, and rightly, begin to take the place of family throughout adolescent and college years. Through friends we develop the psychological and social ability to manage life on our own.[5]

Quoting Anna Freud, Judith Viorst writes in *Necessary Losses,* that it is "normal for an adolescent to behave in an inconsistent and unpredictable manner; to fight his impulses and to accept them; to ward them off successfully and to be overrun by them; to love his parents and to hate them; to revolt against them and to be dependent on them; to be deeply ashamed to acknowledge his mother before others and, unexpectedly, to desire heart-to-heart talks with her. . . . Such fluctuations would be deemed highly abnormal at any other times of life."[6]

Perhaps because the process of becoming an adult takes so long, or perhaps because it is such a perilous emotional journey, adolescent friendships—for better or worse—leave a lasting impression.

Joyce, who is hovering near fifty, still gets teary eyed when she talks about the group of girls she went to high school with in the mid-sixties. "They know your history. There's nobody who knows your history the way old friends do," she says. "Being an only child, it's like they were my family. I knew they were only a phone call away. When we went away to college, we wrote to each other and still do.

"These friendship were so poignant, because we were just getting into our teen years when we met [a few she had known since first grade]. We were breaking away from the confines of our parents and all the rules of home. We were broadening our horizons. What we had in common were our intellects—the fact that we were in the same class, on the same academic track, for the most part. It was the awakening of adolescence, of getting breasts, of starting to have boyfriends that were serious, going to dances. It was the first time we were allowed to do things [on our own]."

In terms of prizing their independence, things haven't changed that much for teens today. A group of thirty-four students I surveyed at a suburban high school vividly illustrate that the process of becoming an adult, of separating from parents, is softened by the natural process of powerfully bonding to friends.

Some of Their Responses

"Friends bring out the person you really are. They are sort of like an extended family. Therefore, you feel safe separating from your parents, because they are like a back-up family."

"Friends are like you, a teen, and know what you are going through. You can relate better with peers. You can talk to them better than with your parents."

"My friends are a whole, separate family on their own. We are extremely close. My friends have helped me mature and move away from the family hold. I also believe that I have had a similar effect on them. It's something we go through together."

"There is a time to depend on your parents and a time to be your own independent person."

"The bond between friends helps to influence the path of life people might take. Each friend you encounter, you create another building block of your own personality, and the building blocks create a person."

Respondents were also asked to fill out the "family-love" scale, adapted from Dr. Bailey's Kinship Scale, below.

Using scores between one and ten, students rated their closest friend, or boyfriend or girlfriend. A score of one means low importance; ten, high importance.

1. Hug me if I'm upset
2. Feel love for me
3. Remember me ten years from now
4. Still like me even if I do something wrong
5. Be available when I need him/her
6. Treat me like a member of the family
7. Be a loving person
8. Feel I am important in her/his life
9. Share a strong feeling of closeness with me

Almost one-third assigned a score of ten to the statement 6: treat me like a member of the family.

Although conventional wisdom predicates that peers have a greater influence over teens than parents, our survey showed that isn't always the case. When asked "Whose opinion matters more to you—your parents or your friends?" more than one-third of the respondents answered "parents." Almost another third answered "both."

Nevertheless, teens overwhelmingly and predictably favored *being with* friends. Nearly two-thirds indicated they'd rather spend time with friends than parents, and most of the rest answered "both."

Sex differences are also part of the teen picture. The Gustavo Nava study, conducted with Dr. Kent Bailey, measuring psychological kinship in students, revealed that the transition to deep friendship or psychological kinship occurs more rapidly for boys than for girls. The data suggested that a fairly coherent pattern of kinship, love, liking, and attachment seems to characterize relations between girls and their closest parent, but not relationships with their boyfriends. By contrast, boys showed a coherent pattern of affiliation with their girlfriend, but not with the closest parent. For boys, kinship with their girlfriend was associated with amount of time spent together and the perceived amount of caring and emotional support they received.

Another interesting variation on kinship came from research conducted by Dawn Lewis and Dr. Kent Bailey. Their study compared female African-American kinship with female Caucasian kinship at the college level, and uncovered some interesting differences between races. Surveying fifty-six African-American women and fifty-six white women on various kinship measures, Lewis discovered that kinship between same-sex best friends is far more powerful among white females than it is for black females. The white women in her study appeared to not have as strong an extended family as the black women; nor had they strongly committed themselves to boyfriend relationships. Thus, for white women, their best girlfriend is an integral part of their live, whereas black women appeared to have a much broader notion of kinship relationships with family and friends.

These findings suggest an interesting question for further

research: "Do Caucasian and African-American females take different developmental paths in making the transition from biological to psychological kinship?" Broadly interpreted, the Lewis data, suggests that African-American college women follow the traditional extended-family pattern where psychological kinships spread widely to same- and opposite-sex friends, while Caucasian women follow a more restricted path, which seems to go directly from parents to best girlfriend and only later do boyfriends, as the primary focus, enter the picture.

Gender, race, and a host of other variables influence teen kinship and friendships, but one fact is clear: With divorce ripping so many nuclear and extended families right down the middle and forcing both parents to work to support two households, teens today are on their own more than ever before. For this reason, the need to create intentional families takes on even more urgency for teens. Take, for example, Mira, a sixteen-year-old suburban teen:

> My friends are like my family. They play an important role in my life. Since I have divorced parents, there isn't someone always there. [Mira's Dad lives in another state and her mom works full time.] My friends provide me with a cushion to fall on when my family isn't there. My best friend, Happy Anne, is like my sister. She also acts like my mother. She looks after me when I am upset. Happy Anne is the most important friend in my life. My other best friend is Trey. He acts like my father. (Trey and Happy Anne are not a couple!!) If he was not around things wouldn't be the same. The reason I know they care for me is that I show them I care for them like a family. We always tell each other to be quiet because we sound like our parents.

> We try to make special days really special. This year for my 16th birthday, Happy Anne and Trey made it the most special day of my life—they made it last for eight days. It all started on Halloween. This year they were out to embarrass me. Well, they did a good job. We went to the mall, and they made me walk around for an hour. Around five o'clock, they made me walk to the music store where this really cute guy gave me a rose. I do not think I will ever go there again. The next day was my [actual] birthday. Trey came to pick me up and said we were going back to his house. [Happy Anne was there], and they made me sit in a room for a few minutes before they let me out. I had a big cake

with trick candles waiting for me. Nice things like that happened all week: I got balloons at school two days in a row and roses. I got phone calls and dinner. This year's birthday was the best ever thanks to them. If I didn't have Happy Anne and Trey my life would fall apart. Sometimes there are things you can tell your parents, but not everything. That's why I need my friends. If you have a group of friends you really care about, they will care for you back, and your life is much easier.

Many young people find kinship bonds in team sports. "Sports families" become their refuge, their home away from home. By participating in team sports teens garner a sense of belonging and learn to trust people outside their biological families.

When you have eleven girls out on a hockey field, "if they don't get along, if they don't trust one another, they are not going to win," explains high school coach Rachel Mead. She works very hard to create team unity by organizing group activities. "I make them do things together. I try to do team-oriented things. Like we have this huge rock down on our field. I stand one person up on the rock and make them shut their eyes and hold their hands above their head. The team has to stand behind them. When they [the person on the rock] falls . . . the girls have to catch them. They're horrified, but they do it, 'cause they know that it teaches them to trust their teammates."

Forming sports families can be a lifesaver for kids whose blood families are not stable, or even intact. Experts say this powerful sense of belonging can offset some of the stress that today's teens live with: the death of a parent, divorce, two-career families, the lack of grandparents, aunts, and so on.

In addition to the enormous pressure to make good grades, be popular, and get into competitive schools, today's teens also face pressure to have sex earlier than in past generations, use drugs and alcohol, and smoke cigarettes.

It's tough to be a kid today. Indeed, according to the 1995 Statistical Abstracts of the United States, a mere 26 percent of American households are made up of two-parent families with children. In addition, the staggering number of blended and step families are also, say experts, a major stressor for teens.

Prior to the industrial revolution, 80 percent of the population lived on farms. There was no distinction between family and work, Dr. David Walsh, writes in *Selling Out America's Children*. Kids worked alongside their parents. They were groomed for what their parents did, and, consequently learned both a skill and family values.

In the past, parents had more power over their children, over what vocations their children chose, and in some cultures over whom they married. Our highly technical, mobile society has changed that. These days, parents aren't close enough to their children to wield such power, which many teens would say is a good thing. But the down side is that the continuity across generations is not as strong as it was historically.

Families also used to be a refuge, where the young were protected from the gratuitous violence and blatant sex that is manipulatively used by the media today to seize young people's attention. Television, with its powerful images and instant gratification, MTV, and our culture's relentless emphasis on material objects have produced a sophistication and a confusion in teens today. This bombardment of media images, plus the reality that even in two-parent families, children today are neglected because both parents are often so busy, shows a true lack of nurturing.

Christopher O'Kennon, in his essay entitled "Leave It to Butthead," states, "While we're all trying to earn a living, no one is bringing up Beaver." Answering the question "Who's raising our children?" he writes: "We certainly aren't. There was a time when our children always had a primary caregiver around. It was usually Mom, but Pop could do a good job, too. Just as long as it was one of them.[7]

"But the economic realities of today's world have steamrollered over that idea for all but the upper-class of our society. Good ol' Mom has been sucked away by the economy, and the children are either left with strangers—who will fake sincerity at an hourly rate [and which may never progress even to a "kin-like" relationship]— or left with that familiar friend, the television.

"As clever as the Power Rangers might be, it's hard to raise kids in thirty-minute chunks of recycled civic duty mixed in with some hearty butt-kicking. Sit and watch television eight hours straight. That's what's raising your children. We're ending up with a bunch of adolescents with short attention spans, a glamorized approach to violence, and a deep-rooted belief that every problem can be resolved in under and hour (and if not, kick the problem in the head).

"Whatever television is teaching, it isn't remotely associated with thinking. In a world of soundbites and sixty-second pitches, the MTV generation is learning that they don't have to have an attention span to be catered to: Madison Avenue will deliver the world in dazzling colors and breathtaking wrap-around sound. So what if it's a meaningless batch of eye candy."

O'Kennon goes on to say that television is not the worst teacher our kids are finding while their parents are off trying to support the family. In many cases they're learning from the social disasters already in place: gangs. "Gangs give a clear message to children," he writes. "Join us and you'll have a family that will care for you, provide for you, and give your life some meaning. We used to have parents for that. . . . The message may be warped, but without the benefit of experience, it poses a very tempting offer."[8]

Although they often promote violence and drug use, gangs also provide a poignant example of modern intentional families; they offer a sense of belonging and nurturing that many troubled teens yearn for. Experts say, any person under the right environmental or emotional stresses may look to gangs, or even cults, for a sense of belonging to family.

While the breakdown of the family can be observed at every socioeconomic level, but especially among the poor, the absence of family support can be devastating. Richmond Sheriff Michelle Mitchell, one of only twenty women sheriffs in the U.S., says that three generations of one family were in the Richmond City Jail—at the same time—grandmother, daughter and grandson. "This is not atypical," she says. "Families provide a service in this community—setting goals and having expectations for members. When you don't have that, you have this chaos that we're seeing now."[9]

Denny Gaulden, who was introduced in chapter 1, agrees, for he's worked in the Virginia Department of Corrections for more than twenty years and sees kids' motivation for joining gangs, and the results, everyday. They're a substitute for family, he says. "If the kids don't have a [family] they'll find other means to get it." Troubled kids reach out for the first thing to come along that gives them even a tiny inkling of some kind of bonding, even if it's a gang.

Gaulden believes that the breakdown of the family is the root of all evil. "Every criminal I see, every inmate I see—it all has something to do with the breakdown of the family."

The Changing Rules of Family

Experts agree that no society, including the smallest society—the family—survives without rules. These rules, which translate into social customs and rituals, provide order and stability concerning marriage, inheritance, and descent. These rules also determine who should live together, whom it's appropriate to have sex with, and how family members are honored and taken care of at death.

While some social rules, especially those that forbid sex with family members, are universal—for psychologically sound reasons, and to avoid genetic abnormalities—other rules that dictate how we choose a mate, the number of times we can marry, family size, authority of gender roles, and burial practices change over time and vary from one culture to the next.

Most traditional anthropological definitions of kinship emphasize blood relationship, genealogy, gender roles, shared cultural symbols, and rules of social exchange. These definitions have been relevant for eons because, for most of human history, kin—blood kin as well as spouses and adopted children—were more likely to share time together over an entire life span, live in the same residence, care for each other when sick, and were most likely to participate in lineage-based marriage, funeral, and holiday rituals.

For many baby boomers, the paragon of the ancestral, loyal, blood family is the Waltons. Memorably portrayed in the 1970s television show, "The Waltons" chronicled a large clan surviving the Great Depression, while eking out a living in the Blue Ridge Virginia Mountains. (And through decades of re-runs, many of today's generation Xers, many from divorced and scattered families, also grew up watching "The Waltons.") The show, based on director Earl Hamner Jr.'s personal experiences, has been enormously popular because it taps into middle America's yearning for a return to a simpler time, when family life was valued and was an integral part of daily human existence.

When the show first aired, a time when the political scandal of Watergate was further shaking people's confidence in government, and a time when society was adjusting to wide-spread social changes of the turbulent 1960s—the tameness of the show struck a chord. John and Grandpa Zeb, the kind family patriarchs, operated a lumber mill. The family was close knit but poor, although that fact was romanticized. The family drama was told through the point of view of John boy, the oldest son. In each episode, he espoused down-home, family morals of togetherness that reigned supreme over materialism. There was none of the sex and violence that abounds on television today.

"It is easy to exaggerate the appeal of the good old days," writes Dr. Lee Salk in his book *Familyhood*. While in the "past there may indeed have been more nuclear families, less pervasive problems of crime, delinquency and drug abuse than today, behind closed doors, within the safe structure of those families, life was far from perfect," he writes. "The taboos and ignorance surrounding sexuality created confusion and anguish for many. For women who wished to work or assume roles in public life, options were limited. Fathers were often isolated from the lives of their growing children, both by the demands of being the family provider and by cultural norms that established the mother as the child-raiser. In many significant ways, the good old days did not offer a lifestyle we would seek to duplicate today, even if that were possible."[10]

And for those who look back to childhood, longing fondly for the good old Mayberry days when Aunt Bea or grandma lived down the street, we might stop and consider what it may have been like for the grownups. Too much of a good thing, say sociologists, may not be that good!

While moderate closeness to family may promote well being, living too near, or in the same dwelling, with each other may produce stress: "In addition to actual crowding, multi-generational households frequently encounter an array of problems, including lifestyle differences, increased household tasks and expenses, and failure to accomplish 'role clarity' among members," Christopher G. Ellison writes. "The presence of extended family members in nearby dwellings or neighborhoods may engage individuals as unwilling participants in family problems and disputes, disrupting the peace of immediate family relations. Such geographic [closeness] may also reduce the sense of individual autonomy and identity."[11]

Looking further back in history at the pre-modern family of

white Colonial Americans, things were not as rosy as they appeared, either. Even then, the family was considered to be an "economic, social and political unit that subordinated the individual to corporate family interests, and subordinated women and children to the patriarchal head," according to Judith Stacey, in her controversial book *Brave New Families.*

> Decisions regarding the timing and crafting of pre-modern marriages served not the emotional needs of individuals but the economic, religious, and social purposes of larger kin groups, as these were interpreted by patriarchs who controlled access to land, property and craft skills.

> Nostalgic images of "traditional" families rarely recall their instability or diversity. Death visited colonial homes so frequently that second marriages and blended households composed of stepkin were commonplace. With female submission thought to be divinely prescribed, conjugal love was a fortuitous bonus, not a prerequisite of such marriages. Similarly, the doctrine of innate depravity demanded authoritarian parenting to break the will and save the souls of obstinate children. . . . Few boundaries . . . segregated the sexes who labored at their arduous and interdependent tasks in close proximity. Boundaries between public and private life were equally permeable. Communities regulated proper family conduct, intervening actively to enforce disciplinary codes, and parents exchanged their children as apprentices and servants.[12]

To borrow from an old Bob Dylan tune, "The times they are a changin'." Indeed, they have changed, dramatically. Today, with women a bedrock in the workforce, our society has become less patriarchal and more egalitarian. In the United States, with its rich cultural and racial tapestry, no one child-rearing practice reigns supreme. And yet another break from the past: today, few of us have a relationship with our first cousins, let alone relationships with an extended clan of second and third cousins, or great aunts and uncles. For a variety of reasons, kinship ties with biological relatives are no doubt weaker than in the past.

One reason for weaker family ties is the fact that many children are not being reared together by both biological parents. It is estimated that only 6 percent of black children and 30 percent of white children born in 1980 will live with both biological parents through the age of eighteen. In 1950, those figures were 52 percent for black children and 81 percent for white children.

While marriage is a powerful form of psychological kinship, there is more stress on marriage today. Modern couples do not spread their "reservoir of affection" across a twenty-five- to fifty-member clan, nor can they count on that clan to help sustain them in difficult times. Vast geographic distances, which can account for differences in personal traits, social customs, ethnicity, and religion, also impede the chances for a sustained union. Historically, marriage partners typically came from neighboring, often similar, tribes; only a few decades ago, they met at their local high school.

Our modern reliance on and our passion for abundant material pleasures also pulls us away from family. Now, instead of hunting or gathering with family members, we go out into a world of strangers to earn money. The pressure fueled by two-career families makes it more difficult to a nurture marriage or parental ties. Indeed, weekends in many modern homes are an exhaustive whirlwind of cleaning, grocery shopping, doing laundry, mowing lawns, caring for gardens, shopping for clothes—all aimed toward getting ready for the next work week, when there will be precious little personal or family time.

Brought about by divorce, death and separation, there are 8 million single working mothers in this country, and 2 million single working fathers, according to a 1994 survey by the U.S. Bureau of Labor Statistics.

Yet another major reason for weaker kinship bonds is our ever-increasing mobility. As we said earlier, too much closeness can be stressful. On the other hand, too much distance can water relationships down to nothing but civil exchanges at holidays, weddings, funerals, and other ceremonial gatherings. Cars, planes, computer travel—all allow us to move away from home base, in ways that were impossible in days gone by.

Geographic ties once bound nuclear and extended families together. Contrast our current mobility with life just more than four decades ago. In 1954, according to William Manchester, less than 15 million adults, or 15 percent of all adults, had been more than 250 miles from home, the equivalent (then) of one day's ride in an automobile. . . . One American in four had not seen either the Atlantic or Pacific Ocean. Although nine out of ten adults had been

on a train, trips by air, though rising in popularity, were still pre-
ferred by a minority. The average worker lived two miles from his
job and could get there in about eighteen minutes.[13]

In the 1990s, travel has created a vastly different cultural and
racial landscape. Anthropologists refer to the rapid mixing of different races as the "browning of America," and predict that in the
future intermingling between Caucasians and Hispanic, African
American, Asian, American Indian, and Middle-Eastern races will
create a kind of "mono-American look" of medium-toned skin,
dark hair, and dark eyes, a look vastly different from the stereotypi-
cal "all-American" look of today: blonde hair and blue eyes. In fact,
population projections estimate that by the year 2050, Caucasians
will barely be in the majority. In time, similar physical appearance, a
collective history and common values will reduce the differences
among minority groups and unite still larger bands of people.

Geographers assert that in societies where there is advanced economic and technological progress, particularly in communication
and transportation, there will also be a corresponding increase in
mobility and migration. In the United States, for example, one
fourth of its residents do not reside in the state in which they were
born, and every year about one out of five Americans moves to a
new residence. Many move in search of higher wages, better jobs,
and general improvements in their quality of life.

Communicating online, Joanie describes her own migration
path: "I've lived in England, Las Vegas, and Alaska during the last
decade. Fortune's been kind. I've had the same family of friends
through it all. If you guessed military, you guessed right. I'm closer
to my friends than most of my relations. Together, we've gone
through triumphs and tears. Births, deaths, job promos and losses.
Baseball champs, near-divorce. We've been through too much
together. They really are more than friends."

In addition to creating physical separation, distance by its very
nature creates emotional distance. We relate differently to people
who are part of our everyday life, people who accompany us to the
hospital when our child needs surgery, help celebrate our birthdays,
take us out to dinner when we get a promotion. People who watch,
in flesh and blood, and participate in our children's growing up
years.

When Becky's husband lost his job, she went to visit her brother in another city. When she mentioned the considerable financial support her friends had given her, her brother responded, "I didn't know you needed help." It had never occurred to Becky to ask her brother for help; nor did he offer.

Indeed, many times we expect the people who are related to us by blood to understand what we need and come to our rescue. Sadly, that doesn't often happen, sometimes even when we make those needs known. On the other hand, some of us are so emotionally entwined with our biological families that when we need their help, they're so preoccupied with their own feelings about what's happening to us that they can't be there for us.

"We are very close. Too close, maybe, because we worry about getting the other person upset or overly concerned," says Martha, talking online, about her two sisters and parents. "Since my family is so helpful and supportive, I sometimes don't like to tell them what is bothering me because it may upset them. I know I can tell my friends. Yes, They will get upset, but I think they get over it faster." Martha, who lives in New York, says she and her best friend have been friends since they were five years old. They're both thirty-two now.

Martha's situation is not unusual. Often, understanding—that elusive quality of emotional honesty that we traditionally expect from blood relatives—we find in friends. (Unless we are exceedingly lucky and find openness and tolerance for pain and success in our traditional families!) But how many of us have been surrounded by loved ones with whom we are genetically related, but to whom we cannot express our deepest feelings because they make our loved ones feel uncomfortable? If we are failing they are embarrassed. If we are succeeding too much, they feel competitive. And if we refer to unresolved difficulties in the past, we are stirring up pain, and our families avoid us until we get over the past. We cannot be ourselves in these relationships.

Lack of understanding and acceptance happens in ordinary and famous families alike. Demi Moore has spoken publicly about her estrangement from her mother and father, both of whom are alcoholic, have gotten in trouble with the law, and have repeatedly embarrassed her. Jacqueline Bouvier Kennedy Onassis had stopped being close to her sister, Lee Radziwill, long before Jackie died. Sibling rivalry—competition over status and money—was apparently the great divide. Diana DuBois, author of *In her Sister's Shadow: An Intimate Biography of Lee Radziwill,* reports that Aristotle Onassis has originally been Lee Razidwill's lover. And although Jacqueline gave money to Lee throughout her lifetime, Jacqueline did not leave her any money in her will, which was a "testament to their frayed connection," according to DuBois. "That frayed relationship was also reportedly why Jackie's children didn't ask their aunt to speak at Jackie's funeral."[14]

Rich or poor, to feel good in relationships, we must master the talent for transcending universal obstacles of jealousy and competition that exist in all human relationships, and we must acquire skills to work through the major, as well as petty, disagreements that will surely surface. To feel good in relationships, we need affirmation. We need acceptance. We need to be heard. How many times do people describe someone they are close to this way: "She was such a good listener," or, "I could really talk to him; he understands me"?

Experts say it is impossible to overemphasize the immense need humans have to be really listened to, to be taken seriously, to be understood. In fact, a major reason for the birth of psychiatry is that many people have no one in their lives who truly listens to them. That thwarted need for someone to listen is the basis for much loneliness and mental illness.

If we say we are depressed and a family member reminds us that we have a great husband and kids, we are not being listened to. Sound petty? It's not. In the midst of over five billion people on this earth, many of us feel very much alone, because all too often our feelings are minimized or washed away by people uncomfortable with feelings. Right or wrong, feelings can create reality. So our feelings, good and bad, ought to be heard and acknowledged. Whether it's through blood relatives or our family of psychological kinship—friends—we deserve to be affirmed.

Red, a mason in his mid-fifties, says he talks to his mother each weekend, but he's not close to her. She never listens, he says. The conversations revolve around her and she usually focuses on the negative. Red's siblings are spread throughout the country. To compensate, Red has found a family in his friends. In fact, he found one of his closest friends when his kids were little and he was coaching Little League. "The mothers would sit up in the stands and visit," he says. "Practice lasted three or four months before the games started.

By the time the season begins, the mothers have grown close to each other. You know, 'Let's go to my house for coffee after the game.'

"It's usually the fathers and the assistant coaches, or the rival coaches, who are good friends, and they bring the wives into it." One of the women in the stands, Bootsie, a friend of Red's wife, kept screaming so loud that Red yelled, "Shut up, sit down, and let me coach!" But they became fast friends. Since then their families have spent many holidays and taken many a camping trip together. Red met his wife when he was in the Air Force stationed in New York. And there, "we developed 'buddies,' " he says. "We enjoyed that more. Families have more of a tendency to criticize than to listen," he says.

A quote from Mother Teresa in *The Sun, A Magazine of Ideas,* sums up our critical need for fellowship and affirmation.

> When Christ said, I was hungry and you fed me, he didn't mean only the hunger for bread and for food; he also meant the hunger to be loved. Jesus himself experienced this loneliness. He came amongst his own and his own received him not. It hurt him then and it has kept on hurting him. The same hunger, the same loneliness, the same having no one to be accepted by and to be loved and wanted by. Every human being in that case resembles Christ in his loneliness.[15]

Our modern need for psychological kinship, however, is not an excuse to adopt kin-like behavior for profit or political power; to abandon responsibility for our children or the elderly because we want new, less-demanding kin; nor is it an excuse for immoral, aging egomaniacs to get rid of older, familiar spouses for newer, exciting models.

As a therapist once said, "*Dysfunctional* does not mean disposable." In a culture where family problems are magnified and family desertions exploited in the media for entertainment—unless there are egregious kinship violations—having a troubled family is not an excuse to abandon our relatives.

Maintaining contact with blood family members gives us a sense of history. When deep intimacy is not possible, because of geographic or emotional distance, maintaining even minimal ties, a civil relationship of exchanging cards and holiday greetings, can be comforting.

6

Kinship in the Nineties

❧

"A good friend is my nearest relation."
—Thomas Fuller

Our rules of kinship are indeed changing to meet our deepest craving for caring companionship. And correspondingly, our choice of kin is changing, too. Dr. Richard Sherman, a clinical psychologist for twenty years, who practices in Southern California, called these new connections "purposeful relationships," in a telephone interview.

Our modern society, with its dysfunctional families, easily dissolved marriages, scattered relatives and exploding population is forcing us to become increasingly skillful in developing "kin-like" relations with an ever-increasing range of individuals. Today, it is important that we develop an open attitude and the skills necessary to survive and prosper in this increasingly larger world of strangers. Intentional families offer us new ways of extending kinship where the old ones are failing.

Sherman sees people who are not blood relatives forming long-term connections to reestablish the idealized family they'd wished for but don't have. He sees clients who are buying houses together, living together, say as two single moms, who aren't necessarily divorced or gay. "Years ago it was unheard of for people who were not blood connected to buy a house together," he says.

But now, the overwhelming reasons people reclassify friends as kin are part social and part financial. Sherman describes two women who are close fiends. One of the women owned a home, but couldn't maintain the mortgage. Her friend moved in and later brought her boyfriend. But the woman and her boyfriend split up. The two women remain living together, however, and have maintained a strong, close platonic bond.

"We're blessed in this country with many choices, and also cursed with many choices," Sherman explains. "In the early and middle part of this century, family bonds were automatic. Unlike today, relatives lived close together in row houses, or lived under one roof. Historically, people also had larger families, which took more time." Each member inherited a lot of responsibility. Often, teens had to work to help support the family, and there the modern debate about whether to take care of aging parents was practically unheard of.

Because people were tied to one another, there wasn't the built-in loneliness there is today, continues Sherman. On the positive side, people without the extended family of the past are selecting companions with whom they share interests and good feelings. Many friends become more like family than people's own family. People communicate with their friends more, and want to spend more time with them.

Besides forging unconventional financial arrangements, friends are relying on each other in many substantive ways, historically reserved for next of kin.

Changes in Descent

Molly's story epitomizes how old, outdated notions of kinship have been replaced by more modern ways of relating. Her husband, Rob, a salesman for a large company, travels around the world. Molly accompanies him several times a year. Whenever they traveled together, however, Molly and Rob worried about their will, which left Molly's sister as guardians of their two small sons.

Molly's parents lived in another state. Rob's parents lived even further away. Various siblings lived around the country. Molly's sister, who was named guardian in the will, lived in the same town, but Molly rarely socialized with her. The two got along all right, but disagreed about values. Molly described her sister's twelve-year-old son as a typical latch-key kid, spoiled and wild.

Finally, unable to live with their choice, Molly and Rob changed their will—just before a trip to Europe—naming as guardians former neighbors and close friends whom the kids knew as Aunt Leah and Uncle Victor.

"When we moved into [our old neighborhood], like everybody else, we moved from somewhere else and family was not there," says Molly. "They [Leah and Victor] lived across the street and one house over. We got to be real close friends."

> Leah and her husband had two boys, eight and ten. They were the nicest children, the ones everybody was envious of. They were the all American-type family. She worked part-time while the kids went to school.
>
> When I got pregnant with Joshua, Leah and I had only chatted as casual friends. She was a baby lover. This was the first baby on that street. For the whole pregnancy Leah was always around, telling me stories of when she was pregnant. When I had a boy (she had two boys), she just went nuts. She was over all the time and wanting to help out. Our friendship really developed. Because she is ten years older, and her husband is three or four years older than she, we didn't start off as girlfriends. She started off as a mentor and a helper. I was on my own having my first baby, and questioning everything.
>
> There's one thing I've learned from Leah that I'm going to keep for when I'm a grandmother. When I would go over there with my children, she'd be so respectful.
>
> "What do you want me to do first?" she'd say.
>
> So many times, I'd tell her, "But you know what to do."
>
> "I know" she'd say, "but I want to do it *your* way."
>
> It made me feel like Supermom.
>
> The first time I tried to go out I left Joshua with her. Right away she wanted to be called "aunt." "Come to Aunt Leah!" she'd say. Then she would come over any free time and visit and say, "I'm taking Joshua," and she'd leave. Just take him. She's very south-

ern: "Yawl go out! Go leave me alone!" This is just how she is. Or, she'd just take the baby, and I'd call to see how he was, and she'd say "What do you want! He's fine!" She's a riot.

When we decided to go to Hawaii—Rob had a company trip when Joshua was six months old—we asked Charlotte if she'd keep him the whole week. She was the first person we wanted to ask. She jumped at it. And I'll tell you, when we came back he was theirs! He was one of them. They ate up every minute. As the kids got older, they were the babysitters. We never had anybody else babysit.

We were spoiled. When we moved [to a bigger house in a nearby neighborhood] and their boys went to college, it was frightful. When I had Daniel, he came early. I called them in the middle of the night; Rob was traveling out of town. They had to come over to take care of Joshua and shuttle me to the hospital. They took care of Joshua until my mom came in town.

Daniel has always been fussy. Somebody had to hold him, usually had to be Mom. He wouldn't even go to Rob when he was a baby. But Leah could hold him. Here it is, five years now, Daniel stands back, not sure of people; clings to me a little more. My [in laws] were up here last week. They tried so hard. Joshua is good going to them. But Daniel has never been warm with my mother-in-law.

Leah and Victor came over one night. You know, they're family, they have to come and visit the in-laws. They know them as well as anybody. Daniel hardly wants to sit by my [in-laws], but Leah and Victor walk in the door and Daniel goes running into Leah's arms. I felt real bad. It's just how it is. [My in-laws] are nice, kind people, very good to the children. They just don't see them as often.

Leah is like me. I am very particular about what I feed my children! Very retentive as far as cleaning and taking care of the kids. It's just who I am. This is probably what gravitated us toward each other. She's got two honor students. She stayed on them with studying. She's raised them really well. Normal people, they just did a good job.

If they aren't home, the second place my sons would rather be is at Leah and Victor's. That's their refuge from the world.

Jill, a professor of astrophysics at a college outside of Boston, has also designated close friends as guardians to her small children, one-year-old daughter, Lucy, and a son Petie, four. Unlike Molly, Jill's reasons for choosing someone outside her family as potential guardians to her children had to do with emotional conflict within the family. In the advent of Jill and her husband's death, they chose friends from church to raise their kids, and chose another friend to manage the insurance money their children would inherit.

Jill, communicating online, says when her mother found out about her will, she screamed, "How can you leave them outside the family?" But Jill felt angry, saying her mother didn't care about what was best for the children, she only cared about how it would look if Jill died and didn't choose her family to raise her kids.

Explaining that she'd love to leave her children with her brother, whom she describes as a "roving archeologist," Jill says she knows his lifestyle is not conducive to raising children, at least not now. As for her sister, Jill says they are so different you'd think they were from different planets. Jill ruled her out as a possible guardian because her sister made it clear she doesn't want kids. As for designating her mother, who's in her sixties, Jill and her husband ruled that out, too.

Jill's story of family conflict is representative of many stories we heard while conducting interviews for this book. On a trip to Florida to visit her mother, Jill described her mom as awful to her son.

> It was really hot, and we were locked in the house for days. We were staying at my Mom's place. I'm never going to do that again. I didn't rent a car, 'cause I thought we could borrow hers. But she kept taking off with the car and leaving us in the house, just saying, "Oh well, I'm sure you can find something to do."
>
> When we would take Petie out to the park, she'd say "Well, I was going to take you to do something." And when we'd want to go out, she'd say, "No they're predicting thunderstorms today!" Florida—they do this everyday. My mother didn't want to go anywhere. She was being weird.
>
> Finally, after three or four days of being locked in the house, Petie didn't want to watch any more videos. He started losing it a little bit. She had a fit! She sat at the dinner table one night and told me right in front of him that he was out of control, that he was a brat.

That he was never going to grow up and be anybody worthwhile, 'cause I was doing a lousy job of being a mother. I really didn't think there was anything my mother could do that would turn me against her, but I was so angry that I couldn't speak to her for about two months.

After that, we were still there for another two days. We barely spoke, 'cause I was so angry. It was horrible. I didn't want to open my mouth and say something I'd regret. Every night when I put my little boy to bed, he'd cry and say, "Why does Grammy hate me?" She wouldn't even come in and kiss him good night or anything. Till this day, her attitude is "Well, he just shouldn't have misbehaved."

He's really hyper; he's a really sweet kid; he's a lot of fun. And he's not a kid who sits well. Now that he's almost five, he's finally gotten to the point that he can sit down for a whole two-hour movie. He could never do that before.

She was really weird even to Lucy, who was nine months old. She was a very shy baby who liked being with Mommy. When I tried to pass her off to her grandma, (she'd only held her once before, when Lucy had just been born, so Lucy didn't remember her), she started crying and my mom handed her right back, and said, "Boy this baby's really fussy!"

My mother knows everything about me. She has the capacity to sink me so deep I could never get out from the hole she could dig for me. It's sad, but I feel like I have to constantly have my guard up with her. I can't be myself with her. She's frozen me at the age of twelve. I finally just had to tell her, "I'm only going to be so involved. The rest of it is up to you. If you want me back in your life, here's what you've got to do: Don't yell at my kids. Don't yell at me. I'm not a little kid anymore. I don't yell and scream at people; that's not the adult way to manage things."

With both my sister and my mother, if we have a disagreement, they just get louder and louder. I'll hang up on them if they do that. It makes me so mad. My heart starts racing. It's just bad for you.

Jill describes her mother as a mess emotionally. "Every time I try to get involved with her, she tries to drag me down with her. And I can't do it! I've got two little kids depending on me, and a pretty stressful job I have to manage. I can't go down into a whirlpool with her."

Jill and her mother eventually patched things up, and Jill says she now has a three-dimensional view of her mom, a more realistic view. Jill explains that she always saw her mother as wonderful person who could kiss all her boo-boos and make them go away. It wasn't fair to her to expect that, says Jill. It was child's view. Jill adds that while her son did not deserve her mother's treatment, Jill herself was acting like a child on that visit, and her mother was treating her like one.

Despite the recurring conflict with her family, Jill says, "The thing I'm really grateful for with my family is that even though we don't get along all the time, at least we try. Even when we're fighting like cats and dogs, we never, ever, disappear." And in an emergency, she says, like when her father died, everybody stops fighting immediately and comes together as a unit.

Jill has about a half dozen friends from college that she keeps in touch with, some via phone and some who live nearby. She also has several graduate school buddies, one of whom "ties with her husband for best friend in the world." Jill has friends from college, through work, and through church.

I have different friends from each of the phases of my life, says Jill. She talks fondly of a friend she's had since she was eleven years old and living in "siege" as she put it, on the Marshall Islands, where Jill's father's business took the family. They were pals for about a year and have written to each other ever since. "She's the kind of friend," says Jill, "where when I see her, we pick right up where we left off. We sit down to talk, it's like we haven't spent any time away from each other."

"It's wonderful. She's very supportive. We're both on Prodigy and write back and forth. We have very similar backgrounds and goals for ourselves." Then, Jill's best friend from college, Claire, lives two miles away. For a long time the two didn't live anywhere near each other—they even lived in different countries—but they still remained in close contact, writing thirty- and forty-page letters to each other about "the men in their lives," says Jill. "She's been an excellent friend, and she's always kept in touch with me. We can sit down and talk about anything; we can yell and scream at each other, and it doesn't matter. We always know deep down we're friends and that's going to be till the end of our lives. We've talked about the trips we're going to take when all of our relatives die and we're the only ones left, and we're going to take old biddy trips together. We're going to go to Paris and then ride the Siberian Railway and all this stuff. She's a wonderful friend."

Another close friend, Lisa, whom Jill says she would call in an emergency, Jill met in grad school. Jill explains their closeness rests on several things: Her friend is spiritual, as is Jill and "she lost her brother too, and had a big long feud period with her mother, like me. She's an astrochemist; I'm an astrophysicist. We see eye to eye on everything."

Besides these close friends, Jill says she also has legions of friends whom she sometimes confides in and sometimes doesn't. Referring to a time when she had complications during her second pregnancy and friends came for several days and cleaned and shopped, Jill says she's always had good luck finding supportive friends and has always been a supportive friend herself. "You only get a short time on this earth, and you should try to make things as pleasant as possible for other people."

"Family is somebody who is an ear to listen, and somebody who's a hand to help, and somebody who loves you for who you are, not just what you can do for them," she says. "To me, friends are a lot more honest [than family]. They can look at themselves, and can say, 'Oh yeah, I've hurt you. I'm sorry.' My mother has never done that. She always says, 'Oh come on. Admit it. You screwed up!' My friends are easier to deal with. My friends are my family."

As we were preparing this manuscript for press, we learned that Jill passed away on January 2, 1996. She was thirty-eight years old and died suddenly from a heart ailment that runs in her family. She left us with her legacy of family-by-choice.

Today, important customs of kinship apply to friends as well as blood relatives. Historically, however, sociologists and anthropologists have failed to incorporate non-genetically related individuals—friends, lovers, co-workers, military buddies, athletic teammates, people bound by mutual suffering, and so forth—into a formal category of psychological kinship, a category inherently possessing rights and privileges, responsibilities and obligations.

The relationship between characters on the television show

"MASH" is a great example of non-genetic, psychological kinship bound by obligation and responsibility. Full of dark humor, the wildly popular show aired from 1972 to 1983, and still showing in syndication. Bonding together in a crisis mentality borne of the 1950s Korean conflict, the doctors and other characters not only provided companionship to each other, they helped one another survive. A more recent television version of medical colleagues forging a psychological kinship under highly stressful circumstances is the mega-popular NBC drama "ER."

Annie provides a good example of someone who has created a family of work friends who are bonded together in a disaster mode. Talking online, she says: "As for my family of choice, I think I went to work in a Trauma Intensive Care Unit because of my past. I seemed to feel comfortable in a crisis. I am very close with all of my natural family except the person who [sexually] abused me. I have never [talked about] the abuse with them. I have also created another family and that was with the nurses I worked with in trauma. In fact, I have been gone for a year-and-a-half from there (I went back to school to get my Ph.D in psychology, but we are still just as close and talk constantly.) It was their encouragement that got me back to school.

"They always want to know when I can come home for a visit; ironically, they forget that where they are is not my [childhood] family's home. It took me four years of working at that trauma unit before I went to therapy to deal with my own issues. In therapy, I realized that the patient in the bed was me. (In trauma units we tend not to look at the faces or remember names; a person is a set of injuries.) That probably sounds bad, but it is a protective mechanism for that environment. I don't know of one nurse in that unit that did not suffer from some form of abuse as a child, but we just try to handle today and look to tomorrow."

Consider this: Two years ago, my eighty-year-old Aunt Teresa, a Bon Secour nun from Ireland, stood on my front porch, practically a stranger. When my father left Ireland, she was only fourteen years old; She would never see him again. As a child, I would occasionally write letters to my aunt and we exchanged photos. She would send religious statues and once or twice we talked on the phone.

To celebrate her many years of dedication to the convent, my aunt was awarded a trip anywhere in the world. She chose to come to America to visit a brother who was still alive, and to meet her dead brother's four daughters—that was me and my sisters. So, over six decades after my father left, two World Wars and one Great Depression later—she would finally meet her American kin.

I felt awkward at first, that is until she opened her mouth. Her lilting Irish accent echoed my father's voice, telling me each St. Patrick's day of my childhood, how, with my golden hair, white skin, and green dress, I was the very picture of the Irish flag.

Throughout that long weekend, my Aunt and I talked incessantly, sharing the story of our lives. She told me how proud she was of how I had chosen to live my life, encouragement I had learned long ago not to look for from family, and told me she was glad I was her namesake and that we were both named for her mother, my grandmother. (My aunt's name, before she went into the convent, was Susan Ahern.) She told me about my Irish grandparents, happy, interesting stuff I'd never known because my father's deep depressions silenced him. With her jewel-like blue eyes and fair skin, she looked like my father, but was such a healthy, warmly spiritual version, it was hard to imagine her related to him. But she was! We shared walks and went to visit a local, vivacious, extremely independent, and surprisingly outspoken clan of Bon Secour nuns. We sat in the warm sun on my back deck and meditated together. One night, we dressed up and my husband and I took her to a fancy restaurant, whose opulence amazed her. Indeed, we enjoyed spoiling her.

When it was time for her to leave, my tears gave away the intense sadness I felt at finding such a kind, trustworthy source of kinship in my life. Yes, despite our vast physical separation across the Atlantic Ocean, we had always shared a genetic legacy. But we had not, until now, shared a psychological kinship—love—a critical ingredient of lasting family ties.

Indeed, love is the distinctive emotional and motivational component of kinship. While kin-like feelings toward others, not classified as kin, may include admiration, infatuation, liking, respect, and fondness, these feelings do not involve love, in the deeper sense of family-love.

The question begged at this point is, At what point does a person become kin as opposed to non-kin? Once a psychological kinship forms between two persons, they are real kin in the sense that each is loved by the other. However, with the emotional satisfaction, companionship, and other benefits of psychological kinship come responsibilities. As the following stories illustrate, establishing a new order of kinship first requires that we classify as family those who will provide the same benefits and live up to the same obligations, including the sharing of resources and emotional support, and financial help, we historically have gotten from biological kin.

Kinship after Divorce

In the past, when a marriage ended, one or both of the wounded parties often moved back to where they grew up, closer to their childhood families. This rule of kinship is surely outdated.

Debra, a registered nurse, divorced, with children ages three and five, lives in a small town on the East Coast. "Cowtown USA," as she puts it, "has a human population of 1,000; bovine population, 6,000."

Debra currently lives 250 miles from her biological family. Speaking online, she explains that she moved away when she got married, partly to get away from blood relatives. Although, she plans to move back to the state where she grew up, she prefers to keep distance between her and her blood relatives. "Long car rides and long distance phone calls, enough to make them think twice about invading my life," she says.

> While our relationships are not perfect, I consider them cordial. The bad memories are gone and my relationship with them is much improved. I find myself more accepting of them, and they of me.
>
> My view of the modern [intentional] family in this era is that it's a necessity and a reality. In times when people do not stay in the same place all of their lives, it seems a natural progression to find people to be close with. While there may be different levels of closeness and support, it is human nature to seek out others, to feel accepted and loved. I believe there is the family we are born into and the family we choose.
>
> When we choose our family, we choose people who will meet our needs and whose needs we can meet, people with whom we can be honest, we can be ourselves.

Personally, the [traditional notion of] extended family seems a bit of a dinosaur to me. I have a large extended family that resides all over the United States and Europe, [and] I talk to one aunt on a regular basis. I prefer my friends.

I have a network of friends who are definitely closer than family. They consist of friends I've met through school, neighbors, and childhood pals. It can be said that our circumstances are rather extraordinary, because we are primarily women without men.

I have gained more insight from my family of friends than I could ever have from my real family. My [intentional] family has helped me through the end of an abusive marriage, and subsequent divorce, put clothes on my children, provided child care, and helped me get aid to complete my education and food stamps to feed my family.

In the event of an emergency I would first contact my friends. We are always available, even in the middle of night. We give each other strength, courage and together form a powerful, cohesive group, each bringing a unique talent or ability. My [blood] family would be hard-pressed to come down unless the situation were extreme. There are also issues in which I prefer to rely on my support network, as they have experienced many of the things I have. The attitude is nonjudgmental, honest, and objective. I would drop almost anything to be by their sides if I was needed.

The woman with whom I am living offered me her home when I finally left my ex-husband. We share the responsibilities of raising our children and we basically function as a family. We are honest with each other and when there are problems, we are able to discuss what we need to do to improve our relationship. We joke about being each other's wives. After all, isn't that what every woman needs? Someone to pick up the slack when each of us is too tired? We do things for each other willingly because we know that they will be returned in kind. There is no pettiness in household expenses, we split almost everything down the middle.

I couldn't ask for a better group of people to call my friends. While the number is not large—ten—it is the quality of the relationships that counts.

In the late 1970s, when women were joining the work force in droves and the divorce rate was skyrocketing, Joyce's husband left her and her two small children for another woman. Her friends—

nineteen in all—were spread throughout the country: in Pennsylvania, Florida, Arizona, California and Virginia. After her husband left, Joyce called one of those friends in Pennsylvania to confide the awful news. Her friend arrived for a long weekend, offering emotional support and comfort. She cross-stitched Joyce a sampler that reads: "A friend is someone who loves you even when things go wrong." It still hangs above Joyce's sofa.

"What I noticed happening during those early years after the breakup of my marriage was that this group of friends, most of whom did not know each other, took me under their wings," she says. "The distant friends seemed to take turns calling me; almost every night, I would hear from one or the other. I felt very loved during a time when I felt so rejected." To this day, Joyce calls these friends her "rescue squad" and keeps in touch with them.

On the day before Easter, the year her husband left, one friend, a children's fashion designer, showed up with a grocery bag full of candy "since you probably haven't even thought about Easter baskets," she explained to Joyce. Her friend also brought a beautifully smocked Easter dress for Joyce's two-year-old daughter.

"One night I became very ill," Joyce explains, "so sick I couldn't get off the sofa. I called the doctor, but he didn't return my call for hours (it was a Saturday night). My neighbors weren't home, and I couldn't reach any of my friends. The children fell asleep on the floor beside the sofa—still in their clothes. When the doctor called back, he called in a prescription to the only all-night drugstore in town, about ten miles away. I called my ex and begged him to go to the drugstore and to come and put his children to bed. He said he'd washed his hands of that and said they had guests. He hung up. One of my friends got home and came over and got the children to bed and took care of things."

Kinship in Unemployment

When Tom's company closed down, he couldn't find a job for three months. He got another job, but that one fell through, and he was unemployed again for five months. Deciding to tackle the difficult task of leaving the retail industry, which had left him little family time, Tom was indeed nervous about supporting his three young children.

During that time he recalls one friend showing up with five bags of groceries. Another friend brought groceries on several occasions. Tom, who is in his mid-thirties, remembers all sorts of anonymous gifts from friends, totally about $1,000. For instance, during the time he was unemployed, his wife put on her coat as they were leaving a Christmas party and in the pocket was a card with $50. No name signed. Numerous Christmas cards containing money showed up in the mail, and many friends left money for Tom and his family at their church.

Also, at Christmas time that year, a most surprising and incredible gift arrived. Years before, Tom's wife, Kim, had babysat an infant for a year while the mother, Shelia, worked. "She is such a warm-hearted person, we hit it off really well, and we stayed friends," Tom explains. Knowing Tom was unemployed, Shelia sent Tom and his family a Christmas card, notifying them that their January and February rent, totaling $1400, had been paid.

Both Tom's and Kim's blood relatives lived several hundreds of miles away in the same northern state. While Tom described his relationship with his family as close, he says they didn't have to help him a lot financially during his unemployment, because his friends had done such a good job. Kim's relationship with her family was emotionally distant and they did not rely on them for help at all.

"Friends can give you a better outlook and more of a strength. You know that family is supposed to be there for you. You rely on your family, you expect your family to be there for you. Anybody who has good relationship with their family would expect that. But not all families are like that. With friends, you don't expect them to be there. They have no [blood] relationship with you. So when they do this, it builds you up so much more. They don't expect anything in return. They do this because they know this is what good people do. We have great friends."

Kinship in Sickness and Death

Where we live, whom we entrust our children to in our wills, how much we let people help us when we are in trouble—all reflect the value we place on kinship, and the value we place on friendship. True, families still feel most obligated to care for its sick members, especially the elderly. According to Nancy Schlossberg, in an article that appeared in *Cosmos: A Journal of Emerging Issues,* "A number of studies demonstrate that women, the wives, daughters and daughters-in-laws, do provide the bulk of caregiving." Women frequently bear the burden of illness even when sick family members are not elderly. But, as the following stories illustrate, this rule of kinship seems to be evolving, as is our society.[1]

Consider the thousands of people with AIDS each year who are cared for by their lovers—today a prominent form of psychological kinship. These lovers, unlike spouses, have no bonds of marriage, nor do they have a genetic or blood bond, yet they are forging intense family ties under the threat of death.

Mark, from Missouri, is representative of the growing trend of non-blood family caring for an ailing loved one. In a personal e-mail letter to us, Mark, who also is HIV positive, tells his story about nursing his lover, Dale, from 1991 until his death from AIDS in 1993.

> I did not do it alone! I had friends, and I had some wonderful professionals to help me. Yes, Dale had biological family—that is to say, his father is still alive and was helpful in a limited sense. He could not care for Dale Jr., directly as [Dale] Senior is over eighty years old. He did what he could financially and bought a car for us to use when our old one died.

> I did most of Dale's primary care for the first six months, during which I had to retire from my job, because doing both was doing me in. What I did was give him IVs, and his daily meds, made sure he ate, and got to the bathroom, emptied his vomit pan and urinal when he couldn't make it to the bathroom. Nurses came by to check his condition or an IV I couldn't get to run.

> Then [Dale] got a little better and did not need much care aside, from help with IVs. It lasted until about the middle of August 1992. In early 1993, Dale developed CMV Retinitis and lost peripheral vision in his right eye. He had to be on an IV for the rest of his life, twice a day at first. About this time, I asked for a nurse. I was wearing out. I have AIDS, also, and the load was just too overwhelming.

> I was an emotional wreck. Sometimes I hated Dale for being sick, many times I cried. I had tested positive sooner, and thought I would be first. I loved him but sometimes, I couldn't stand to be

with him. That shell of a human being wasn't really Dale to me. In truth, I would wonder who was going to do this for me, when he was slipping so fast. Yet I wanted to do this.

I had to sleep over at the hospital each time Dale went in, about six times all together. He usually was vomiting when he went in and the night shift at the hospital was insufficient. If he'd had to wait for an aide, he would have choked to death on his own vomit, because he was too weak to rise out of bed on his own. So I stayed.

I hated that hospital almost as much as he did; it came to a point where he refused to go back. Because he was afraid, [I] fought to keep him at home so he could die there. As a person without insurance, he had to use this horrible hospital. All treatments were done at home in 1993.

He had broken a knee and was bedridden. We already had two shifts [of nurses] coming in. When I finally decided to bring in twenty-four hour nurses for him, he wouldn't accept it. He wanted me on the night shift yet insisted I stay up for the days also. So I left. I told his LPN that I was going to visit my mom for a couple of days, and she would have to call and get a third shift. By then, her rapport with Dale was good, and I did leave and returned more rested. Dale never kicked [up] about the third shift again.

He died a few months later. I was there, since he died at home. Well I was lost for almost two years, just floated through life. Dale was family to me. I may have had some problems with his habits, and we had our share of arguments, but he was my soulmate. I could no more have left him permanently than I could cut off a limb. I loved the man, body and soul. I got AIDS first, remember, and he had every chance to leave me and find somebody else. In fact, when I first found out, I thought he should. Instead, he stayed and cared for me when I got sick. Thankfully, I am not too sick most of the time, just weak and fatigued. How could I do less for him?

Mark signed the e-mail: "Have a good life. Peace and long life."

Although sometimes a spouse, parent, or daughter might do the primary caretaking when someone is ill—friends may nonetheless become a crucial source of moral support.

In an era when so many daughters and sons are not emotionally—and sometimes not even geographically—close to fathers (because of estrangement, divorce or for other reasons), Kitty's tale offers hope that we can indeed find surrogate kin to nourish us when it is absent in our biological families.

> When I was a little girl," Kitty says, "I used to go to church alone a lot. I remember crying silently one Sunday watching a daddy in front of me hold his child in his lap. I wasn't sure why I was crying, I just knew there was an ache in me somewhere that hurt at moments like that. After graduation from college, a man I dated introduced me to a couple in their early fifties, who seemed to love me from the moment they met me. Don would sit with me at their kitchen table, while his wife, Susan, poured coffee. Often, we would talk through tough decisions or tearfully wrestle with a problem that felt bigger than me. Don's eyes never wandered as I spoke. His care for me was genuine and fatherly.
>
> At some point, he would cover my hand in his while Susan would hold the other one and he would pray a beautiful and loving prayer for me. He wasn't one to offer cheap advice, but if I needed it, he had the good, sound stuff I could count on. Today, whenever I flip through my wedding album, I always notice with fond memories the image of Don in the background as I walked down the isle with my real dad, whose legs were trembling that day because of his alcoholism. And when I recall how much I longed to have a strong, capable, reliable dad beside me that day, I am thankful that in another way, I did. And it was because of our friendship that I finally knew what it must have felt like for the little girl in front of me at church to have her daddy's arms around her.

Often giving support is as nourishing to our souls as receiving support, as this short poem tells:

> The only reward of virtue is virtue;
> the only way to have a friend is to be one.
> —Ralph Waldo Emerson, *Essays on Self Reliance*

Because kinship is often reciprocal, when Don needed help, Kitty was there for him, too. Six years ago, Don had a heart valve replaced with a pig valve, and Kitty dressed like a pig, went to his hospital room and performed a skit, informing Don (who is interested in family genealogy), of his new swine lineage.

When Don had the valve replaced recently, Kitty decorated his hospital room with eight humorous posters—each made from family-photo head shots superimposed over pictures of models' and athletes' bodies. Kitty says a clerk at a local copier store, who had just moved into town, and had no family nearby, was so inspired by her project that he offered to help pay for enlarging the photos.

In his classic novel *Sons and Lovers*, D.H. Lawrence depicts life in an English mining town—long before the days of universal health insurance—where a buddy system was the only safety net people had. Back then, if a breadwinner got sick or was injured in a coal-mining accident, co-workers passed the hat each week to raise money for the victim's medical expenses and to keep the family afloat. In today's complex society, we increasingly need friends and a wide circle of community to help us survive. With health insurance companies reducing their costs by frequently disqualifying life-saving medical treatments, Judy's story of inspiring friendship is indeed timely and poignant. Diagnosed with cancer at thirty-five, she would die without a special kind of bone-marrow transplant. But her insurance company, deeming the procedure experimental and trying to save money, refused to cover it.

Judy is the mother of an adorable, blonde-haired, third-grade angel. They live in a typical middle-class suburb. The neighborhood has a winning swim team, a popular women's club, and is recognized locally for its annual Halloween celebration and Easter egg Hunts. At Christmas, most families participate in the old tradition called "Luminaries," where residents line the streets in front of their houses with small white bags anchored by sand and lighted white candles. Guided by the glowing trails, families walk or drive to the community association clubhouse for caroling, hot cider, and a visit from jolly old St. Nick.

It is the kind of neighborhood that over the years came to the aid of several families with medical emergencies, the kind of neighborhood that would come to the aid of Judy as well. A local fund-raising campaign, spearheaded by a neighbor and friend, raised $25,000 in one week. Yes, one week! Judy's colleagues at work also raised $25,000, and friends from her hometown of Emporia, Virginia, raised another $5,000. This generosity from friends allowed Judy to obtain the life-saving medical treatment she needed and, surprisingly, left her with no medical bills. Money left over from the fund raising was used to help other patients afford expensive cancer treatments. Indeed, it's comforting to know that the spirit of friendship is thriving today and can be a powerful safety net in America.

Judy is not alone in her reliance on non-kin to see her through an illness. When Nancy's husband, Bill, was diagnosed with pancreatic cancer, her sister and a couple Nancy and Bill knew, all went out to dinner, "to settle in with the news."

Except for her sister, Nancy's family is spread across the country. Bill's family wasn't close by either. Nancy describes herself as an open book. "Everybody knows everything [about me]; I don't usually keep it in," says Nancy. "My sister's the opposite way."

Nancy's husband was sick for two years.

"You know how it is. It starts out, everybody hovers around you," she says. When my husband had surgery, friends from the choir and [other] church groups came and brought boxes and boxes of food. Nancy was staying at the hospital a lot, going back and forth. Her two sons were still at home, having just graduated high school.

Bill belonged to a spiritual group at a large, suburban Catholic church, and would meet with them on weekly basis. While Bill was in the hospital, they visited him regularly. "That was his greatest comfort, I think," Nancy says.

"My family called and everything," adds Nancy, "but with [my friends] being here they were able to do the physical visiting and all that."

Bill's first surgery was during Christmastime, Nancy says, describing a visit from her choir friends: "They brought donuts and cider and serenaded us. They stood on front porch and rang bells. It was wonderful."

Toward the end of Bill's illness, Nancy and her family had to move. "We lost our home trying to get his medical bills paid. Just lost everything we had," she says. "Health insurance did pay a lot of stuff, but his income was gone, and he had no life insurance because he had changed jobs.

"He could not move things physically. He was to the point where he was not able to walk around very much." Nancy called a friend to ask for help moving. "Eleven guys and three trucks showed up," she says. Nancy and her husband moved to another house, still near their church. The parents of a choir friend rented it to them at reduced rate.

Meanwhile, Nancy worked part-time at church, where she routinely received anonymous gifts of money in the mail. On her desk, she often found generous gift certificates to a local grocery store.

"At Christmastime we got five turkeys; we lived on turkey for about a year after my husband died. I never said anything about it, but people knew things were tough. I guess somebody must have found out he didn't have insurance. At the memorial service, I got a couple of gifts of $500 each to help cover funeral expenses. At the memorial service, we had over 500 people. What was more amazing is that I knew most of them. I didn't realize I knew that many people, 'cause you don't see them collectively. All eighty-five members of the choir were there, and all their families.

Bill had wanted to be buried in Indiana, his childhood home. So a friend of Bill's drove Nancy and her sons there to save her that expense. At the memorial service, friends donated money to pay for Nancy and hers sons to take a leisurely train ride back from Indiana, so Nancy could spend some much-needed time with her sons.

When her husband was alive, Nancy and her sister usually got together for holidays. But when she called her sister the Easter after Bill died, the reply surprised her. "Well, we're going up to see Kerry [her daughter.] We figured you were going to be with your friends."

"I've always felt holiday-time was family-time," Nancy says. "Especially since I had no other family here but her. That's about the only time I got to see her.

"From then on I felt like I was inviting myself if I went over there. I've had to sort of make family the other way around. I want more connection [with my sister], but I'm not getting it, so I don't want to force myself on them anymore. Sometimes it upsets me, because, you know, especially the first couple of years, I felt like I really needed to have family [around]. I felt because she was here she would want to do that. But I was mistaken."

Such reliance on psychological kinships during illness is not isolated: increasingly this phenomena of friends substituting for kin is reflected in the media. Who can forget Hollywood's 1988 tear jerker, "Beaches," a film of friendship extraordinare? Bette Midler's and Barbara Hershey's characters kept a friendship alive for decades, through fun and tough times. When the one friend became ill, the other cared for her until the very end, and became the guardian of her daughter. The love the two friends shared developed into a true psychological kinship, complete with obligations and benefits.

Indeed, portraits of psychological kinship in the media are plentiful. In a 1996 episode of "Boy Meets World," the popular NBC television series, the principal, Mr. Feeny, tells one of the students that "you don't have to be blood to be family." And Deborah Laake, in an article in *New Woman,* describes her ordeal with cancer at thirty-nine and the nongenetically-related family she has created. Divorced, childless, and living in South Carolina, Laake writes that she has found a new security "from the friends who have wept for me, fed me, done my laundry repeatedly to the bottom of the bin, and for six months slept in the room next to mine on the nights of chemotherapy treatment."

Before she got sick, much of Laake's blood family had been angry at her for defecting from the family's strict Mormon religion. Although her eldest brother and her mother offered emotional support throughout her illness, they and her ill father were unable to provide any of the day-to-day help Laake required.

She now sees herself as someone who "loves and is loved," she writes. "That has been proven a thousand remarkable ways this year, although not by the traditional displays from family. . . . I was cared for by friends through a long period of need, and the experience has changed the foundation of my life. . . . I believe that my strongest bonds of friendship will bear the weight of a lifetime's seasons and demands; that they are the real thing of connection, not the second best."[2]

In an essay in *Between Friends: Writing Women Celebrate Friendship,* Susan Kenney talks about the friends who supported her during her husband's long sickness. "They came often, in ripples, in waves, a creative tide of helping hands and hearts . . . caring for us and about us. Not always the same people, some going out of our [group] for one reason or another and others coming in to take their place, still a constant, steadying presence in our lives. . . . These friends became our extended family. Often acting invisibly or behind the scenes, and almost always unasked, but even in our saddest and most frenzied moments we noticed their reaching out with countless acts of kindness and support, so that we never lost the feeling that, as the father in *A River Runs Through It,* says, 'there was always someone there with the part that was needed.' "[3]

When the people we love die—our parents, spouses, companions—it is often our friends who see us through the roughest periods of grief. These days, it's easy to identify psychological kin: They're the ones we ask to ride in the hearse along with our blood relatives. A tradition usually reserved for next-of-kin, through this invitation, we classify our dear comrades as family.

Psychological kin are being acknowledged in obituaries, such as this one we found in our local newspaper: "Mrs. Josephine Blanton, of Richmond, died Wednesday, March 1, 1995. She is survived by a beloved friend, Mrs. Betty N. Lawton of Richmond; several nieces and nephews." It used to be, such obituary notices applied only to gays and lesbians. Not so any more. Similarly, with families living so far apart, close friends are asked to give testimonials today, or even the eulogy, because they often know the deceased better than the family.

What Makes a Family

If geography, finances, legal contracts, and social customs are not the strongest arbiters of family today—what makes a family? In his book, *Familyhood,* esteemed author and psychologist Dr. Lee Salk writes that what constitutes a family are those "who provide love, care, and emotional support for one another."

Citing a comprehensive study on family values, conducted by the Mellman and Lazarus organization, Dr. Salk writes that most Americans consider emotional or functional elements more important than structural or legal elements in defining a family. To the question, "Which of the following comes closest to your definition of the Family?" respondents replied in following percentages:

A group of people related by blood or marriage or adoption? 22%
A group of people living in one household 3%
A group of people who love and care for each other 74%

Indeed, more than four out of five agreed with the statement: "My closest friends are like family to me." And almost one half thought of people at work like family.[4]

Salk also writes, "These numbers make it sufficiently clear that we have come to accept alternative lifestyles within our definition of family. Perhaps in response to the indisputable fact that large numbers of traditional marriages and families have not survived the evolutionary challenges of modern life, he continues, the majority of Americans are focusing more on the interpersonal function of family than on the institution of family."[5]

Consider Jen's story. Every time her husband, a computer expert, got a new assignment at work, it meant a move for the family. His latest move was the most painful for Jen. Uprooted with two small sons, she missed her network of friends. Her husband's job kept him busy day and night, and Jen grew increasingly restless. Within months, she decided to divorce. For a brief period, she moved back to where her parents lived, back to where she grew up. But soon she took her sons and returned to the intimate circle of friends she'd left behind when she and her husband moved.

"As marriage becomes less of an obligation, an institution developed around a need for financial security and a requisite for child raising," Salk writes in *Familyhood*, "and more a choice for companionship and love; as family takes on a startling broad meaning in public perception, Americans are reaching toward the deepest human needs to measure joy and satisfaction. . . . People are saying that family doesn't just mean the immediate relatives. Family means everyone who loves and cares for you, and whom you love and care for in return."[6]

What Makes a Parent?

In recent years, a series of notorious adoption and child custody battles has forced our society to also reckon with the question: what makes a parent? Indeed a parent may be one who copulates and creates a child. But most people agree that a mother, a father is one who walks the floor all night, holding a colicky baby. One who nurses a child through a high fever or braves icy roads to fill a prescription. One who faithfully checks homework each night and wisely navigates the tortuous emotional tugs of protectively holding onto a child and letting go when it's time.

Indeed the almost universal reaction to famous custody cases is yet another indication that the rules of kinship are changing and evidence of our culture's growing preference for bonds of love over legal ties, for nurture over nature.

Among the first was the Baby Jessica adoption case, which dramatized in the media the debate over which is more important in determining custody: psychological parenting or shared genetics.

Two-and-a-half-year-old Jessica was taken from the secure home of adoring, adoptive parents and returned to her biological parents—all because of a legal technicality. Jessica's birth mother, Cara Clausen, had conceived Jessica just as she was breaking up with the baby's father, Dan Schmidt, a trucker. Cara didn't tell Schmidt about her pregnancy, and instead told her next boyfriend, and soon fiancé, that he was the father. He and Cara willingly signed away parental rights to Jessica.

Several weeks after Jessica was born and living in Michigan with her adoptive parents, Jan and Roberta DeBoer, Cara told Schmidt he was the real father and soon went to court to have her parental rights restored. She and Schmidt later reunited and married. Because Schmidt had never signed away his rights, baby Jessica's fate was to be decided by lawyers.

The courts refused to put any weight on the fact that Cara had tricked both Schmidt and her fiancé. The courts also disregarded Schmidt's irresponsible parenting in the past—He had fathered a son in a previous, albeit brief, marriage and hadn't seen the child in nine years. Schmidt described the conception of his second child (also before Jessica's birth) as a "one night stand." What's more, his refusal to pay child support forced both mothers of his children to court in an attempt to get Schmidt to support his children. All this baggage even before Jessica.

Ignoring these startling, clear signs of irresponsible parenting, the court wrenched Jessica from her parents and turned her over to strangers who had only a biological link to her. Within a year, baby Jessica had a new name, Anna Lee Jacqueline Clausen Schmidt, and a new identity, as well as two new parents. To the court, genetics proved to be more important than the child's best emotional health. Popular sentiment supported the adoptive parents. In fact, 87 percent of respondents to a 1994 survey by *Glamour* magazine said the courts were wrong to send two-year old Jessica DeBoer back to her biological parents. As one respondent put it, "The DeBoers were the only loving family Jessica knew. How can anyone expect a child that age to understand why she's no longer allowed to live with her mother and father?"[7]

Psychological ties are developed at a critical period in toddler-hood when children, through their parents' consistent presence, learn a foundation of trust in the world. Professional literature suggests that these attachments persist throughout life. Psychologists almost unanimously agree: when that caregiving is not consistent, the child is set up to experience powerful terror of abandonment in later adult relationships.

By awarding Jessica to her biological parents, the courts ultimately valued ceremonial blood ties over Jessica's critical psychological development, and ignored any potential long-term emotional damage. In an issue of *Parents'* magazine, columnist Leslie Bennetts blasts the court's decision: "The essence of parenthood is adulthood, and the essence of being an adult is taking responsibility, both for your own actions and for your child. Cara and Dan Schmidt have never taken such responsibility. No one forced Cara to give up her baby! That was her idea. It was also her idea to lie about the child's paternity. She is the architect of this entire tragic mess. Nor is it someone's else fault that Dan has been such a pathetic excuse for a father.

"Loving parents understand that they must, at times, sacrifice their own desires in favor of their children's needs. The Schmidts have refused to put Jessica's interest first, and so the unsuspecting toddler may have to get used to a new home, a new family."[8]

A baby born into this world cannot choose parents who will provide the physical necessities as well as the emotional nurturing and love necessary for later sound mental health. A baby born into this world cares little if those needs are met by a genetically related parent, a foster parent, adoptive parent or surrogate parent. What's important is that the child is cared for consistently. That's what makes a parent.

The notion that blood and genetics somehow implies ownership of children is surely becoming outdated. The debate is starting to intensify in the wake of these tough adoption cases in America. The ability of biological parents to win back custody of a child placed for adoption varies from state to state. While Canadian courts fully consider the legal rights of biological parents, they tend to emphasize the child's physical, psychological, and emotional welfare. And based on those criteria, the adoptive parents generally win out, according to an article, "Homeward Bound: An appeal Court chooses Nurture over Nature," written by D'Arcy Jenish in *Maclean's* magazine.

Another media example of our culture's changing kinship rules comes from *Time* magazine. Focusing on the famous Jessica case, the article raises the question of children's rights in determining what constitutes a parent.

> In many states the rights of biological parents are all but inviolable; only in extreme cases are the courts willing to terminate a parent's right to custody. But as stories emerge of children who are plainly suffering the consequences of being treated more like property than people, the tide has begun to turn.[9]

The story of Gregory K. in Florida who brought the debate onto the national stage, when he successfully sued to "divorce" the mother who had abandoned him in order to remain with the foster family he had been living with for nearly a year is one example of the tide turning.

There is no definitive answer to what makes a good parent. Intelligence doesn't always endow people with the capacity to love, neither does money. Being a professional versus a blue-collar worker doesn't automatically endow one with the requisite caretaking instincts needed in parenthood, either. While statistics suggest that children reared in troubled families will have difficulty parenting their own children—and certainly abused children frequently grow up and abuse their own children—coming from a broken home doesn't guarantee poor parenting skills either. Referring to my family, my sister once said, "We are the broken of the broken families," but we both grew up determined not to make the same mistakes we saw our parents make. And after fifteen years of marriage, so far I haven't. But while we can't precisely quantify or define what makes a good parent, we can make educated predictions based on people's track record as adults—their consistency; their honesty; their ability to manage their own lives responsibly; their ability to provide a secure physical environment; their ability to form lasting relationships— these are the things children need or should have modeled to them. These, rather than a shared genetic pool, are the things judges and psychologists must weigh when determining what makes a parent.

Vera Duke, an attorney who specializes in family and domestic law, says the trend in adoption cases nationwide is indeed moving toward ruling on a child's best interests as opposed to parental rights. As result of the Baby Jessica case, Duke says some states have reduced the time period in which biological parents can challenge adoptions. While this legislation elevates the child's best interests in the adoption process, it will not prevent a Baby Jessica incident from occurring again. However, a few states, such as Virginia, have made the child's best interests a paramount concern in adoption battles.

Duke is adamant that the rest of the nation should follow suit by demanding legislative reform. She says all state adoption statutes should carry a "saving" clause, which would force judges to perform a "best interest analysis," regardless of whether the parents possess the legal right to challenge an adoption. Duke says that Iowa, which gave Baby Jessica back to her natural father because his rights had not been terminated, did not have a "saving" clause in its adoption statutes. When a court is forced to do a "best interest analysis," it can legally determine that if a child has lived with her adoptive parents, for say two years, and has formed a psychological and physical bond, it would be in her best interest to remain with her adoptive parents.

As public and media reaction to these battles show, our society is leaning more toward psychological kinship in custody cases where biological kinship is malfunctioning. Indeed, in the *Glamour* survey, when asked which should count for more in adoption disputes—the parents' rights or the best interests of the child—95 percent of respondents said, the "best interests of the child." Children should not be treated like property, said one respondent.[10]

While psychological kinship has not historically been as morally or legally binding as blood relationships and marriage, psychological kinships increasingly offer security, flexibility, proximity to loved ones, and an emotional shield in stressful times. Thus our psychological kinships are becoming powerful mediators of social behavior, especially in today's mobile, industrial society where the immediate family includes little more than spouse and children. Since human beings have evolved from small bands where everyone in the clan was family, it is not surprising that we now find solace and joy in the psychological kin we are acquiring in our world of ever-increasing strangers.

Psychological kinship is not designed to replace a warm, loving biological family that emotionally and physically nurtures its members; rather, psychological kinship is an important resource for folks whose family lives far away or is not able to provide necessary emotional or physical support. For those who fear that intentional families signal the death knell for an already shaky blood-family system, think again. In many instances, psychological kinship can actually improve genetic relationships.

Ted Kalontz is executive director of Onsite, a nationally-respected facility in Tucson, Arizona, for people healing from family trauma that has impaired their ability to form intimate, honest, reciprocal adult relationships. At Onsite, Kalontz says, the first thing people learn to do is set up a network that can sustain them emotionally through the healing process. He says most of Onsite's clients never had, and still don't have, appropriate family support.

So clients are placed with a group of people who are able, as much as humanly possible, to offer them unconditional love like a family is supposed to, and who can be there for them, even when they aren't perfect. Learning to identify their feelings and communicate emotions clearly and without blame is a big part of learning how to relate to their new intentional family.

"It's surrogate brothers and sisters, surrogate aunts and uncles, guides and mentors. Unless people find intentional families, we keep looking for [emotional support] in people who can't offer it," Kalontz says during an interview, referring to many blood families.

But if you can build a support system of friends, Kalontz believes you can then go back to your family and enjoy what they have to offer, even if what they offer is limited.

"In those limits there are little gold nuggets," he says. But if you're looking for the deep intimacy, the main vein, in your blood families, and it's not forthcoming, Kalontz says you will tend to resent your family and ignore "the gold nuggets."

7

Cyberfamilies

The Secret

Got so much inside of me
That no one will ever see
It's all the fault of those
Stupid people
Who think they know the way we
should be
Funny, seems that they will be
The ones judged one day
For putting so much ridicule
on innocents like
You and Me.

All my life no one could tell
The difference
As far as they knew I
Was the daughter they wished
Theirs would be

Would it crush them
To discover God
Had made me different
Than They
Would it give them a new cause to
fludder
to pout
To be disgusted
Sure they know what is and isn't.

Some days are good
Some days are bad
Most are spent enjoying friends
Wishing some of them were more
But the pretty little secret
Still hides behind a door.

—Caroline posted this poem online,
on Prodigy's gay and lesbian bulletin board

"What I was most struck by as I researched the way human beings interact on the Internet, were the support groups," says Dinty W. Moore in a telephone interview. He is assistant professor of English at Penn State University's Altoona campus, and author of *The Emperor's Virtual Clothes: The Naked Truth about Internet Culture.*

"There are thousands of different groups, from depression to skin disease to grief to divorce. I was skeptical. Certainly no one is going to get the kind of support they need on this kind of thing, on the Internet. I thought it was a cold, sterile, faceless medium. I was dead wrong. I talked to hundreds of people and read thousands of messages attesting to the fact that the kind of support they are getting is real, and helpful.

"What I finally discovered, which I thought most interesting, is that it's not so much that people are getting help on the Internet, it's that they wouldn't have gotten it otherwise. People might not feel comfortable going to their minister, a YMCA or wherever, and sit around a table with a total strangers, saying, 'You know, I have these crazy thoughts. I'm worried about this.' They probably wouldn't even tell their sister.

"But the Internet makes it safe. They'll log onto groups where people are discussing whatever it is that concerns them, whether it's mental, physical, or sexual, and they'll just eavesdrop for a couple of weeks until they're comfortable enough with the idea that they are not alone. Within a few weeks they'll ask a question tentatively, or make an observation without signing their name. Then, depending on the person, three weeks later, three months later, three years later, they're totally out of the closet. They're on this bulletin board, trading information, trading opinions, signing their name.

"It's a sort of coming-out process that wouldn't happen off-line, because these people are so reluctant to tell anyone, in anything but the safest environment. They would hold this inside of themselves forever. But the Internet is allowing them to reach out."

Online communication is not just a fad, say the experts. Nearly four out ten American households now have personal computers. Twenty-five percent of high school and college students are online, and the number is escalating, fast. Seeking emotional support is just one reason people go online; gathering information is another. online services are also sort of a worldwide canvass where creativity blossoms. People exchange poems, drawings, short stories—many devised spur of the moment and some painstakingly created. Tuning into the electronic support groups, where anonymity and pain comingle, the creativity is especially intense and prolific. When perusing this original art, what is striking is the universality of human experience expressed. Although separated by time and physical space, we all feel sadness, joy, rage, and terror. Cyber-art can inspire us, and despite vast distances, stir up these universal feelings.

In addition to pop art, there are an enormous number of electronic bulletin boards, or club houses, for political activists, bikers, antique clock collectors, or even pastors. Besides work-related, and special interest bulletin boards, there are also loosely connected communities, where anonymity reigns and fun is the bonding agent.

"Prodigy, which is not the largest online service for computer users, happily reports that its subscribers now spend 1.2 million hours every month 'chatting' to one another," Don Steinberg writes in the magazine *Virtual City: Your Guide to Cyber Culture*. Online you can chat live, which means communicating with others in a conversation, in real time. You can post or respond to notes on public bulletin boards, which people in bedrooms, offices, and dens across the country can read and respond to at their leisure. Or, you can chat more privately by sending your message directly to people's personal e-mail addresses. At a variety of online sites, people are discussing a broad range of topics—from hobbies, to sex fantasies, to exotic dream vacation spots, to favorite cars or favorite drinks. It's kind of like talking on the phone, but you often don't know the person and your words are written, not spoken.

Steinberg explains that about half of Prodigy's chat space is given over not to topics like sports and hobbies but to an area called 'Pseudo,' an online personals section, composed of live discussion groups focusing on people's desires. These groups advertise offbeat titles, such as "Indecent Proposals" and "30s and Looking."

"About 1,500 people pass through Pseudo's chat areas everyday, sometimes for regularly scheduled events, such as Saturday night's 'Weird Film Chat' . . . But mostly they play out fantasies in rooms like 'Vampire Pub II,' where a regular guy can be a lusty female vampire, or vice versa," writes Steinberg.[1]

People develop friendships (and sometimes make enemies) just as they would in other social situations, writes Christopher O'Kennon in *Style Weekly*. "Anyone with access to a modem can do the electronic equivalent of strolling into a favorite cafe and looking for friendlies.

"There are huge numbers of people wandering around, and they're more than willing to listen to you," according to O'Kennon. "Before you know it, you get the impression you're somebody. Cyberspace communities are almost as close-knit as real world communities, sometimes more so. After all, anyone can belong, not just the charismatic elite. Because we can't physically see each other in cyberspace, no distinctions can be made based on age, sex, national origin, or how closely someone approaches the current bodily goal set forth by the entertainment industry. Individuals with disabilities—be they physical or emotional—that normally might make it difficult to form new friendships, find that the virtual communities of cyberspace treat them as they've always wanted to be treated: as thinkers and fellow human beings, not merely the sum of their apparent parts."[2]

When writing *The Emperor's Virtual Clothing,* Dinty Moore interviewed Bruce, who belongs to a virtual community of people who live in suburban Philadelphia. The BBS, as the community is called, has about fifty active users who connect regularly to discuss movies, sports, politics.

There wasn't time to go out and meet with friends, Moore says. There wasn't time to have dinner parties. By the time the kids were in bed, it was almost his own bedtime. But for a half hour each night he could log on this bulletin board. He could have conversations he enjoyed and keep an intellectual connection with other people.

"It was the only way he could do it," Moore explains. "He didn't necessarily prefer it to sitting around a big table eating Chinese food and talking to people. But that didn't happen anymore. His life was too busy."

"I didn't understand that," he continues. "I thought, 'why don't you just get together? Why would you want to do this?' And the fellow pointed out, 'For a lot of us, who work eight hours a day, commute two hours a day, and have children, we just don't get out anymore. This is the only way we really get to carry on a social life. You can manage it.'"

Brian C., talking online, also found his cyberfamily on electronic bulletin boards. "On one bulletin board, I was talking about childhood problems with family and asking how others reacted," he says. "I formed a real good relationship with this one woman, and we became 'online siblings.'

"I mostly connect with only that woman. I've never met her. We live several states apart. We talk about lots of things, like hobbies, emotional stuff, how our parents would never understand us, or when they would fight and things like that. My 'online sis' has provided me with a great amount of support, and I have supported her. Getting e-mail from her always makes my day a little brighter.

"I get more support from my cyberfamily than my blood family. My real family is very difficult to talk to. My definition of family is a group of people who provide love and support. These families need not be blood; sometimes blood families fight a lot or live far away. Intentional families can provide support almost anytime, and these families can provide the same amount of support as a real family."

Indeed, if you spend a few weeks navigating the information highway, you can see for yourself that throughout the online universe people are having fun and many are seeking solace by bonding with similar souls. While the virtual communities that organize around hobbies, work, talk of politics and shared passions, are a valuable part of many people's lives, it's in the support groups that the feeling of kinship resonates the most.

Not surprisingly, one of the most active family communities is the gay and lesbian bulletin board. Perhaps because mainstream society has historically rejected gays and lesbians because of their sexual preference, they have been pioneers in creating alternative communities. In that way, the gay and lesbian community is a kind of model for conventional society, which is just getting around to creating intentional families and psychological kinship.

"Many of us have had to seek out new friends and new family, when our real family or what we thought were our real friends turned their back on us because of what we are," says Richard Vanaman, a member representative for Prodigy's Gay and Lesbian bulletin board, speaking online from Las Vegas. "It is popular to refer to a member of our gay community as family. A gay owned and operated business may be referred to as family-oriented. Everyone of us is a member of a very large family, where we can always rely on that support and information available to us through the network.

Knowing I can turn on my computer or pick up my phone and knowing that I have a friendly ear waiting is absolutely essential.

"The people I meet on bulletin boards and information services, as well as my non-cyberspace friends, are all very supportive. I consider them my family. I turn to these people when I have a crisis or decision in which I need more input; but even more important, I don't need a reason to write or call them, because they are my friends. They have helped me get through an abusive relationship, coming out to my sister, the death of a friend, quitting smoking, and even helped me to put the romance back in my relationship. I receive more mail and calls from my friends in the family than I ever have from my biological family."

Eric Marcus, in a foreword to Nancy Andrews's 1994 book, *Family: A Portrait of Gay and Lesbian America,* writes:

> Like all human beings, gay men and women desire the comfort and love that "the family" ideally provides. We wish for our families to be a place of security, a refuge from the chaotic, threatening world around us. Yet, as homosexuals, we are likely to fear that if the families in which we were raised discover who we really are they'll no longer love us, that they'll banish us from home. . . . But we are not without family. Some of us have been lucky enough or have worked hard enough to remain part of the families in which we were raised. Others have created their own families—their chosen families—in place of the ones they've lost or fled. And as gay people, we are all part of that very large family of lesbians and gay men who yearn for a safe world in which we can live with pride and dignity.[3]

Caroline, who authored the poem at the beginning of this chapter, and who has recently begun logging onto computer bulletin boards, has a good relationship with some members of her blood family, but she has also created a cyberfamily. Communicating online, she explains that although she cannot tell her father of her sexual preference, because he and his wife are Jehovah's Witnesses, she is close to her sisters and her mother. They have been supportive. But she still feels the need to find additional support by connecting with folks on the gay and lesbian electronic community, who have felt the things she has felt, and who can identify with the challenges she is constantly facing because she is a lesbian.

A member of the National board of Directors for the Gay and Lesbian National Task Force, Don Davis, says he has lived all of his life in small towns in the South. (He asked that we use his real name.) Davis didn't come out until he was twenty years old and says he wonders how differently his life would have been if at fourteen he had access to a bulletin board that provided support and information on homosexuality. He believes he would not have experienced the deep feelings of oppression that marked his early life.

Davis, who stands 6'7" tall and looks like a Republican banker, says he defies the stereotypes.

"I don't have an artistic bone in my body and I can't do anybody's hair," he says, followed by a bellowing laugh. He and his lover have been together for fourteen years. Davis, who holds a responsible position with the local government in Williamsburg, Virginia, where he lives, has been online for several years now and is part of a huge network of friends and political allies around the country. Because of his passion for political action, Davis says he's more involved in cyberspace than most people.

"I met my best friend online. He was a graduate student in journalism. We struck up a conversation one night, and spent time talking about political issues and issues we were interested in.

"When I met him he was an ambiguous personality, if you will, but predominantly straight . . . engaged to be married. I accepted that and went on, because I was very interested in the political, journalism side of our conversations. As time went on, he started slowly coming out of the closet, telling me: 'You're not what gay and lesbian people have been to me all my life. You have a legitimate and substantial role in life, a real mission and sense of purpose. I never met people like that who were gay and lesbian.'

"That relationship continued to evolve. I knew a lot of activists in [his town] and they connected him with the gay and lesbian community face-to-face. As time went on, he graduated from college, decided to move to Washington, and I helped find him a place to live. He now works in public relations and is a volunteer in the National Gay and Lesbian Task Force.

Davis, who is thirty-five, says in a lot of ways it's been a mentoring relationship. "He's twenty-years old and was very late in coming out, compared to a lot of people today. Davis adds that the relationship has never been a physical one; nevertheless, it's been one of the most loving relationships he's ever had.

Davis tells another fascinating "cyberstory" helping a sixty-year-old man, online, figure out how to come out to his eighty-one-year-old mother. "I was able to walk through the whole experience with him," Davis says. "His mother could no longer take care of herself and he didn't want to put her in a rest home, so he moved her in with him. He had been publicly living a gay life for the past twenty-five or thirty years, but he'd never told his mother," Dan explains. She lived in another state, so it wasn't important that she know. But suddenly their lives collided.

"For him, the experience of coming out was very different than it was for me fifteen years ago. You're sixty years old and you mother is twenty years older than you are. And you're still stuck with the conventional thinking. You've got sixty years of a relationship that's been based on something that is not your reality. And it's challenging.

"I've never spoken to the man on the phone; I've never met him. Everything happened online," Davis says.

Davis helped his online friend decide how to reveal his secret to his mother. "It went through all sorts of gyrations," says Davis. "But now she really wants to understand, and she's really challenged by it."

Alexa, a book editor in Boca Raton, Florida, has a different reason for seeking comfort and emotional support from a virtual community. She belongs to a computer network for people around the country with Crohn's disease. (A doctor's certificate is required to get on this registered bulletin board.) Crohn's is a disease characterized by inflammation of the intestinal tract, primarily affecting the lower bowel. The disease causes bloody diarrhea, is excruciatingly painful, and can even be life-threatening.

"Family is supposed to mean unconditional love and acceptance," she says, talking online, "but few are lucky enough to have that in their life. One reason I think the bulletin board, BB, is so popular, is because people with this awful, painful, embarrassing disease, find others just like themselves who have "been there, done that," in terms of both treatment and acceptance. There is a lot of support, and it seems to be much more than lip service. When one of us goes into the hospital, it's like a call to arms. E-mails, cards, and letters start flowing. Spouses and family members are encouraged to participate. It's a family in its own right."

When she got pregnant, which can be extremely dangerous for Crohn's patients, Alexa posted the news on the Crohn's bulletin board and got twenty-seven congratulatory messages from "cyber aunts and uncles." Her pregnancy worsened her condition, and she was hospitalized for eight days. Throughout that time, her husband went online each night to update members around the country about Alexa's condition.

Alexa explains that about twenty-five people, whose names and lives she knows, make up the "regulars" on her board. She says there have been two marriages on the Crohn's bulletin board. Each month, the members pick a central location and hold a big meeting. They swap photos, videos, and resource material, and even have their own newsletter.

Alexa logs on to the BB at least five to eight hours each week and says that most of that time is devoted to answering e-mail and checking in on her bulletin board. "Speaking in computer space is completely different," she says. "We have cyber jokes, symbols and so on."

"There are many times when my BB friends were really there for me. When we are on treatment, we might sleep three or four hours. There were times when I was up for twenty-four hours straight because the dosages I was taking were so high. It's an amphetamine-type reaction. I used to post on the insomnia topic, or other more light-hearted ones, and "gab" with friends till three or four in the morning—if only to keep from watching endless reruns on TV.

"The first night I posted, I could not walk. I introduced myself, told them how ill I was, and desperately asked, 'Does anyone ever get better?'

"There were twenty responses, all of incredible sensitivity. The words these people used were *my* words. People understood what it was like to not sleep, to be sick all the time. I sat there and cried with relief. Prior to that, it was my daughter that kept me from killing myself, I think. But after that I had so much hope and comfort. I could talk about fear. Anyway, that night really stands out to me. I remember it like it was yesterday.

Alexa recently gave birth to a son, is back to work, is writing an inspirational book, and is doing just fine.

Another online community with a real, close-knit family feel to
it is the Sexual Abuse BB. Because of the extremely private matter of
sexual abuse, some members use different names and don't reveal
much of their history or feelings. Nevertheless, they may contribute
poems or stories that inspire or comfort other BB members.

Annmarie is one of those cyber artists, but she wishes to use her
own name, because writing poetry and sharing her words online has
help her overcome shame she used to feel about what happened to
her; she doesn't want to hide anymore, she says. Annmarie has written poems about her cyberspace support group and written of her
anguish about being infertile. Annmarie also wrote a poem about
her friend whom she met through the Sexual Abuse bulletin board.

For Miss Vicki

Oh! What a friend I have found
while treading over shaky ground,
our lives so different, yet so parallel
We both had lived our private hell

She, too, walked on tender feet
Was it fate that we should meet?
We both had made the ultimate sacrifice . . .
lost childhood innocence would be our price
I found comfort in the words of a stranger,
and speaking truth no longer seemed a danger.
In a sense, she took my hand
picked me up, helped me stand.

She is someone I truly trust
there's nothing we haven't discussed
With her I have nothing to hide
She knows of the darkness inside.

She knows my deepest secrets,
something I shared without regrets,
For she, too, knows it all too well
We've both lived the same hell.

Who would have ever guessed
I could be so richly blessed,
to find a friendship based on truth and love . . .
she is, to me, an angel from above.

Annmarie and Vicki began corresponding via e-mail in 1994. That progressed to phone calls and regular letters. Just about a year ago, Annmarie flew out to Michigan to meet her friend in person. "We had never even exchanged photos, but I knew I would know her the moment I saw her, and I did. We spent four days like teenagers at a slumber party. We've moved beyond the abuse that brought us together and have gone on to form a very strong friendship."

Finding others who have endured sexual abuse is critical for survivors. For a time, in news commentaries and literature, it became fashionable to denigrate the proliferation of support groups, where people share deep, painful feelings about their abusive childhoods. For example, in Sheri Reynolds' novel *Bitterroot Landing*, the protagonist, who was abused as a child, first investigates a support group, then shuns and later mocks it. (She overhears the group at the church where she lives and works as a custodian.) Instead, the woman gleans wisdom from the statues she imagines talking to her. The voices, metaphorically speaking, are her own inner wisdom. This is a lyrically written and wonderfully imaginative story. Unfortunately, a hallmark of people from troubled families is that they isolate, which exacerbates their problems. And people from abusive backgrounds frequently have developed an internal monologue filled with fear and despair. Finding sources of love and encouragement strengthens, rather than weakens, the powerful healthy inner voice often buried within us. And as that inner voice grows more hopeful, grows louder and stronger—we can then learn to nurture and comfort ourselves with learned optimism. Thus experts overwhelmingly agree that regardless of whether it's socially fashionable, reaching out to others—whether you do it online, offline, with a family member, minister, friend, therapist, or support group—reaching out and talking about feelings, about what happened in your past, is as standard a cure for trauma as chemotherapy is for cancer.

But just as with the gay and lesbian community, unfortunately, many sexual abuse survivors can't talk to their families and lose that source of support. Family members either side with the perpetrator or don't want to believe the sexual abuse happened, mainly because it would require them to take action. Even in families where the abuse is not disputed, say experts, families often reject sexually abused members—they are too painful a reminder of what everyone wants to forget. It is common in these families to "shoot the messenger," because nobody wants to face the message.

Holly e-mailed us with this comment: "It's hard to say about my 'bio family.' I speak with them often enough, at least part of them anyway. But to say 'close,' no I don't think so. I have been through a lot with my ED [eating disorder] and SA [sexual abuse]. My family knows of both, but have more or less chosen to deny their existence. It is the best they can do—I am beginning to understand that. I think that since this last near-death relapse of the ED, they are coming to terms with it, but I doubt they have any inkling that it is not a problem that goes away once medical conditions stabilize and weight gain arrives.

"The family I have built here on the P [Prodigy online service] is a family that believes in my strengths and accepts my weaknesses. They allow me to be real . . . to show the parts that are hurting. They ask questions and help me to heal. In terms of everyday life, I guess you could say that when my biological family comes to visit, I spend hours making the house spotless and organized. When one of my P family comes to visit, I leave the house as is—lived in and messy. Love and Peace, Holly."

Not everybody, embraces cyber relationships with such enthusiasm, however. While she says online communities can be a wonderful resource, Dr. Suzanna Walters, a professor of sociology at Georgetown University, cautions that participating in online relationships as a form of intimacy can be a mistake.

Walters, in a telephone interview, likens online communities to the proliferation of talk shows, where strangers get on "Jenny Jones" and weep in front of people. "I think it's sad," she says. "It's a sad commentary on our inability to find embodied, humane ways of connecting with each other.

Some observers note that one of the attractions to cyber communities is that they create fewer obligations than traditional friendships—a critical factor in relating today. Indeed, we are a work-focused, not a family-focused society. Walters adds, "The Internet becomes a way for people to create community, to find like-minded people. But it can never substitute for the intimacies that occur with physical proximity," she says. "We are embodied as human beings. We aren't just what we type into computers. We take up physical space. When intimacy gets detached from that physicality, there's the potential for a kind of alienation. The people you are communicating with can become an object. They don't become a flesh-and-blood person."

While some folks, such as Walters, fear online communities are reducing human relationships to electronic bleeps in cyberspace, there are others who disagree." Charley Murphy, quoted in an article in *Common Boundary*, says, "I have a technological optimist in me that says this [the Internet] is a seed that may well be one of the things that counter the entropy, the tearing apart of our communities."[4]

Holly, mentioned above as a member of the sexual abuse bulletin board, echoes that sentiment: "They [friends] may not be with me in a physical sense, but their love comes through the screen and touches me in ways that no one else could. In a way, I feel it is even a more honest relationship than someone you meet in person. For the person responding to you is doing so without knowing whether you are white, black, Indian, or Hispanic, Catholic or Protestant. There are no cultural biases to get in the way. They only see the true me, and yet they still want to be there. That in itself is honest and rare."

What's more, for Holly and many others, many cyber relationships do become flesh and blood relationships. As a result of having an online family, Holly says, "I have gotten to talk to people in states thousands of miles away and see parts of the country that were otherwise unknown to me.

"In July, my husband and I wanted to go on vacation for our five-year anniversary. So we went to meet, in person, one of the people we met on the BB. We had never really talked on the phone, and did not know what each other looked like, but it was the most natural meeting of my life. I felt as though I was entering a safe and warm environment. It was by far a fantastic, love-filled vacation. I look forward to being able to visit other friends from the BBs."

Walters believes that if online communities become a substitute for meeting people and for being with people in the flesh, it would be "terrible." If it's a secondary way of connecting, of getting and sharing information, it's great. If it becomes a substitute, where people spend hours and hours [online], it's to their detriment. All the time they're doing that, they're not being in public spaces, not going to movies, not being in the world, not engaging with friends, flesh-and-blood people."

Another concern Walters has is the anonymity factor. "You have no way of knowing if the person is who they say they are," she says. "There is such incredible room for deception. Obviously there have been cases where people, men, tried to lure girls into meeting them by masquerading as someone they're not. But there's also a real danger of misrepresentation, a kind of construction of a fantasy self that is disturbing."

Indeed, anyone who has gone online has heard stories of cyber deception. And headlines in local papers around the country are beginning to reflect proliferating deceit. "Computer pen pal is charged in county. L.A. man met 13-year old at Chesterfield schools," read one headline in the March 28, 1995, edition of *Richmond Times Dispatch*. Take a look at the opening of the story:

"A 13-year old Chesterfield girl, surfing the Internet with her computer believed she had found the perfect pen pal when she linked up with a 19-year old Los Angeles man last month. Their computer conversations went on for more than 30 days before he suggested they get together. So on March 16th, the man flew to Richmond and told the girl to meet him at an elementary school.

"But the man wasn't exactly who he said he was, police said. The self-described condom salesman was really 32, and he possessed 'a big, spiral-bound notebook that had the names of girls in other cities across the country,' said Chesterfield Police, Lt. Ben Mize.

"'He hadn't really proposed anything,' Mize said. 'But I know in fact that he kissed her on several occasions. We felt like he was probably up to something else.'"[5]

Even I have witnessed firsthand one brand of this new wave of cyber deception. One of the mentors on the gay and lesbian bulletin board was helping me set up public notices to invite feedback on cyberfamilies, the week the Kyle Krittan story broke. Kyle was a gay teenager living in the boonies of Nebraska, who, despite the challenges life dealt him, seemed to have it all together. His online persona was engaging, articulate and breathlessly optimistic.

I logged onto the computer one morning to find a public notice from Kyle's dad informing the online community that Kyle had just been killed in a car accident on the way home from a high school football game. He was hit by a drunk driver. Kyle's father invited online friends to share their memories of Kyle, which the father said he would read at the memorial service. "We know that [Kyle] is already telling God how things should be run and is making the other angels laugh, but we do ask for your prayers for our family," Kyle's Dad wrote.

I said some prayers. I thought of my own two sons and spent the whole day wondering about the insanity of raising our precious children, only to have their lives accidentally, unnecessarily, and instantly ended. Ended by something totally out of our control.

The news of Kyle's death zapped rapidly over the gay and lesbian bulletin board. Across the country, computer monitors lit with public notices by bulletin board members expressing sadness and outrage that such a terrible thing could happen to a refreshing, innocent kid like Kyle.

One member, in awe of this youngster, reached into his electronic memory files to retrieve Kyle's own public notice just a few weeks ago, which described how he told his father that he was gay. His parents came off as the most understanding, sympathetic parents on God's green earth. It was like a nineties version of "Leave it To Beaver"; you could just imagine ole June and Ward welcoming the Beave back into fold, for they cared not a bit that he was gay. "You know, God doesn't give us our children," Kyle quoted his father as saying. "He only loans them to us for a while, but your Mom and I both feel that God loaned us a very special person when He loaned us a gay child. We will do everything in our power to make it as easy as possible for you to be gay."

Unfortunately, this electronic model of family acceptance quickly unraveled. When some of the online members tried to find out more information about the accident, it became apparent that there was no accident; there was no funeral. Kyle was a constructed fantasy. Somebody made him up.

Before Kyle blew his own fuse, bulletin board leaders had been so taken with his inspirational words that they had invited him to become an online mentor. That meant that his real identity would have had to be verified. Kyle found a convenient way to avoid that, the bulletin board leaders suspect, a way that was emotionally devastating for members of the gay and lesbian bulletin board.

"Misrepresentations in cyberspace, as in real life, work on a sliding scale," says Richard Vanaman, in an e-mail from Las Vegas. "Gay BBers might not feel betrayed if Kyle had posted as a gay man, though he was a lesbian. But what if he'd been an FBI agent trying to entrap some Kentucky fried chickenhawk [pederast]. The Prodigy users greatest fear was that Kyle had hoodwinked all his cyber friends by inventing an 'identity' that didn't match his identity at all, and that they'd wasted their love and admiration on a lie. . . . But on the info-highway, everyone has a fictional component. Sensitive netheads who seek to verify their virtual friends can get the rug pulled out from under them."

"What is noteworthy about this type of disillusionment is the way the electronic community goes about healing itself," Carolyn Shaffer and Kristin Anundsen write in *Creating Community Anywhere*. When members express their emotions, and respond to others' comments in a sort of "group soul searching," this facilitates the community process.

Referring to fake suicides online, similar to Kyle's saga, the authors write, "Members could communicate their feelings when they felt them, at any time day or night; they tended to speak more honestly and freely than if they were confronting one another face to face; and everyone involved could 'hear' the others' comments exactly as they had been made, without the distorting effect that occurs when stories are passed serially from one to another."[6]

That sequence of events is precisely what occurred after Kyle faked his demise online. Weary, but wiser, bulletin board members understood that cyber deception can be real, and that they must be wary of it. But in many ways, the Kyle crises brought online members closer; it didn't stop them from posting, from continuing to share their deepest feelings about life and about themselves. It didn't stop people from wanting to connect with other people.

Says Don Davis, "One of the things most of us yearn for is an intense emotional attachment with someone whom we respect and we trust. Cyberspace really allows us to get that kind of emotional relationship without having to go through all the guff one traditionally goes through to get there: meeting one another, dealing with how he looks and how I look, and then dealing with where we go. And how many times do we go out before I start telling him secrets, or he starts telling me secrets?

"In cyberspace, you pretty much can connect quickly and find out a lot about the other person's intellect and what they say their value system is. And just like in real life, you never really know. But after a while, again like in life, you will discover the truth."

For centuries, folks have been expressing themselves and discovering the "truth" through a variety of mediums, from cave paintings, to the beating of drums, to the modern pecking of computer keyboards. Peter Hawes, author of the *Common Boundary* article "Casting a Wider Net," likens the spawning of the electronic age to a time when "the written word began to supplant oral storytelling."

"The internet, with its boxes, cables, wires, and satellites, is a materialization of the spiritual connection that we already share with our fellow humans but have been given little cultural permission to celebrate. What's happening," he says, quoting one expert, "is an electronic neurosphere that is going to change philosophy, theology, the way we think about ourselves. I mean literally a global mind field that is spawning a new culture."[7]

So, caught up in this world migration onto the computer, obviously the problems people *can* encounter online aren't stopping them from logging on—just as divorce statistics aren't slowing down the number of young couples heading to the altar. Take Patricia, who, responding to a bulletin board notice about cyberfamilies, e-mailed us this message:

"We recently acquired a computer, and I am very new to [this] network. As I have gone throughout the different posts and read replies, I noticed a miraculous thing . . . a wonder in today's society—people reaching out to other people and actually caring! The people here in California do not generally know their neighbors and it can be lonely. But here strangers become important and beloved friends.

"Creating friendships here provides people with a sense of belonging. The amount of support and love is awesome. People post here not only to gain for themselves, but to share the positive thoughts and energy they have. It feels good to know that your bulletin bolstered someone on a gray day. It is a place where you know that your contribution to this little universe matters. And your presence is valued. A place where people welcome you and miss you when you're gone.

"Maybe it sounds like people who go to the bulletin boards have no life. But they are really any one of us who works, raises a family, shops, has hobbies, goes to school, has pain, or wonders how others cope. This world could use a stronger sense of family and belonging."

8

Afrocentrism

Magical Kinship

❧

"Sisterhood is the one way black women have survived. We have had to depend on each other. And the weight, the value, we give to our friendships is so large that once it is given, once the hands are taken, it is very hard to lose. You can give up a lover much easier . . . In times of trouble there are about seven women in the United States I can call at any hour and say, 'Now. Now. I need you now.' And they will come. No questions. No objections. Nothing would keep them from me, or me from them."

—Maya Angelou[1]

Winter sunsets are among my favorite things. Looking around my middle-class, suburban, wooded neighborhood, I stand beneath a great arch of watermelon dripping color in a frozen lilac sky. Each sunset is different, and as part of our evening ritual, I take my small sons outside to wonder at these impressionistic masterpieces etched in nature.

I am amazed. In the summer of 1957—when my mother brought me home from the hospital as a newborn—we came home to a public housing unit. In the projects I mostly recall cinder block dwellings and grimy, littered highways. I don't remember ever seeing woods flaming in fuchsia and orange as the sun's descending glow ignited the trees.

We lived in the projects until the early sixties when I was five years old, because my father, who suffered from paralyzing clinical depression in his late fifties, was unable to provide for better living arrangements. Some doctors theorized that a severe head injury caused my father's depression. Other doctors theorized that the severely strict brothers who ran the Catholic grade school my father attended in Ireland brutalized him. This trauma, they asserted, left him vulnerable to depression. My mother, however, believed that when my father left his cloistered, familiar Irish neighborhood in New York City to look for more stable work, the loneliness and isolation, exacerbated by the responsibility of having four young daughters late in life, triggered a genetic predisposition to depression.

Although my mother worked full-time throughout my childhood, I still vividly remember walking with her to a neighborhood community center each week to pick up government-issued orange surplus cheese, powdered eggs, and milk, which we needed to survive.

When I was in kindergarten, my family moved up—and I mean up—to a blue-collar black neighborhood, and I fell in love with the family next door. I desperately wanted to be Tia Thompson. I secretly envied Tia as she sat on the front stoop in her Sunday best after church each week. Her raven, wavy hair freshly twisted in three fat braids, always decorated with brightly colored barrettes and satiny ribbons that matched her soft lacy dresses. Confined to the steps so she wouldn't get dirty, Tia looked like a round-eyed china doll. It's just that her face was a lustrous ebony instead of the familiar rosy white. Mostly, I remember how her hair, and the skin rimming her face, always glistened from the Vaseline her mom used to tame Tia's wild mane.

Once in a while, if my sisters and I were very lucky, Tia's plump, light-skinned, soft-spoken mother, Gloria, would let us into their house to play. But she need only frown once if we got too loud in that immaculate house with its soothing, peach-colored living room walls.

Tia's father, Harry, was the closest I ever had to a father figure. He was a fourth-grade teacher at one of the elementary schools downtown. I conjure his appearance fondly: a short, stocky man with a wide, mustached grin that lit his dark brown face. I still recall what a strict disciplinarian he was; but I, who had known only chaos at home, craved the loving structure he provided for his family.

Although I was an overly responsible kid, I was also hot tempered and on the wild side. Mr. Thompson was forever trying to talk some sense into me; I don't think he ever realized, though, how much took hold. Especially when Daddy's dark spells hit. I remember one summer afternoon in 1968, when my sister Deirdre was nine and I eleven. The consummate tomboy, I was outside playing kick ball with the neighborhood boys when Dee Dee came running. She was crying hysterically, because Daddy was in the basement trying to hang himself. A bomb of adrenaline detonated in my body as I flew back to the house with her. When I got inside Daddy was standing on a kitchen chair fumbling as he tied a piece of clothesline to the water pipes overhead. I could see that rope was attached to a noose he'd made around his neck.

Deirdre pleaded with him to stop, but I yelled. That was mostly my job as a child, to get daddy out of bed, feed him, and make sure he didn't hurt himself. Shaking, he put the rope down and went upstairs. I ran for the phone to call Mom at work, and Daddy was back in the hospital by nightfall. For a while, anyway. Knowing Mr. Thompson was next door didn't end my fears, but it sure helped.

And Mr. Thompson, as we respectfully called him, helped out in emergencies. Like when I got hit by a car in first grade and lay in the middle of an oil-drenched street with one shoe blown off, it was Mr. Thompson who hovered over me, keeping the crowd back. When I momentarily gained consciousness and begged to be taken inside the house, my trembling father tried to lift me as my hysterical mother screamed in the background. But Mr. Thompson took charge: He stopped my father, leaned down softly to reassure me and ordered my mother not to let anyone pick me up until the ambulance arrived.

I recall in the early grades, sitting week after week in my dreamy, candle-lit Catholic church listening to the priest perform the stations of the cross. Frequently bored, I'd escape by imagining Mr. Thompson as my daddy.

Tia was my best friend at home, but my best friend at my white

Catholic grade school was Paula. We've been friends since first grade, and we are still in touch. Every year, she writes me a letter on my birthday, signed "Your friend always," and calls at Christmas. Her third daughter is my Goddaughter. Besides Paula, though, I was not accepted by other girls in my Catholic school because my family was poor. Because my family lived on the wrong side of town. Because my chocolate-colored wool school uniform was frequently stained, rumpled, and torn. In terms of friendship, economics was the great divide; the fact that my schoolmates and I shared the same color skin was irrelevant. And when I slipped my peanut butter-and-sugar sandwich, wrapped in a napkin, out of my coat pocket for lunch, I, too, knew I didn't belong. These kids had pretty lunch boxes decorated with Barbie dolls and loaded with deli sandwiches, TastyKakes, and fruit.

But after school, however, once I'd traversed the two miles back to my black neighborhood, I was home! It was truly a case of kinship across racial lines; the normally rigid color barriers were blurred by the fact that we were all poor together. And despite our collective poverty, summertime in that neighborhood was pure joy: Each morning a sunny brilliance lured me out of sleep as I automatically leaned over to grab a Nancy Drew book from the stack by my bed. Stretching like a lazy marmalade cat, I'd snuggle down into the cool sheets, deliciously escaping into some fantasy world until a grumbling stomach drove me downstairs for a bowl of Coco Puffs.

Then, out the door I'd spring, for a day of building clubhouses out of plywood, and terrorizing the young, white hippies who had organized in a nearby row house to launch grassroots protests of the Vietnam War. They called the project "Vietnam Summer." And what a thrill sneaking with a handful of my friends into the basement of their headquarters to spy on those college-boy rebels. It was our duty, as we believed grown-up rumors that these protesters were actually communists trying to divide Americans on the issue of Vietnam.

Spying, though, soon turned into basement "racketeering," which meant banging an old beater piano and screaming in unison: "We're having a party! We're having a party!" until the long-haired, white iconoclasts swarmed down and threw us out on our butts: Me, the wiry white girl, and my group of black friends.

But before every racketeering adventure, my friend Bernard and I would hide some willing kid in an old filing cabinet, so he wouldn't be thrown out with the rest of us. And as soon as the young men got back to the critical job of organizing protests—our hidden compatriot opened the basement door for another round.

In between our mischievous fun, my face was warmed by the tranquilizing sun, as I hung out laundry and gazed at the sky. I thought I had everything back then.

Because, you see, although I was born the palest shade of white, I had "soul"—that elusive black coolness that meant I knew how life really worked.

The best memories of my childhood involve roaming the streets of that ghetto. Sure, like all kids I got into childish fights with my playmates. And though name calling sometimes degenerated into "honky!" and "nappy-haired nigger!" like with most kids, our fights blew over quickly.

My own neighborhood had a notoriously high crime rate, but what was invisible in the statistics were the thousands of good black people who surrounded me. You see, growing up, I saw mostly hard-working black people who wanted the best for their children and who wanted, like me, to own pretty things, to have a place of dignity in the world.

Which is why I could never understand why my white school friends looked down on black people. Walking to the store for penny candy, I was always soothed by the black harmonies ringing out from Baptist Churches on most every street corner. When my beloved, red-haired dog, Patsy, died, several of our neighbors came over and sat with us late into the night, consoling us over coffee and one of my mother's famous cinnamon cakes. It was a black woman at my mother's job who lent her money to buy a piano for my sister, Sally, who took classical lessons for almost a decade. It was a black girl who was my sister's best friend. Almost every weekend, Sally went to stay with her friend's family which had clawed its way out of the projects and moved to a predominantly white suburb. They were my sister's "other family." My sister told me once that it was through these special people that she'd learned what a loving family was all about.

My own extended family had long abandoned us because of the mental illness and poverty that dominated our family. My aunts and uncles were busy pursuing careers, raising children, and saving to buy decent homes and send their kids to college. Contact with my family was simply an embarrassment for them and a call to helping arms, which they perhaps had no time or energy to heed. Most of my father's relatives still lived in Ireland, where my father was born. But the relatives who lived in America, we rarely saw. I vividly remember my Uncle Richard's barely masked pity as he crumpled bills into my hand during one of his few visits from Upstate New York. He had just returned from visiting his brother, my father, at the state hospital, and even as a child, I could read the disgust on my uncle's face as he looked around our black neighborhood and shabby row house. At the time, I couldn't have cared less, because all I could think about was the ten bucks.

Not long ago, I sent my Uncle Richard's daughter a card and some pictures of my family. Although she is my first cousin, and close in age, we have never met. When she returned the greeting with some photos of her own, I was amazed to discover that she looks tall, athletically built and red-headed, like me. We could've been sisters.

But instead, my sisters and brothers and my extended family were Mr. Thompson, his family, and the other black folks I grew up with. The warmth, closeness, and kinship in that poor community inspired me, nourished me.

True, African-Americans certainly have no cultural link to a perfect model of kinship—any more, perhaps, than the passionate, loyal, affectionate Greek, Italian, and Spanish native cultures—known historically for placing preeminent value on family ties and friendship. But today, African Americans are the largest minority in the United States—12.6 percent of the population, according to U.S. Statistical Abstracts.[2] Examining their extended family relationships can be fruitful, because in some important ways, African-Americans have held onto models of kinship from their native lands. Models that are a source of strength and that serve the African-American community well.

Harold M. Rose, whose study of the spacial patterns of black Americans was reported in *Ethnicity in Contemporary America: A Geographical Appraisal*, explains that blacks represent one of the original groups involved in the making of America. Their presence in North America dates back to 1619, and today the population of

African-Americans in the United States is larger than was the whole nation's population in 1850.

"But what is important," he writes, "is the developmental sequence that has led that population to acquire an *internal* identity that is rooted in a sense of peoplehood:

> Blacks today not only represent a population group distinguishable in terms of a set of biological traits, but more importantly it represents a population whose experiences in America have promoted a *social bonding* that has led to a unique group culture.
>
> This process has fostered not only a racial identity, but an *ethnic* identity as well. It is not possible to indicate when an ethnic identity began to emerge. But, by the close of the Civil War it became obvious that blacks no longer represented a population group that had simply evolved from a common racial stock.
>
> Because race in the United States has historically represented a more powerful social construct than has ethnicity, the ethnic qualities of the black population have been given only limited attention by scholars.[3]

Alexa Case, who developed and taught a federally funded program in the seventies on visual literacy in the inner cities, said in a personal interview that what caught her attention about the black culture was the fact that "everybody was everybody's cousin."

Case says she didn't understand that until she discovered their sense of interconnectedness. African-Americans have a sense of familial ties, she says, whether the ties are genetic or not. "Often [inner-city] children were raised by grandparents, by someone who was their 'uncle,' or by people who were assuming a role as guardians; but you never could tell whether there was a biological connection," she explains.

In contrast to her own suburban perspective, Case says African Americans "know how to makeshift. They are naturally more tribal." A white single mother, for example, emerging from a nuclear family, might feel more isolation, she says, "but African Americans instead draw in uncle so-and-so to make a family."

In Terry McMillan's best-selling novel *Waiting to Exhale,* which was recently made into a movie, four black women are searching to meet a man who will take their breath away. As men drift in and out of their lives, the four women adhere to each other like extended family. When thirty-six-year-old Bernadine's husband leaves her for a white woman, it is Bernadine's friends, Gloria and Robin, who help pick up the pieces. Gloria's thirty-eighth birthday party is one of the few times in the book that the friends are together at the same time. Slightly drunk, they get around to discussing their friendship, which is a lot like a family. When one of the women says the only thing they have in common is that they all have no men, Gloria replies:

"So what? Men ain't everything. When are you gonna realize that? I'm having a good time sitting here acting silly with you guys, and do you think if any of us had a man we'd be here doing this?"

"That's precisely my point, Savannah," [another of the four friends] said. "If. But we don't. And let me say this up front. If I had a man and it was your birthday and you were going to be over here by yourself all lonely and shit and Robin and Berandine called me up to come over here to help you celebrate, I'd still be here, girl. So don't even think a man would have that much power over me that I'd stop caring about my friends. And that's the truth."[4]

Near the end of the novel, a health emergency involving Gloria draws the women together in hospital room. A hospital employee asks the women who's responsible for Gloria. "I think we're all responsible for her," Berandine said. "She's our sister. Please tell us she's going to be OK."[5]

Gerald Early, director of African-American Studies at Washington University in St. Louis, and author of an essay published in *Civilization* magazine, asserts that black separatists have every right to rage against a western multicultural liberalism, because "liberalism set free the individual but did not encourage the development of a community within which the individual could flower." In his essay, Early explains that African-Americans who prefer the company of other African-Americans, and who glorify kinship ties in their native homeland, honor African nobility, and mourn a lost paradise in Africa are simply wishing to "retrieve a place for themselves in their own community." A refuge in a white-dominated culture.[6]

Indeed, finding a place of refuge is central to many people's lives, today—black people, white people, and people of all shades in between. For in our modern era, the color green (the color of money, and standard of living), more than race or cultural heritage, seems to determine the intensity of kinship bonds. The more wealthy and industrialized one's culture, the more likely blood kinship bonds will have deteriorated. For example, one hears folk stories of Westernized Japan, where elderly people resort to "renting" families for the holidays. Kinship bonds have degenerated to the point that the elderly are perceived as expendable and often abandoned.

That's why elevating African-American kinship as a model for extended family connectedness is valuable, because despite living in a highly industrialized country African Americans, more than any other group, have preserved a more natural mode of affiliation. Unlike many white families, contemporary African-American kinship is not organized primarily around the nuclear family—an organization rapidly becoming the trend in most industrialized countries. Many African-American families also provide multiple caregivers for their young, and many have retained more of an extended family than is observable in other westernized cultures. Members of African-American families also play more roles and exchange roles more easily within a family.

Richard Majors, Ph.D, former researcher for the Urban Institute in Washington, D.C., and author of *Cool Pose: The Dilemmas of Black Manhood in America* and *The American Black Male: His Present Status and Future,* says African Americans have unique kinship bonds.

In direct contrast to the way most white men treat each other, African-American men, who are often strangers walking down the street, will make contact and most likely ask, "What's up, Brother?" This embracing, and immediate "Fictive Kinship," according to Majors, stems from blacks' shared experience of slavery and oppression. And, he says, from the black solidarity movement in the sixties.

Fictive Kinship is as strong a bond as physical attraction, Majors says. But in this case, you're not romantically attracted; you've had a shared history of similar pain. Majors says that another contributor to African Americans' ability to easily extend kinships bonds to large groups of people is the fact that many blacks are raised by an extended family of grandparents, uncles, aunts, and so on.

"I was raised by my grandmother," says Majors in a telephone interview, "and a good deal of my friends were raised by grandparents, uncles, or another relative. My best friend's mother is raising a third generation of great grandchildren."

According to Majors, economic instability and single-parent families are strains on the African-American community. But a recent study Majors conducted suggests that married black males are actually more traditional, in terms of men being the breadwinner, than white males are. When given the opportunities and the resources, black males are good fathers, and they rate being a good provider as very important.

But slavery broke up the family, says Majors, and disproportionate numbers of black men die or are worn down from economic conditions, stress, hypertension, depression, and violence—all of which are reactions to the horrific living conditions black men endure.

Experts also cite the growing wage gap between the upper classes and the poor as another reason why marriage among poor and inner-city people does not appear to be a good option. Real wages (adjusted for inflation) have fallen 35–40 percent since 1970. Two people struggling and not making it financially makes no sense, especially if much-needed government assistance is denied because a person is married. Criticizing government assistance in this instance is akin to blaming the safety net on the high-wire act at a circus for catching folks who fall in. And automatically assuming most people want to fall in the net is sheer lunacy. My mother never intended to fall into the net of government assistance, but without that surplus food we got each week, my family would have starved.

Indeed, the net may have some holes. But before we inhumanely whisk it away (which hurts mostly children) wouldn't a moral alternative be to look at the structural problems in our economy that are causing people to fall into the net? For example—the dramatic drop in real wages in this country, or the fact that millions of blue-collar manufacturing jobs that pulled many blacks out of poverty in the sixties have gone overseas. Rather than acknowledge the vast, structural economic divisions in this country, many would rather blame the victims, shoo them off welfare, train them and hustle them into job market.

But "job training for what?" Theresa Funiciello asks in her controversial book *Tyranny of Kindness: Dismantling the Welfare System to End Poverty in America.* "If the strongest workers in the labor force (white men) continue losing relatively better paying jobs (i.e. steel production, automobile, manufacturing, middle management and even finance) and continue a downward spiral into lower-wage [service and trade] work, it is not too difficult to guess who will get pushed out altogether. Women and men of color."

And writes Funiciello, the trend toward rote jobs created by robotization and computerization diminishes "mid-level positions and disintegrates the ladder of opportunity that remains the myth of entry-level employment." The growing service sector, such as AT&T, traditionally dominated by women and men of color, is also rife with technological displacement. "Recordings will do the talking from now on," she writes.[7]

Facing ever-diminishing economic opportunities, marriage among poor, inner-city blacks is proving a less viable strategy for survival than it is for other ethnic groups. An article in the *New Republic* asserts that divorce rates that peaked in the seventies and eighties have actually slowed over the past years. But the author, Ruth Shalit, goes on to say: "Today, the most obvious instances of family instability and breakdown are in the (mainly black) urban underclass, where the problem is not divorce, but the failure of families to form or remain intact. Two out of three black children and one out of five white children are currently born out of wedlock.[8]

While marriage as an institution seems to be abandoned by many inner city poor blacks, the extended family ties of African Americans are often a valuable and critical source of kinship.

A plethora of literature highlights the multifaceted role of the extended family in the black community, particularly for the elderly. Sociologist Christopher Ellison of the University of Texas-Austin writes:

> The members of black extended families participate in broad support networks, often exchanging financial aid and an array of services (e.g. housing, household tasks, etc.). Research on a sample of urban black women suggests that while these exchanges of goods may have emerged as an adaptive reaction to deprivation among lower class blacks, close extended kin relations persist today even among upwardly mobile black families.

Unlike social support among friends, supportive exchanges among kin are governed by strict norms of reciprocity. Recent evidence indicates that material support is the predominant form of support received from family members. In contrast to resources acquired from other sources (government agencies, friends), the receipt of aid from family members does not appear to carry a social stigma, provided that the recipient is willing to offer future assistance to other members of the kinship group.

In addition to exchanging money and services, family members are typically in frequent contact with one another. Often members live close enough to visit regularly. Black family members provide companionship and emotional support for one another, and the extended family can constitute an important mental health resource. The available evidence suggests that among blacks, kin are more common as members of social networks than non kin, and extended families are more prominent among blacks than among whites.[9]

Paco is a good example. A thirty-year-old hair stylist, Paco describes his childhood African-American family as "pretty close." He is number four out of nine kids: Six sisters and two brothers from two different marriages.

"We all live in a proximity of about ten minutes apart," he says. "My sister, she lives just across the street. My brother, he just moved from across the street; but he's still five minutes away. They help out when they can. My sister keeps the kids [two daughters and a son) at no charge. I'm off on Mondays. My Mom keeps them one day a week—her day off. My sister keeps them the rest of the week.

"I have one sister in the Army; she's in Washington State, but I call her all the time, so my phone bill is astronomical. She just had a baby, so I've been talking to her about every night. She had complications, so we've been keeping in close touch.

"Most of my relatives on my father's side, I'm closest to. When I was growing up, it was the exact opposite; I was closest to all my aunts and uncles on my mother's side. Now that I've gotten older, they've moved away and now I'm closer to my aunts and uncles on my father's side. I'm from a divorced marriage.

"Family is very important for me. I work in a salon. I'm just starting out, and I can't afford day care. My family knows that, and they help me out any way they can by providing day care and putting the kids on the bus when I need them to.

"I'll do my sisters' hair and we exchange services. If you can't depend on your family, who else can you depend on?"

Although Paco says extended families "are more prevalent in the black community where blacks try to stick together," he explains that he used to work in a noodle factory and also saw a strong extended family network among the immigrant Korean culture. But with two parents working and teens having more freedom these days, Paco says he's begun to see ties weakening in black families, as well as in other race families.

Dawn Lewis has written a thesis and begun work on her doctoral dissertation, with Dr. Kent Bailey, on the differences in biological and psychological kinship between African-American women and white women. (Lewis was listed in the 50th anniversary edition of Ebony Magazine as one of the fifty African-American "Leaders of Tomorrow" in America.) In her work with Dr. Bailey, Lewis has found that kinship is more highly related to self-esteem for African-American women than for white women.

This finding, Lewis says in a personal interview, lies in a distant past of the African American—the extraordinary worth African culture places on family in its native land.

> Even in Africa, we believed in the concept of extended family, in the sense that your whole neighborhood is also your family," says Lewis. "If you talked to a black person they wouldn't say "This is my biological or my psychological [family]." Basically they would say, 'This is my aunt'; they would say 'Aunt Sue,' even if she wasn't biologically related. Or if it was a half sister, they'd say, 'this is my sister.' It goes all the way back to African times where we felt that family was more than just a nuclear family. It can [include] cousins, your aunt, your godsister, your godmother.

Ancient Africa

As my childhood experiences growing up in an African-American neighborhood illustrate, I, too, once felt a part of the large extended family of the African-Americans Lewis describes so well—even though I shared neither skin color nor an ancient heritage. It is easy to understand why I once yearned so much to be part of this "other clan," if one examines African-American roots. For it is in that heritage, we can trace the original roots of an ancient African "kinship magic." The roots of that mysterious something that makes deep human relationships, that makes "love" so fulfilling, and spiritually satisfying. Africa is the evolutionary home of all members of the human race. In that sense we all share African roots.

The immediacy and power of Africa for the indigenous African, and for those transplanted around the globe, is phenomenal. A deep spiritual longing of the African-American for the land and culture of his ancestors is especially keen, and is a central feature of African-American psychology.

Self-esteem, self-efficacy, and personal identity are inseparable from the "Africanness" of an individual, and the Afrocentrist Molefi Asante argues that blacks must come to terms with their African consciousness in order to be fully centered and fully true to self. Africa comprises many peoples, but all share a larger, cultural umbrella that unifies them as Africans.

As the great anthropologist and Africanist Colin Turnbull writes in his book *Man in Africa:*

> Wherever one looks in Africa . . . certain similarities emerge. There is a focus on social personality rather than on individual identity. This is learned in the normal way as a member of a biological family that is itself almost invariably a cooperative economic unit. This same family also serves as a model for wider social relationships, ultimately embracing the whole society, be it a band, tribe, or nation. This feeling of "kinship" is embedded in the culture . . . complemented by a sense of spiritual unity brought about by the focus of ideological attention upon the natural environment . . . taking it also as a model from which to fashion social and intellectual order. This creates societies that are . . . essentially democratic and essentially egalitarian. . . . Almost everywhere you travel . . . you are likely to find biological kin, each with its own separate circle of familial, economic, and political relationships. So everywhere you go, the myth of the tribe as a single biological unit is reinforced by a measure of actuality, and the ideal of familial relationships of obligation and privilege—and affection—is maintained.[10]

Thus, the African family, tribe, and nation is tied to the land and the natural order of things. In "Africanness" there is a warmth, spontaneity, and natural kinship that is lacking in modern societies that are held together by political coercion and rule of law. Turnbull bemoans that fact that many Western and some Eastern nations have lost the natural social order of Africa, where the moral imperatives of kinship and the social personality give way to technological complexity, so-called progress, and what he calls "security resting in a bank balance rather than in one's neighbors and kin."[11]

A Culture in Crisis

Turnbull wrote these words twenty years ago, and, unfortunately, many Africans of today have lost touch with their "Africanness" in the famine, political turmoil, and tribal hostilities that have characterized Africa in recent times.

Africa has been in economic crisis since the late 1970s, and there has been a precipitous deterioration in the well-being of the majority of Africans. Africa probably has the fastest-growing population of any region in the world, and the rate of increase rises about 3 percent each year. The twin plagues of economic malaise and a ballooning population have produced a continent characterized by high rates of infant mortality, short life expectancies, poor physical and emotional health, massive external debt, grinding poverty, exploitation of women and underutilization of the talents and resources of women, and widespread human rights violations, military dictatorships, and rule by power.

As Africa stands face to face with the demands of modernity, a constantly changing world, and the information revolution, the poverty-stricken citizens of Kenya, Ethiopia, Somalia, Nigeria, Ghana, and many other sub-Saharan countries now long for the Africa of the past—the ancient Africa of family, kinship, community, and spiritual connection with the land. It is one of the great tragedies of our age that the modern African must struggle to retain, yet often loses, the African spirit of community that so characterized the evolution of our human race over the last five million years.

In our hearts all human beings are Afrocentrists, in the sense that we share an African ancestry and a deep, subliminal affinity for the continent. Even outsiders are fascinated by its dark mysteries, mighty beasts of the jungle, and the warmth and vivacity of its people, in large measure, perhaps because in the deep recesses of our minds, we understand that our kinship psyche evolved from ancient Africa. For it was on that continent that the spirit of kinship was born, flourished, and was later handed down to all of us.

Genetically, the African, the Eskimo, the Laplander, the Englishman, the German, the Mongolian, and the Pacific Islander are all equally related to our most recent ancestors, *Homo sapiens,* but the indigenous African had a special geographic advantage over the rest of us: he grew up at "home," while the rest of us had to make our way in many strange lands. Forging our way in these unfamiliar lands, we may have lost much of the family and kinship magic that the native African possesses in such abundance.

Slave Families

Remains of our evolutionary ancestors have been found mainly in eastern and southern Africa, but the ancestral home of the majority of today's African Americans was West Africa. As little as 2,500 years ago, people living along the Niger River planted crops, caught fish, herded cattle, made tools, and created art in a time of plenty. Until about 2,000 years ago there was little contact between West Africans and the rest of the world . . . but their Edenic (Eden-like) world could not last forever. Around the time of Christ, Berber people from north of the Sahara began to cross the desert on camels to trade with their brothers to the south. A time of prosperity followed, and several great West African empires rose and fell, culminating with the great Ghana empire around the year 1000.

By this time, Arabs had expanded their trade with West Africa and it was not long before Islamic religions and Arab scholars began to change the cultural landscape of Africa. Islamic influence grew during the Mali Empire in the 1300s; by the 1500s, doctors, judges, Muslim priests, and other learned men were common sights in the African king's court. Centuries of lucrative trade and economic interdependence with the Arabs extracted a cost of monumental proportions, however. One of the chief Arab exports to Europe and other parts of the world were African slaves.

Slavery had been common in Africa before the Arabs, but its practice bore little resemblance to the slave trade that thrived a century later in America. The African slave was typically a prisoner of war, often integrated into the group as "psychological kin"; there was little in the way of abuse, torture, or needless exploitation. Some slaves even served as advisors to kings. And certainly there was no permanent class of slaves created at birth.

How things changed when Arabs first took African slaves with them to conquer parts of Portugal and Spain in the fifteenth century! In the following centuries, slavery would become one of the great tragedies of human history and the great destroyer of the kinship culture and kinship magic of the West Africans.

Children, teens, and adults were literally kidnapped—torn from their homes by force—and brutally transported in the stinking, crowded holds of slave ships to strange lands where new families had to be reconstituted from aggregations of people accidentally thrown together. Kinship magic had not been totally lost, but the struggle to keep it alive was a mighty one, helped along by stories of a common past, dreams of loved ones, and visions of a beloved land so recently and obscenely lost.

A Golden Age

The psychology of the modern African American, then, is one part tied to the continent itself; one part to the golden age of kinship in Western Africa; one part to the bittersweet memories of a reconstituted kinship culture during slavery; and one large part to the new world of America. You see, the African American is precisely that: an African in America. The most highly educated and socio-economically successful American black cannot help but look wistfully back to Africa on occasion. But as the phenomenal success of Alex Haley's *Roots* showed, even people of non-African heritage are fascinated by the African story.

As the poet Langston Hughes reveals in the following poem, the image of Africa is dear to the African American:

So long,
So far away
Is Africa.
Not even memories alive
Save those that history books create,

Save those that songs
Beat back into the blood—
Beat out of blood with words sad-sung
In strange un-Negro tongue—
So long,
So far away
Is Africa.

Subdued and time-lost
Are the drums—and yet
Through some vast mist of race
There comes this song
I do not understand,
This song of atavistic land,
Of bitter yearning lost
And touching each other natural as dew
In that dawn of music when I
Get to be a composer
And write about daybreak
In Alabama.[12]

Dawn Lewis, whose research correlates African-American self-esteem with family ties, echoes Langston Hughes's harkening back to the past to rediscover the importance of kinship ties in the African-American culture. In a personal interview, she stated:

"It all comes back to the origins of African Descent. [We] really believe in the concept of the village raising a child. One person represents us," says Lewis. "In African times we always did things together. Rituals are something that's coming out in the African-American culture. We're taking some of the symbols from Kwanzaa and applying them to our daily lives." (Kwanzaa is an African-American celebration in which communities give thanks for the past year and prepare for the new year. Fifteen to twenty million African Americans participate in the annual December celebration.)

To reinforce cultural identity—once a cohesive force in African culture—rituals are starting to become more important for girls and boys in America, Lewis adds. Rituals are a way of claiming people from your history and claiming an identity that makes you proud. "When we think about rituals, we're looking at structure and we're looking at unity," she explains. "Rituals mean you are someone of the village and you are representing us, and now you're going from a boy to a man, a girl to a woman. And [it's] not just a sense of, 'We're going to move you out of the village.' Africans focused on the process of initiation, rites of passages, going through different ceremonies. The whole village would be there. Everyone would watch, not just the immediate family. [Rituals] say we're proud of you."

Margaret Musgrove, in her book *Ashanti to Zulu: African Traditions* describes that cherished, ancient ritual in Africa—the coming-of-age initiation. "In Chagga, Africa, children grow up in groups of the same age and sex. Often a group takes a name that sounds brave or proud. The children work, play, and go to school together. In a special initiation ceremony they all become adults at the same time. Chagga priests perform this ceremony in traditional costumes, and sometimes the children's faces are painted. After a big celebration the children are considered adults."[13]

Echoing Lewis's observations, experts say African Americans are indeed bringing past traditions to life in America. Suggesting a powerful new use of psychological kinship, this "national movement [of rituals] is helping young black men cope with the difficulties they face from stereotyping and other societal pressures," writes Erin Burnette in an article published in the American Psychological Association's *Monitor.*

> Rites-of-passage and mentoring programs—started about ten years ago to target the problems of African American males—are providing solutions. Through initiation rites, the programs reinforce values such as self-respect, responsibility, and dedication to family, community, and each other. • • •
>
> Programs, such as Chicago's "The Young Warriors" are aimed at teaching kids what it means to be an African-American male. Six to ten participants attend group sessions and community activities during the school day. Forming a sort of intentional family, other mentoring programs require a teacher, parent, or community member to spend ninety minutes with a child each week doing activities such as field trips, movies, arts, and crafts, and community service.[14]

It seems, "Western societies have lost the traditions once used to initiate boys into manhood," the article asserts, quoting Rhoderick

Watts, Ph.D., who was a researcher and psychology professor at
DePaul University when this article was published. "Initiation rites
now consist of getting a driver's license, getting drunk, and having
sex. Rites-of-passage programs use traditional practices from Africa
and adapt them to the contemporary needs of young men in urban
United States communities."[15]

Black Kinship at Higher Socioeconomic Levels

"Rituals are not for everyone, though. Not everybody wants to
claim Africa," Lewis continues.

She says that blacks in higher socio-economic groups are now
starting to feel more isolated [from other blacks]. While they may
still have stronger ties with family compared to other races, they are
moving, she says, like the rest of the country, toward a more
Westernized mode of weakened kinship ties.

To combat this alienation, Lewis says many African Americans
are forming cultural groups, such as "Jack and Jill." A modern
brand of "intentional family," Jack and Jill is a national group for
black parents to meet each other to reinforce their children's cultural
identity. African Americans want a better education for their children, Lewis says, and will send them to predominantly white
schools, but then join Jack and Jill to unite them culturally.

Religion is also an important social unifier for African-
Americans: "Church, out of everything, is always going to be where
you see the black culture," explains Lewis. "Spirituality is very
important. If they're going to be isolated in their personal environment, as far as residence and education, church is a real big thing
that is always coming up in research [as being critical to blacks.]"
Lewis adds that the emphasis on spirituality in the African-
American family "goes across social-economic lines."

Much can be learned from African-American models of natural
kinship, from the way African-American kinship is evolving in this
country: As more blacks prosper and move up the economic ladder,
as they participate more in our country's high-tech communication,
as they begin to take more advantage of global travel, and as they
move away from their families to take better jobs, they will be in the
same boat as the rest of America.

Connecting back with our biological family, or connecting with those of a similar ethnic or racial makeup is critical to maintaining a feeling of heritage, a knowledge of cultural identity, and a sense of place in the world. For human beings, at essence, are a tribal people who naturally seek community, kinship, and love. I am reminded of this warm, nourishing notion of kinship on Sunday afternoons when my husband and I bicycle along a gorgeous, twenty-mile route bordering the James River in Richmond.

Racing up and down hills, my spirit glides aloft the wind, and I am instantly transported back to the ghetto of my childhood—where I first learned the joy of playing, running, and riding a bicycle. A ghetto where, in spite of poverty and a troubled family, I had a home, I had a people, I had a place I belonged.

Back in that neighborhood, where the poor huddled together, I learned that kinship has less to do with color of skin, heritage, religious faith, or blood bonds—and more do with our minds, and with our imagination.

9

Genetics of Racism
Shattered Kinship

"Watch your thoughts; they become words.
Watch your words; they become actions.
Watch your actions; they become habits.
Watch your habits they become character.
Watch your character; it becomes your destiny."
— Frank Outlaw[1]

"Watch your beliefs; they control your thoughts."
— Gary Fenchuk[2]

Searching for kinship, emphasizing our separateness, our exclusiveness, and luxuriating in the instinctive love of our own kind is basic to the human species. So yes, it's natural and healthy for ethnic, religious, and racial groups to celebrate their differences. And if we go with the premise that ignorance breeds fear, then multiculturalism—exposing people to a variety of cultures and teaching respect and understanding—is vital to coexisting in our racially diverse society. But if we focus too much on our uniqueness, if we get too caught up in our differences, we can become separatists.

Ever hear the old saying: "The best way to make a friend is to share an enemy"? Well, that is the malignant side of kinship.

In Toni Morrison's Pulitzer-Prize-winning novel, *Beloved,* the main character, proud, beautiful Sethe, escaped from slavery but is haunted by its history. That haunting takes the metaphorical shape of the ghost of Sethe's toddler daughter, Beloved, who comes back to avenge her own mysterious death. Beloved's death symbolizes the sheer horror of slavery, as Sethe laments:

> That anybody white could take your whole self for anything that came to mind. Not just work, kill, or maim you, but dirty you. Dirty you so bad you couldn't like yourself anymore. Dirty you so bad you forgot who you were and couldn't think it up. And though she and others lived through and got over it, she could never let it happen to her own. The best thing she was, was her children. Whites might dirty *her* all right, but not her best thing, her beautiful, magical best thing—the part of her that was clean. No undreamable dreams about whether the headless, feetless torso hanging in the tree with a sign on it was her husband or Paul A.; Whether the bubbling-hot girls in the colored-school fire set by patriots included her daughter; whether a gang of whites invaded her daughter's private parts, soiled her daughter's thighs and threw her daughter out of the wagon. She might have to work the slaughterhouse yard, but not her daughter. And no one, nobody on this earth, would list her daughter's characteristics on the animal side of the paper. No. Oh no.[3]

Morrison dedicated her novel to the "sixty million and more" victims of slavery. One of the worst kinship atrocities in human history, slavery arose and flourished because of a separatist philosophy, an erroneous belief that certain segments of our society were inferior, and therefore should not mingle with the larger, dominant society.

While studies show that groups sequestering themselves build a spirit of unity, bolster self-esteem, and help victims triumph the effects of prejudice, taken too far, sequestering can limit choices for finding psychological kin in our increasing world of strangers.

We have seen how kinship can be forged despite color of skin, heritage, religious faith, or blood bonds. As I explained earlier, I once loved and bonded to the black family who lived next door to me in the ghetto. Fundamentally, kinship involves our minds, our imagination. By opening my own doors of perception, essentially, I was able to forge a psychological kinship across racial lines. You see, the bigger picture here is that at its most basic level, kinship is a product of *classification,* of choosing.

Once classified as kin, a person is incorporated into a system of mutual obligations and benefits that is held together by the glue of love. He or she is now a part of something bigger than the self. Only death or such an egregious offense as a serious betrayal or horrific abuse can undo this classification.

Take Mark Twain's classic tale of Huckleberry Finn, who floats down the Mississippi River with the escaped slave, Jim, to a new life and freedom. Throughout the book Jim acts like a father figure to Huck—an ironic twist, because Huck's status as a white person, despite his youth, gave him authority over Jim.

Indeed, the raft serves as the household for this family of two runaways. Young Huck, in a canoe, tries to tie the raft to a river-bank. But he gets lost in the thick fog. Later, he climbs back on board the raft and pretends to be asleep. He's trying to trick Jim into thinking it's all been a dream. When Jim discovers the lie, he is angry, yet the reader sees clearly Jim's affection for his young master.

> When I get all wore out wid work, en wid de callin' for you, en went to sleep, my heart wuz los', en I didn't k'yer no mo' what become er me en de raf'. En when I wake up en fine you back agin', all safe and soun', de tears come en I could a got down on my knees and kiss yo' foot I's so thankful. En all you wuz thinkin' 'bout wuz how you could make a fool uv ole Jim wid a lie. Dat truck dah is trash; en trash is what people is dat puts dirt on de head er de fren's en makes 'em ashamed.[4]

Later, we see the depth of kinship in Huck's feelings for Jim. Jim has been recaptured into slavery and Huck begins to feel guilty for help-ing Jim escape in the first place. To clear his conscience, he writes a note to Miss Watson, Jim's former owner, telling her where Jim is in the hopes that she can reclaim him. "I felt good and all washed clean of sin for the first time," says Huck after writing the note. "I knowed I could pray now."

But Huck's conscience won't let him off the hook that easily. He begins by conjuring up the memories of all the good things Jim has done; the things a father might do for his son:

But I didn't do it straight off, but laid the paper down and set there thinking—thinking how good it was all this happened so, and how near I come to being lost and going to hell. And went on thinking. And got to thinking over our trip down the river; and I see Jim before me, all the time, in the day, and in the nighttime, sometimes moonlight, sometimes storms, and we a floating along, talking and singing, and laughing.

But somehow I couldn't seem to strike no places to harden me against him, but only the other kind. I'd see him standing my watch on top of his'n, stead of calling me, so I could go on sleeping; and see him how glad he was when I came back out of the fog; and when I come to him again in the swamp, up there where the feud was; and such-like times; and would always call me honey, and pet me, and do everything he could think of for me, and how good he always was; and at last I struck the time I saved him by telling the men we had small-pox aboard [the raft], and he was so grateful, and said I was the best friend old Jim ever had in the world, and the only one he's got now; and then I happened to look around, and see that paper [the note informing Miss Watson of Jim's whereabouts].

It was a close place. I took it up and held it in my hand. I was trembling because I'd got to decide, forever, betwixt two things, and I knowed it. I studied a minute, sort of holding my breath. And then says to myself—'All right, then, I'll go to hell'—and tore it up.[5]

The classification that produces kinship occurs unconsciously, or with minimal conscious awareness. It is a natural response that operates through brain mechanisms particular to a given species. But through experience, natural kinship can be extended to persons other than biological relatives. We love our mates as if our blood coursed through their veins, but in reality we share no genetic tie to them.

Yes, We live in complicated world of kinship possibilities. Psychological kinship represents a flexible category of kinship—a category in which non-kin can be used to extend the biological family or to substitute for the biological family when the need exists. In theory, *anyone* could become kin if we choose to classify him or her as family. The boundaries of kinship are definitely flexible, and we can change them if we so desire.

Human Herding

Our modern cities and ever-expanding suburbs provide opportunities for building creative kinships and engaging in kin-like interactions with acquaintances and strangers vastly greater than in the past. But, before we can begin to classify, to choose, our kin without regard to the color of their skin, their ethnic heritage, or their religious or sexual orientation, we must first face our ancient fear of strangers, our inbred wiring that drives us to be prejudiced against anyone different.

If genetic differences between humans and their closest primate, the chimpanzee, is a mere 1 percent, the genetic difference between races, though they may appear very different, is actually infinitesimal.

Anthropologists speculate that early human beings were designed for relaxed, intimate relationships with a substantial number of highly familiar biological kin, and a smattering of less familiar members of the extended family or band. Because strangers were not that common, a human being's natural response was fear. Only when strangers proved friendly was the internal danger signal turned off, and only after a period of carefully assessing their intentions were strangers eventually admitted to the band.

Our ancestors were wired to first assess intentions, then to classify strangers as "us" or "them" as quickly as possible; what our forebears were not designed to do was love strangers at first sight. Strangers were considered dangerous until the facts proved otherwise.

Today, evolutionary psychologists believe that hostility may very well be inborn, a genetic hangover from ancestral environments where meeting up with a stranger typically meant a battle resulting in the threat of sudden death of one or both parties. Experts believe of host of interworking genes influence our fear of strangers. There are probably other biological factors, too, such as hormones that promote aggression, and other variables we simply haven't discovered yet. No doubt prejudice is a learned cultural behavior, but our genes may well prove to be the springboard for this troubling behavior, and culture, the perpetuator.

But for these "fear stranger genes" to exist in the modern psyche, they must have evolved as an adaptive strategy and survived disproportionately throughout human evolution. This ancient mind-set of fearing *all strangers,* however, is unnecessary in today's global village.

True, our inner cities can be dangerous if we appear too different, too vulnerable. But walking in the mall, rushing through the crowded business districts of our city, strolling down our suburban streets, driving to the grocery store—we encounter thousands of harmless strangers on a daily basis. Yet, we still cling to our mistrust of "different" people.

If we are to choose to live more deliberately, to fashion our own loving families and to discover a new kind of harmony with fellow human beings, prejudice as a natural impulse is something we must guard against. Natural instincts, you see, are often relentless and amoral, and provide a poor basis for justifying the rightness of our behavior.

For example, anthropologist Dr. Helen Fisher asserts in *Anatomy of Love* that the natural impulse to mate, stray, and mate again—namely serial monogamy—may very well be an adaptive reproductive strategy evolved throughout primate and human history. This pattern is evident in our society's high divorce rate, explains Dr. Fisher, which is not at all new to the Twentieth century. In ancestral environments, when this impulse evolved—dependable, intensely bonded clans existed to care for the offspring of parting lovers. This reproductive strategy most likely evolved to vary the gene transfer through successive generations—a variety that would increase the likelihood of human survival over the long run.

How could nature guess that large, nurturing biological families would give way to the tiny, isolated, nuclear families of today, where divorce creates excruciating abandonment terror or devastating economic chaos for jilted spouses and deserted children? Just because the impulse to mate with a variety of people is innate, that doesn't make it right, especially in an era where the there is no extended clan, so children desperately need both parents' guidance and support—emotionally and financially—to grow up healthy. While we cannot always control our feelings or thoughts, our base impulses do not have the power of an almighty god.

Only by recognizing the powerful ancient biology that drives such feelings can we choose whether or not to follow instinctive reproductive patterns, believes Fisher. Indeed, we can decide to walk away from temptation much more easily when we know the luring rush of romantic and sexual feelings is not true love, but the echo of our primitive genetic legacy to mate, stray, and mate again.

This same reasoning can be applied to our genetic heritage that drives the impulse toward prejudice. At one time, our innate warning system was critical for survival. But today, when we don't hire an African-American because we already have the "token" black in our department; when we refuse that bank loan to someone because they belong to an ethnic group we perceive as inferior; when we deny someone entrance to our club because they believe in a different religion; when we cringe because a family of a different race family has moved into our neighborhood; when we bemoan the flood of immigrants, despite the fact that most of us had ancestors who were once immigrants, we are simply giving in to primitive animal instincts imprinted upon our DNA millions of years ago.

Although studies show that many of us in society have become more sophisticated about not advertising our racism, or for that matter, our sexism and homophobia, many of us still cling to these old prejudices.

The verdict by a mostly black jury in the landmark trial of O. J. Simpson first and foremost punished a botched murder investigation. But as one of Simpson's leading defense lawyers, and as many black observers, noted, racist America was also on trial. Around the country blacks' empathy for O. J. Simpson and their enraged reaction to the issues of prejudice raised in his trial clearly demonstrate that the oppression and racism of the past, and the present, has not been forgotten, nor has it been forgiven. Indeed, for many blacks, justice equaled, not simply *truth* in the murder case of two dead white people, but the history of a people still raw from the pain of inequality and injustice over the last several centuries.

In forging a clan mentality, the Simpson jury, as well as angry blacks around the country, are hardly alone, the *Wall Street Journal* reports. "Thirty years ago, two all-white Mississippi juries refused to convict white supremacist Byron De La Beckwith of murdering civil rights leader Medgar Evers. [Mr. De La Beckwith later ran for lieutenant governor of Mississippi with a campaign slogan that he was a "straight shooter."] . . . And in the white enclave of Simi Valley, a jury in the Rodney King trial ignored dramatic videotapes of a brutal police beating and accepted a Rube Goldberg explanation that the white cops really weren't brutalizing Mr. King. That jury, with 10 white, was the flip side of the Simpson panel."[6]

Although black-white race relations are clearly better than they were thirty years ago—these trials clearly show we are still a divided and a tribal country.

Recognizing the harmful side of human herding, Paul Henderson, a black former public defender, switched sides of the legal profession and became a prosecutor. According to an article in the *Wall Street Journal,* when Henderson's own mother asked him why he would want to do that, Henderson, obviously aware of innate in group/out group dynamics, replied: "It's very scary for me to think that black people are going to be prosecuted, sentenced, and judged by people who don't look anything like them and [who] don't understand their experience."[7]

What is truly fascinating is that these tribal conflicts, at their core, have less to do with racism than they have to do with human beings' inborn tendency to divide and herd into in groups and out groups.

Our country's billion-dollar-a-year, mega-obsession with sports—including television, radio, and online chat programs, and including professional sports paraphernalia and equipment—is an excellent example of this instinctive division—a lust for competition.

Obviously this modern, albeit harmless, tribal warfare occurs in endless variety, but the divide-and-conquer mentality that characterizes all in/out-group conflicts is quite predictable. Perhaps the most familiar example of such a confrontation is the notorious "battle of the sexes," still being played out on colleges campuses of the all-male Virginia Military Institute and the Citadel in South Carolina.

Essentially, the conflict is not about whether single-sex education is better at promoting self-esteem in either sex. Rather, it is about women combating the entrenched male networks that historically form at those schools and tenaciously persist after graduation.

When denied access to these schools, more than half of the population—women—are excluded from powerful kinship bonds tied to political, economic, and cultural success in our society. No matter how you look at it, this is immoral. A 1996 edition of National Public Radio's *Marketplace,* citing a study by a New York research group, "Catalyst," shows that the number of women CEOs at Fortune 1000 companies was two. Yes, two. Women in the study pointed to male stereotyping of women and the "old boy network" for the lack of top executives.

All-female schools, regardless of how much they bolster self-esteem, *do not* have access to the enduring, mostly-male corporate and business networks that dominate the U.S. economy. And sexism, you see, is simply another variation of the ancient human inclination to herd.

Indeed, this barbaric legacy is so basic to our species that even when the most powerful dividers—gender and race—are not an issue, human beings will find other ways to divide into clans and exclude a group they perceive as inferior. Observe children playing on a playground and you'll see how naturally they split up, cleave together, and attack a different group. The outlawed, but nonetheless entrenched, caste system in India is a good example of adults—of the same race—clinging to this archaic herding behavior. The British fanatical obsession with social status is also a perfect example.

A poignant example from Japan's past illustrates this important point: even when racial differences are not the issue, enduring, inborn mechanisms in the brain the *Homo sapiens* will give rise to primal herding dynamics. Interestingly enough, this study, reported in Philip G. Zimbardo's and Floyd L. Ruch's text *Psychology and Life,* also shows that the differences these isolated groups exhibit can be the result, rather than the cause, of discrimination.

> In Japan, since Medieval times, based on the myth of biological inferiority, there has been systematic segregation of a pariah caste known as the Burakumin. Not racially different, or visibly distinguishable from other Japanese, they can be identified with certainty only by their registry of birthplace and residence. Over the years, however, they have been segregated as untouchables, crowded into squalid shacks in ghettos, and limited in whom they can marry, what work they can do (only menial jobs), and how much education they can have.
>
> Generations of segregation and inferior status have created differences. Their speech patterns have become different and now identify them as does the speech of the lower-class Cockney in London. Regardless of their abilities, their papers (identifying their occupation and place of residence) prevent their escape. Not surprisingly, there is a greater delinquency and joblessness, higher school absen-

teeism and dropout rate, and lower tested IQ scores among boys who live in the Buraku ghettos. These are regarded as signs of "innate racial inferiority" and used to justify the necessity for further discrimination.[8]

Scientists believe this kind of innate hostility toward dissimilar people lies in all of us, waiting to be aroused by the example of our peers scapegoating outsiders and our natural desire to herd.

For assimilation of Americans to occur, writes Jesse O. McKee, editor of *Ethnicity in America: A Geographical Appraisal,* certain key factors encourage or discourage the process. Two of these include: cultural and physical similarity of the two, and the desire of the minority group to assimilate and willingness of the majority to allow them to.

McKee explains that numerous migrants from Northwest Europe, as well as other white migrant groups, have had an easier time of adapting and being accepted into the mainstream. Research efforts include the use of a social distance scale, frequently referred to as the Bogardus scale. The seven items used to rate the acceptance of certain racial and religious groups are listed below. Each phrase, or ranking completed the sentence: I would accept (a certain group)

1. to close kinship by marriage
2. to my club as personal chums
3. to my street as neighbors
4. to my employment in my occupation
5. to citizenship in my country
6. as visitors only to my country
7. would exclude from my country

The survey, administered to white respondents as well as blacks, Jews, and Asians, over a period of forty years (1926, 1946, 1956, and 1966), reveals striking similarity in the hierarchy of acceptance of various groups. Although some groups have moved up or down in the scale over time (the Japanese, Russians, and Italians, for example), the general order has been for white Americans and persons of North European descent to be ranked in the upper third of the distance scale, while Eastern and Southern Europeans occupy the middle third, and racial minorities (even though they've been in

America since its founding) the bottom third. When certain racial (blacks) and religious (Jews) minorities have been surveyed alone, they did place their own group high on the scale.[9]

This prejudice has profound repercussions: Its appalling depth becomes obvious when you learn of studies showing that blacks, Hispanics, Asians, and American Indians are more likely to live near hazardous waste sites, according to an Associated Press article, "Environmental Injustice Cited."

"A member of a racial minority has a 47 percent better chance than a white person of living near such facilities," according to a report issued by three organizations: The Center for Policy Alternatives; The Commission for Racial Justice; and the National Association for the Advancement of Colored People.[10]

Think about it, if aliens descended upon the U.S. tomorrow and traveled around, city to city, one of their likely questions would be: Why do the darker people, for the most part, live differently from the lighter people? Why do they have less? And you know, it would not be an exaggeration. It would be an observation; and an accurate one.

The Economics of Prejudice

I cannot tell you how many people of conservative persuasion have told me that my life is evidence that anyone can surmount prejudice, pull themselves up by the bootstraps, and rise above a poverty-stricken childhood. The notion is so silly, I laugh.

I remember my father telling the story of his arrival in the United States in the early twenties, when signs discriminating against the Irish were posted prominently in the windows of many business establishments. The signs read "Mics need not apply." To combat this prejudice, many of the Irish immigrants changed their names—from say, "O'Quinn," to simply "Quinn," or from "A'hearne" (the original spelling of my family's name) to Ahern, or even Hearn. Children of Irish immigrants usually did not possess the Irish brogue of their parents and often in one generation, armed with new names, the Irish were virtually indistinguishable from the majority of first American arrivals: the English.

The source of my amusement is that while I was indeed raised in a ghetto, my mother's English heritage and my father's Irish background furnished me a typical, fair, Anglo-Saxon attractiveness. That and my strict catholic-school education, which shaped my work ethic, my manner, even the grammatical structure I use to communicate, masked my childhood upbringing in a ghetto. Thus, unlike many minorities, I was able to fit in among the dominant Caucasian society—though surely not enough to break the corporate glass ceiling of the male-dominated Fortune 100 company where I worked for many years.

While I do not wish to diminish my own arduous efforts climbing out of poverty (most likely I will be paying off school loans until my small sons enter college), but I've also heard these same conservatives say that minorities, through the same government loan programs I used, can obtain a "good" college education, like I did. As most of us know, a good education begins long before college. And the old herding dynamics largely determine who gets access to that "good" college education.

When my sisters and I were young, my mother loved to tell the story of how the grand Monseigneur Dwyer saved our family: how, without his help, we girls would have had to attend the sub-standard public schools in our poor neighborhood. She told the story of how one night she heard a knock on the door. When she opened it, she saw a large figure, draped in wine-colored robes—a priest— standing before her; a black limousine and driver waited in the background.

The man gallantly extended his hand and introduced himself: "I'm Monseigneur Dwyer from Christ Our King Church, and I've seen your little girls with their daddy in church. After inquiring around, I learned they don't go to Catholic school, and they haven't made their First Holy Communions." He paused, looking at my sisters and me, and asked, "Mrs. Ahern, do you want your children to go to Catholic school?"

My mother was Episcopalian, believed Catholicism was barbaric, and would not set foot in a Catholic church. But she knew darned well that a Catholic education was better than any education I would have received in the ghetto. She informed the Monseigneur that she could not afford to send us to private school. But he told her he would take care of that. Mom added that she could not afford four uniforms and books for us, either. He explained he would see to that, too. My mother said that as long as Monseigneur

Dwyer was alive, she never had to pay a cent for us to go to private school. After his death, when the nuns got nasty about our non-paying status, my mother paid what she could, and they never kicked us out.

What seemed so strange is that I never saw Monseigneur Dwyer go to one black family in my neighborhood to see if they wanted a free, private-school education. I will, however, give Monseigneur Dwyer the benefit of the doubt and say that most of the kids in my neighborhood perhaps never went to my white Catholic church two miles from my house. So perhaps Monseigneur didn't know any black children who, like us, were in dire need. And he didn't go looking for any, either.

Looking back, I realize how superior my education was. In sixth and seventh grades, rebelling against my mother's wishes, I attended the public school in my neighborhood. I easily got As, because my class was studying topics, such as grammar and fractions, that I'd learned much earlier in Catholic school. And in eighth grade, when I finally crawled back to Catholic school (the rioting and threats of violence made learning impossible), I was lost in the pre-Algebra my school mates were already tackling. I never caught up. Not until geometry in high school, where you start over from scratch with completely new concepts, was I again able to get As in math.

True, I'm only a sample size of one—certainly not statistically significant. But every year in my local newspaper, I read that inner-city students are scoring significantly lower on standardized tests than their suburban counterparts. And I am not alone in observing that things haven't changed much for inner-city children of minorities in my town. Nor are things changing in many inner cities around the country, despite the Brown versus Board of Education ruling back in 1954, which guaranteed all races access to an equal public education.

Capitalism, by its very structure, creates winners and losers. The lack of a quality education among minorities, generation after generation, fuels the loser category in our economy. While there is indeed a growing African-American middle class, the preponderance of minorities still living in poor, inner-city neighborhoods across this country is evidence that ethnic tribalism exists. These shameful in/out-group dynamics and the dilemma of prejudice are some of the most challenging problems that face human beings. At the root of this prejudice is the hatred of people outside our perceived tribe. And, while the emotional consequences of that hatred can be agonizingly painful, the economics of prejudice can be deadly.

A 1995 *Los Angles Times* article reports, "A majority of white America has fundamental misconceptions about the economic circumstances of black Americans." According to a national survey, most white respondents think the average black is faring as well as, or better than, the average white in such specific areas as jobs, education, and health care.

"That's not true," the article goes on to say. "Government statistics show whites, on average, earn 60 percent more than blacks, are far more likely to have medical insurance and more than twice as likely to graduate from college."[11]

Many of us are so saturated with the news and statistics detailing racial inequities, we don't pay much attention any more. They're like old photos on the living room wall—you just stop seeing them after a while. But some of us—sometimes, the youngest of us—aren't jaded by such dismal facts and continue to notice the obvious prejudices that still exist. I was having a backyard catch with my son one day, when and he threw a real "curve ball."

"Mom, why are all the garbage men black?" "Out of the mouth of babes . . . ," an apt saying if ever I heard one.

"They're not all black," I answered, trying futilely to remember the last white garbage man I'd seen.

The parade of headlines in local papers reflects a very real, very painful, startling contemporary truth: "Loan Denial Rate Is Still High for Blacks: The Impact of Race on Mortgage Lending"; "Area Ad Agencies Still White Houses: Minorities Say Entering Field Is Difficult"; "State's Infant Mortality Rate Decreases: But It's Worse Than National Level, and Deaths Are Higher among Black Babies."

National Newspapers echo much of the same: A *Wall Street Journal* headline: "Self-Employment Rates Differ Greatly among Racial and Ethnic Groups." According to economists, 30 percent of men from Israel and Korea own their own business in United States. By contrast, only 4.4 percent of African Americans are self-employed. It seems that differences also exist in the types of businesses, owned. African-American businesses tend to be in less profitable arenas, such as restaurants, personal-care stores, and auto-repair shops.[12]

True, Reconstruction after the Civil War first addressed the blatant discrimination denying blacks the most basic freedoms (voting, for example) outlined in the Constitution. And the Civil Rights movement of the fifties and sixties banned institutional discrimination in the south—"Jim Crow" laws designating where blacks could eat or go to the bathroom, even what race they could marry. Despite such progress, as the modern newspaper headlines suggest, the occupations of many blacks, and the racial demographics of the ghetto have not changed significantly in the 130 years since the Civil War. Economic segregation, which Martin Luther King, Jr. called *de facto* segregation, persists.

King first articulated this type of segregation when he traveled north in the sixties. He discovered that while northern blacks were not oppressed by discriminatory Jim Crow laws endemic in the South, they were nonetheless discriminated against by virtue of the inhumane poverty that existed in the northeastern states. Economic segregation is as egregious and harmful as racial segregation, and, once again, is yet another variation on our primordial pattern of divisive herding.

What Can We Do?

Before we can begin to address the emotional/intellectual and cultural components that drive prejudice, as we've said earlier, we need to address the severe economic problems that enslave minorities. David C. Korten, writing eloquently in an article in the magazine *Tikkun*, believes we can replace our present "economy of meanness, with economies of meaning." In his article, he asks the pivotal question: what are characteristics of an economy that would meet both our material needs and serve to create the ethos of caring relationships and of ethical, spiritual, and ecological sensitivity essential to life in a good society?

Korten explains that our prevailing cultural myths that society must choose between a free market economy or a state-planned economy (such as that the communist disaster in the former Soviet Union) paralyzes us from moving toward an economy that protects our fragile environment, and allocates resources in a much fairer way than our present system, which creates a huge gulf between winners and losers.

"Our own history is one of many sources of alternative examples," writes Korten. "During the post-World War II period, in which a large and prosperous middle class was a defining feature of the Western industrial nations, the market functioned within a framework of rules set through a democratic public process. The institutions of government, market, *and* civil society functioned in a reasonable pluralistic balance."

But now, according to Korten, deregulation and globalization have freed the market place and destroyed any humanizing balance. For example, he explains, in the absence of government intervention, "successful competitors gain ever greater monopolistic advantage through their accumulation of economic political power. Now the competitive market economy is being steadily replaced by a centrally planned global economy managed by an ever-more tightly integrated alliance of global corporations."[13]

Korten asserts that there is no need to eliminate markets, trade, and private ownership, but rather than allow the continued development of global economies that anonymously concentrate power and wealth in the hands of a few, we as a society could focus our collective energies on building strong, self-reliant local economies that root ownership and the management of precious resources in democratically governed communities, which recognize all peoples' inherent right to the basic means of creating a livelihood.

Korten adds that the cornerstone of a healthy society is such a globalized system of local economies that thrive on life-affirming values of sufficiency, caring, cooperation, and reverence for life, instead on our current system, which rewards individual self-interest, materialism, greed, and opportunism.

There's no way around it—today we all need money to survive and thrive. Let's face it, money buys not only our basic sustenance, such as eating and shelter, but also comfort, privacy, safety, and accessibility. Our ancestors didn't have to shell out money for these things. Also, unlike our predecessors, every time we leave our house today, we need money to do almost anything—even to enjoy nature: we must buy gas to travel to rural settings, and often we are charged admission to enjoy what was once our natural home—a landscape of grass, trees, and an open sky.

So yes we need money to live; but embedded in what Darwin called our "social instincts" is the powerful urge in human beings to acquire resources, land and status—which in ancestral environments likened the chance that our genes would make it into the next generation. Just as we naturally desire to have sex more than the few times we wish to procreate—similarly, the ancient legacy to want more, more, more material possessions is what leads humans, say evolutionary psychologists, to keep acquiring wealth far beyond what they need to live. A democracy that tempers, certainly not eliminates, this genetic compulsion to acquire ever-more resources is humane and moral, because it recognizes the social consequences, namely increased violence and bloodshed, that occur when powerful in-groups gobble up most of the economic pie, leaving the poor, often minorities and women, to forage the leftovers.

Addressing the injustice of our current socioeconomic structure is the first step toward solving the problems of prejudice in our great country. But we cannot begin to solve the problem of prejudice until we acknowledge its depth. Prejudice will never go away unless we face its roots buried in our genes and stop the behaviors we enact daily, such as economic segregation. Only then can we find genuine ways to advance the destiny of the human species by transcending our basic herding instincts.

Retreating from people we perceive as different is usually not the answer. As any social psychologists will tell you, social segregation prevents normal interchange and destroys, or blocks, communication. This in turn—in the larger society at hand—allows rumors and stereotypes to go unchecked, fantasies to surface and blossom, and the "strangeness" of the group, real or perceived, to increase over time.

Research has shown that contact between antagonistic groups can promote better intergroup relations and lessen existing hostilities if—and only if—many other factors are favorable; mere exposure doesn't help. In fact, it is more likely to intensify existing attitudes, Philip G. Zimbardo writes in *Psychology and Life*. Changes as a result of contact are most likely when the contact is rewarding rather than thwarting, when a mutual interest or goal is served, and when the participants perceive that contact was the result of their own choice.

This may explain why many enlightened national companies and large universities offer diversity training programs to provide employees with information on different races, cultures, religions and even on people with different sexual orientations. Indeed, information breaks down emotional barriers, and once we realize that people who appear different, in fact, share many of our own fears, dreams, onerous responsibilities, and goals in life—we begin to see them as part of our in group; often fear and scorn disappears, which promotes a better working environment.

As human beings with our evolving intellect, sense of morality, a wondrous capacity for spirituality, and most important, free will—we can indeed choose our kin today, based not on a herding instinct, but upon warm, loving connections. At the same time, we can recognize that our primitive wiring is no longer useful in today's world of strangers. We can teach our children about their individual, rich, wonderful heritages, and we can teach them about the dangers of human herding—the destructive side of kinship. We can teach them that placing too much emphasis on differences maintains invisible barriers between all folks, and that genuine understanding and acceptance come only when we work together, play together, grieve together, grow together, and form psychological kinships by sharing life's uplifting, soul-bonding moments together.

Through these creative kinships, we can all move toward the spirit of a global village where our enemies are no longer other people, but poverty, the undereducation of children, pollution, and universal diseases. Even as we strive to celebrate our differences, we can also reach for that place of magical kinship where we are all family—the family of humankind.

Anderson and Hopkins, in *The Feminine Face of God,* describe this process of creating connectedness with others by a Hebrew word, "tikkun." It means to heal, to mend what has been broken, to transform.

> The legend, the source of this word, goes: "In the beginning of the world, the abundant divine light was held in primeval vessels." But somehow—no one knows how—the vessels were shattered, and discord and confusion spread everywhere.
>
> The great task for human beings, the story tells us, is to repair the ancient vessels, to gather together the scattered light, to call home all those who have been lost or in exile, to heal the separation and bring peace to our world.[14]

10
Making Family
Creating Close Relations
Not Genetically Linked

"Better to light one candle than to curse the darkness."
—Asian proverb

In his classic science fiction novel *Slapstick,* Kurt Vonnegut, Jr. depicts a futuristic world where the government arbitrarily gives tens of thousands of people the same middle name and instantly declares them family. The book is the memoir of Dr. Wilbert Daffodil-Eleven-Swain, a one-hundred-year-old ex-president, who proposes giving everyone new middle names so they will become part of an elaborate extended family. But a plague and other calamities render the plan worthless.

The book's subtitle, *Lonesome No More,* gives away the overriding theme of the book, which is that our Westernized culture is filled with people who feel alienated, unwanted, and without meaningful direction.

A critical analysis in *The Dictionary of Literary Biography: American Novelists since World War II,* explains how *Slapstick* mourns the loss of family in modern life:

Vonnegut talks about that large old German family in Indianapolis from which he is descended, and how it gave love, comfort, and stability to its members. Once most Americans had such families. But now the generations are separated and the remaining nuclear family is overloaded with the burdens once assumed by a larger and more heterogeneous group. The new problem with modern Americans, he [Vonnegut] concludes, is that they are lonely.

Once they are so abused, they lose value to themselves and to others. In big families, or artificial extended families, such as Vonnegut proposes here, such people are still loved, valued, and cared for.[1]

Thankfully, we do not live in a futuristic world where the government forces the regeneration of lost family structures through some brave new world plan. Of course, it would be wonderful, as today's conservatives admonish, if families could act more like they used to. Indeed, wouldn't it be miraculous if families everywhere could clean up their act and be responsible for their own children?

The roots of most maladies plaguing families today lie in poverty, mismatch stress, or untreated trauma in the parents' own childhood, which they predictably re-enact with their children. There is no quick fix, but we as individuals have some power to effect change. Imagine the lives we might change for the better!

If each us were to reach out in our community—perhaps to a friend of our own child, or to a neighborhood family in crisis—or if we could reach out through a volunteer organization, such as mentoring programs sponsored by local schools, surrogate grandparenting programs, Big Brother/Big Sister programs, and so on, perhaps we could help relieve the ailing family structure in our great country. Imagine the implications that such surrogacy and psychological kinship would have on inner-city crime, and on the loneliness, anxiety, and violence of evolutionary mismatch stress.

During a crisis, such as divorce, job loss, or emotional illness, people often withdraw out of embarrassment and fear. The family closes ranks and becomes a closed circle, cutting members off from other, often healthier perspectives. Also cutting members off from friends who can be a rich source of comfort and reassurance that family members, caught up in the current drama, can't offer. When we obsess about our problems in isolation, they become exaggerated, spiraling us downward into a seemingly hopeless abyss. It is only when we drag our worries out into the light of day, into the sphere of examination, that they lose their power over us. Friends are invaluable at times like these, if only to remind us that they've been there too, and survived—just like we will.

When I look back over my own life, I realize that, in addition to severe mental illness, my family endured unrelenting poverty, domestic violence to the point of police intervention, numerous parental suicide attempts, and unrelenting substance abuse. The first memory I have, from age two or three, is of being held upside down by my ankles as my head was bashed into the ground. This happened because I had been playing with the water heater and shouldn't have been. Punishments got worse as I got older and evolved into the kind of tortuous child abuse that would get people locked up today.

And although the effects of that trauma will likely be with me until I die, there were clear instances where people—Jewish, black and various shades of white—came into my life and transformed it. The love from these people nourished me, and filled me with hope, by showing me that life does not have to be experienced the way I lived it in my family.

Creating our own families is a way of reinventing ourselves, no matter what kind of background we come from. It is a way of adding purpose to our lives and creating self-esteem. "You don't necessarily get what you need through biological luck," says Dr. Gina O'Connell Higgins. Indeed, she sees many people in her private psychology practice who have intentionally created psychological kinships. They have "prized them and cultivated them," she says, "the way a gardener would tend a garden."

Such close ties are integral to maintaining our mental health and sense of well-being in today's society. Indeed, studies have shown that people with close intimate friendships tend to have fewer illnesses, better immune systems, and lower levels of stress. People with close friends tend to be stronger, more supportive, and more hopeful, and they tend to enjoy a greater sense of belonging than people without close friends.

Friendships truly are good for the soul. It seems the Bible was right all along: "Friendship is the medicine of life!"

Unlike the characters in Vonnegut's novel, we have a choice. We have many opportunities to decide whom we will classify as psychological kin. Of course how we do that is entirely up to us. The ways to find an intentional family are as endless as there are types of friends. Social groups, 12-step and support groups, volunteer organizations, churches, work, hobbies, leisure activities—anywhere you meet people.

The author and columnist Judith Viorst explains during a telephone interview, "You are picking your friends, people you are choosing to spend time with, because of shared interests, feelings of warmth and caring."

"Among intentional families I know, there is, as there is in blood families, a tremendous sense of coming through for each other. Sometimes even more so."

While Viorst says she and her close friends look forward to lavish New Year's parties and dinner parties, "it's not that we just share good times and holidays. If our group has a friend sick in the hospital, we all make meals for her husband to put in the freezer, and to have when she comes home. We take care of each other."

"That's true for a lot of my clients," says Dr. Leslie Butterfield, referring to her clients who have found a family in support groups. "I have seen an incredible sense of solidarity, of helping one another out. When someone is ill, these are the people who come to their home, bring them food, walk their dog, pick up their mail. They really do function as a family."

Seniors

Of all of us who need psychological kinships and intentional families, it is perhaps the elderly who need to create new kinships the most. Dr. Nancy K. Schlossberg, writes in an article "Till Death Do Us Part—The Growing Need for Family Care" that the elderly population is increasing dramatically in this country: "An increase in people sixty-five years of age and older—went from 4 percent of the population in 1900 to 12 percent in 1987, with a projected increase to 21 percent in 2020—more than one fifth of the population."

According to Schlossberg, a major problem is that "low fertility rates mean fewer adult children will be available to care for the elderly. In other words, as the percentage of elderly doubles, the percentage of young people—caregivers of the future—will decline dramatically."[2]

Dr. Henry Simmons, a professor of religion and aging at the Presbyterian School of Christian Education in Richmond says that today, older people usually die of organ failure rather than secondary infections, which once caused people to die at a much younger age. Thus, with people living longer and dying sicker, seniors desperately need to form intimate ties with people nearby.

"I work with old people," Simmons says. "Looking at the social fabric of our society, old people don't have families. Their parents are often dead; their children are divorced or have moved away. There is no flesh and blood to rely on. And late-life divorce is not rare."

Many seniors are widowed, which can be another painful lost source of kinship; Here, too, close friendships can make all the difference. Web's Story is inspirational.

Thirteen years ago, Web's beloved wife, Mary Ruth, died of a cerebral hemorrhage. It was the night of their thirty-eighth anniversary. "We fell asleep holding hands," Web remembers. "I not only lost my wife; I lost my best friend."

Although he is in frequent contact with them, Web's three adult children live in other states. Culturally and with his disposition, Web, who is 75, says he should have found another wife. But although he met several women with whom he felt an "ancient bond," it never led to marriage. Slowly, Web says, he came to accept that he would probably never marry again.

"As I've gotten older, I've become more of a feminist," adds Web, who is a retired engineer from the DuPont Company. "I seem to be attracted to lovely ladies who live by a freedom as necessary to them as breath."

"I'm not trying to possess anyone anymore," he says. "I'm trying to share myself, which is what love is all about." Web explains he met his group of friends primarily though two national groups: the Great Books Club and the Academy of Life-Long Learning. "These dozen [women] are collectively very much like a wife. All the favorable things. They give me what I need."

Web says his life is much brighter since he's developed a large group of friends. Although the relationships are nonsexual, Web says all his friends are women, because he started out looking for a wife. From search to search, though, he developed deep friendships.

While Web says he would never have missed the wonderfully close relationship he had with his wife, he realizes that if he were married now, he probably wouldn't have rich, close relationships with such a diverse group of people. "Oh, the joy of being within a family," he says, describing a birthday party he shared with friends.

Although he sometimes says he misses that warm body next to him at night, Web says that when he lays his head on his pillow, comforting thoughts, not the images, of the three women he is closest to, spin around in his head until he falls asleep.

"It's not a bad way to go," he says. "Although this is not what I thought I wanted." Referring to the process of creating close relations not genetically linked, Web says, "I feel like I've discovered something no one else knows about. Where I am [today] is, for me, wonderful!"

Indeed, forming an intentional family is critical for seniors, but not just to form social networks. Increasingly, intentional families are necessary when seniors can't live on their own anymore. In *Creating Community Anywhere,* the authors, Carolyn Shaffer and Kristin Anundsen, assert that housing will be a major issue for seniors of the future: "By 2030, the U.S. Census Bureau estimates, more Americans will have reached the age sixty-five-and-over bracket than will be under the age of eighteen," they write. The authors refer to this as the "elderboomer bulge."

"Already the surge in the number of elders has accompanied a decrease in the amount of affordable housing available. Even those elders fortunate enough to own their own homes may find these increasingly difficult to maintain, as they (both homes and the owners) grow older. And, because families today are often so separated by physical and emotional distance, moving in with relatives may prove impossible or undesirable. Where everybody is going to live, and with whom, loom as challenging questions."[3]

No doubt, psychological kinship will be a vital part of how seniors live in the future. Unrelated seniors moving in together, sharing resources, and creating community, is one solution that is already spreading rapidly across this country.

Margaret Harmon of the National Shared Housing Resource Center, estimates that some "350 programs nationwide now offer everything from roommate matches that pair elderly homeowners with single moms, to dorm-like group residences," *U.S News &*

World Report recounts. And "thousands of inquires pour into the center annually."[4]

The article also profiles seniors who are opting to join a commune-like cluster of private homes, where they may eat in a common dining room several times a week. Of course, large institutions like the renowned Sun City retirement communities will be a mainstay of kinship care for elders. And, say experts, even large institutions can nourish the growth of community if they are managed with the right structure and attitude.

How the elderly will live and whom they will live with have mostly to do with the types of connections they forge in their younger years. Incredibly vibrant, ninety-one-year-old Mary Virginia Powell, a retired office worker, says, you need to make one new friend a year, preferably younger than you are. That way you will not outlive all of your friends.

Mihaly Czikszentmihalyi, in *Creating Community Anywhere,* is quoted as saying, "In adolescence, when so many interests are shared with others and one has great stretches of free time to invest in a relationship, making friends might seem like a spontaneous process. But later in life friendships rarely happen by chance; one must cultivate them as assiduously as one must cultivate a job or a family."[5]

Betty Booker, reporter/columnist and editor for the "Prime Living" [seniors] section of the *Richmond Times-Dispatch,* has been researching and writing about the elderly for twenty years. She says creating intentional families among older people has a lot to do with size as well.

When 20,000, or even 600 people live in a community, it's difficult to develop a cohesive sense of family. But if you have a three-story retirement community that has a homey feel, people often automatically develop a system of taking care of each other. And people will naturally socialize together.

Another common phenomenon, says Booker, is "aging in place." She says many people are moving to a small apartment complexes or retirement buildings in mid-life—places where everybody is in the same boat. They stay on and begin to "age in place." Then, when they begin having difficulty taking a bath or cooking, or if they have an episode of illness, they will get help from friends they've made within the building, and these friends can prolong their independence.

Booker tells of one intentional family that came up with creative ways, on small amounts of money, to socialize. A group of seniors on fixed and low incomes decided to get together for dinners, but instead of everybody taking turns making a complete dinner, the group decided to recreate depression-era, cheap meals, where everybody brought something. "And they ended up with things like bread pudding, for desert. Things like cornbread, beans, pot liquor, and mixed greens. You can have a perfectly satisfying meal and spend twenty-five cents," Booker says.

The important point here, Booker says, is to be creative. Be intentional about creating new kin.

"Adopting" the children or grandchildren of friends or neighbors is an increasingly popular and essential role for seniors today. Many schools are setting up "mentoring" programs that allow seniors to impart knowledge and care to the children of their communities.

Boys and girls need people who care about them in their lives, Booker says. They require it. That is a role uncles, neighbors, teachers, grandparents and godparents can perform. They can adopt these children. They can communicate with them, call them, send them birthday cards and presents, and Hanukkah or Kwanzaa presents. They can participate in their lives, being a strong, grounding, touchstone place. A place of security and constant unjudgmental love for children who have a deficit of that. The children, in turn, grow to have a sense of rootedness, which they may not otherwise have.

Therapist Linda Sapadin says that when seniors feel they have something to offer to the community, they are more willing to reach out. And she says that the baby boomers who are turning fifty today are dramatically changing the concept of old age. The old-grandmother image in the rocking chair just doesn't fit anymore, she says.

Boomers were the generation known for challenging the status quo, she says, and that will probably be true much more as they get older: They will create a new sense of what it means to be elderly. Clearly, she says, they've already created a new sense of what it means to be over forty.

Indeed, baby boomers may very well help make psychological kinship and intentional families a huge, entrenched part of families of the twenty-first century.

An increasingly popular way for seniors to find supportive kinship is by joining an online community. SeniorNet began as part of a 1986 research project in San Francisco by Dr. Mary Furlong, who is president of the nonprofit organization.

SeniorNet is an international community of computer-using seniors who share a similar goal: to meet and enjoy the friendship of older adults with similar interests. Over 20,000 seniors are paying members of SeniorNet and about 100,000 people have been through SeniorNet learning centers around the country, where seniors take computer classes designed specially for them.

SeniorNet members live in every state and in several foreign countries and they range in age from fifty-five to ninety. Most seniors access SeniorNet through America Online (AOL), a computer service.

Members provide mutual emotional support, they debate economic, social, political, and religious issues, as well as issues relating to aging. And seniors learn together by participating in discussion groups that focus on topics ranging from bird-watching, gardening, pets, sex, recreation, writing, travel, and so on. SeniorNet offers three hundred discussion topics.

Fran Ollweiler, talking with us over e-mail, is a volunteer "Cyberhost" for SeniorNet. "I am a sixty-eight-year-old woman," she explains, "who has a pretty good opinion of herself, but little did I think that after I retired from an active life as a freelance photographer, I would become a computer nerd. Going online has changed my life dramatically. I have always been very friendly and outgoing, but I have been married for forty-eight years to a wonderful man who is just the opposite. Going online has allowed me to make friends from all over the world with whom I can share the good, the bad, and the ugly parts of my life. Most I have never met, and never will meet, and even the anonymity of being online is very appealing. This is something I can do day or night, and the fees, if you remain in the SeniorNet area [of America Online] are very reasonable."

Ollweiler adds that the people she has met online, who have shared their ideas, feelings, etc., are very kind, supportive and loving. "And they are smart." Being online has opened up new avenues of thinking about things.

Gail, who is fifty-five, e-mailed us about her journey into Senior-

Net. "I have made several e-mail friends about my same age. One women is in Connecticut (a retired teacher) and she is moving next month to a town south of me, in Florida.

"When I first got the computer [about five years ago], I was finding so many interesting things and people. Once I put the potatoes on to cook for supper and forgot them. I smelled something burning; it was the potatoes. So now when it gets near supper time, I shut the computer off so I can make supper without getting into trouble."

Gail says that when she gets up in the morning, she does her chores first and then "the rest of the day is mine to play and learn on the computer. The hours go fast. It seems there are not enough hours in the day. Life has been good to me. I have been married for thirty-six years, and it has been great. And, I have four children who have turned out well. Now it is my turn to have time for myself."

Glo also spends a good deal of time online. And she says it's been productive, contrary to the "get a life," line she often hears people say when they notice someone is online a lot.

"I am seventy-two, and married to a retired psychiatrist," says Glo, speaking to us through e-mail. "I have four children and seven grandchildren. Three of the grands live nearby, but the other four live in different states, and we communicate via e-mail. I like the spontaneity of being able to reply right then and there. My two oldest grandsons are in college and postgraduate school, and they have been my gurus over the years. Two of our grandchildren LOVE to be able to send me small messages each day.

"The first thing I do each day is climb the stairs to my loft to check my mail. It's fun, especially since the only mail one tends to get via snail mail [U.S. mail] is junk mail.

"I don't need the support outside of my family, although I know a lot of people online for whom this is the only support they have when they are lonely.

"I have met perhaps two hundred people in person, whom I first met online. Some are as close to me as people I have known for decades IRL [in real life]. I have found that one can sense what a person is really like by what they type on the electronic page . . . My hunches have always been right.

"It has been a wonderful experience to be able to reach outward at a time when we [seniors] are losing friends through death, family moving away, and so on."

Glo says she's tried other chat rooms, but mostly sticks to the chat room for seniors on AOL, where she knows she can meet with familiar friends. "That's the only way you can create community," she says, "by getting to know one another. It's like talking over the back fence, or on the village green."

Making Family

"In order to get out in the world and to be part of the world—to be part of something larger than you—you are going to have to take chances," says author Judith Viorst over the phone. "Maybe some people will disappoint you. Maybe some people won't be as loving and generous to you as you are to them. There has to be acceptance that all relationships, both blood and non-blood, are imperfect, are flawed. If we can find areas of pleasure and comfort in each other, we should be very grateful for that."

As we've seen throughout this book, rooted deep within our genes and our collective human psyches lies a desperate yearning for warm caring bonds with other human beings. But our modern fast-paced lives, where hectic careers, divorce, job relocations, and scattered families reign, have left many of us without the natural heritage of family once considered a birthright.

But we have much to be hopeful about. Nature, with its ingenious ability to adapt and recreate, is showing us, once again, that it cannot be suppressed. Indeed, one of the natural laws of physics is that energy cannot be created or destroyed; it is only changed from one state to another. Thus, if extended blood families are not meant to be the mainstay of modern life, the family will not die out. Rather, it will simply find new ways to change, grow, and mutate. And intentional families and psychological kinship are at the forefront of this marvelous adaptation of the human spirit.

Perhaps you are close to your biological family, but they do not meet all of your diverse needs for companionship and intimacy. Perhaps you love your blood family deeply, but they live too far away to be a source of comfort in your busy, stressful, daily life. Perhaps your family has been a source of emotional pain and you don't see changes in their troubling behavior; and being around them makes you feel afraid, sad, or unhealthy. Although running out and creating an intentional family in one week is unlikely—it will perhaps be possible in the future to reach out and build an intentional family, like the many, many people in this book.

Authors Carolyn R. Shaffer and Kristin Anundsen, provide some pointers, and I've added a few, for developing new kinships in *Creating Community Anywhere*:

1) Decide what kind of social network you want. Some of us lead such busy lives, caring for children, earning money, and performing community services at school and so on, that we have room in our lives for only a few special, intense relationships. Do you desire a sense of family from these relationships—a mixture of adults and children who feel comfortable with one another and who are willing to work, listen, cry, and play together? Or do you respond more to the peer community model, a loose network of adults who meet regularly for fellowship? Consider talking with a friend or family member about your ideal model for a family-like bond. When you can define and quantify what you are looking for, it's often easier to find it. This is a critical first step in generating a circle of friends that feels like community.

2) Clear time in your life to nurture your growing friendships. Conscious community takes time and perseverance, as well as openness to personal sharing. Take some time out to review how you spend your time; or better yet, keep a log for a week or two. Are there some solitary, passive, or consumption-oriented activities you would prefer replacing with social, active, participatory ones? Television is one of these passive, addicting activities that can eat up hundreds of hours a year. Ask yourself, "How essential are my current pastimes compared to participating in community activities, or compared to weaving a web that feels like family?" Also consider how you can convert routine tasks and errands—such as cleaning house, grocery shopping, or gardening—into community-generating encounters with friends or family members.

3) Remember to acknowledge and honor whatever needs you have for solitude, recognizing that alone time can help you be more enthusiastic about reaching out and building community in your life.

4) Most of all, seek kindred spirits.

I remember twenty years ago being a frightened teenager who went off to college at the University of Delaware, only twenty minutes from my home. Being from a troubled family, I craved structure and was absolutely terrified of change. Any kind of change! College was a whole new world, full of very different people and very different landscapes. It seemed I was crossing the globe.

Wandering around my dorm on the first day, I met a friend, Laura, who had moved from another state. She grew up in an upper-middle class Jewish family, so we had entirely different histories. We also looked dramatically different—she had wavy black hair and very pale skin, and with her riveting almond-shaped blue eyes and striking ethnic features, she looked like the slender, long-necked, mysterious subjects in a classic Modigliani painting. I, too, looked ethnic, but in a completely different, Irish, sort of way. Yet, sensing some unexplainable kinship, I quickly gravitated toward her.

We hit it off immediately. She had the same high-energy personality, and the same frank, lay-it-on-the-line style of communication. She had a quirky sense of humor and was extremely emotional, sensitive, and analytical. Just like me.

The next year we got an apartment together, and throughout college, we were inseparable. Over endless cups of tea we shared many a soul-searching conversation and many confidences.

Even though today we live in different states and are each busy working and raising two young sons, we keep in touch. As my friend said recently, "You are my soul in Virginia. When we talk, it's as if we've never been apart." She understands and accepts me, more than any member of my blood family. I understand her spiritual journeys and musings, because I've traversed similar roads myself.

I come from a tall family with poor circulation, and am forever cold. One year in college, for Christmas, Laura bought me a warm, flowered quilt. Now, that blanket is worn, the flowers faded to pastel, and the cloth is almost threadbare. But that blanket is with me wherever I go in the house, summer and winter. Most of the writing I did for this book was done with that blanket wrapped around me. It's so soft and comfy and filled with my touch, that my boys are forever sneaking it off to their rooms to snuggle with it—that is, until I snatch it back.

This year, Laura sent me a Christmas card. Enclosed was a long letter, signed "Love always." I believe that, for we are kindred spirits.

So, yes, when looking for an intentional family, seek people with similar experiences, but also seek people with different experiences. Most important, seek people who respect your differences. Those who, even if they aren't "totally together," are willing to labor on the nitty gritty elements of a sound relationship: communication and building trust. People willing to share their feelings, to be emotionally honest, when thorny, uncomfortable problems in a relationship arise. And they will arise, for no relationship, with its ebbing needs and desires, will be in tune all the time.

Seek people who accept your problems and suffering without minimizing and trying to fix or rescue you. We grow more quickly when we are allowed to make mistakes and glean the necessary lessons from those mistakes, ourselves. Seek people who don't condemn you for *feeling* the way you do.

In turn, love your intentional family friend, as Scott Peck in the *The Road Less Traveled,* defines love: "extending your will to help another person grow."[6] Whether you believe a specific kind of growth is best for the other person or not, if that's what they want, help them. That's real love. It is a rare kind of love, but it's out there. Many of the people in this book found it. None of us has to be lonely anymore. Whether you are young or old, with blood family or without, married or single, whether you work outside the home or in the home—you can find it too, as long as you keep on searching.

The most important thing to remember about forming intentional families, says Dr. Leslie Butterfield, is that *you* have to initiate it. The old adage fits here, she says, "If you want a friend, you have to be a friend first."

Notes

Prologue

1. Associated Press, "Singer, Entertainer Dean Martin Dies at 78," appearing in the *Richmond Times-Dispatch* (26 December 1995), B-3.

2. Rodger Doyle, "House to House," *The Atlantic Monthly* 271–72 (March, 1993), 95.

3. Ellen Graham, "Craving Closer Ties, Strangers Come Together as Family, *Wall Street Journal* (4 March 1996), B1, B5.

4. Judith Viorst, *Necessary Losses* (New York: Ballantine Books, 1986), 197–98.

5. Sherry Ruth Anderson and Patricia Hopkins, *The Feminine Face of God,* (New York: Bantam Books, 1992), 222.

6. John Gray, *Men Are from Mars: Women Are from Venus* (New York: HarperCollins Publishers, 1992), x.

7. Susan Kittenplan, "Nannies Dearest," *Vanity Fair* 58:1 (January 1995), 62.

8. Carolyn Shaffer and Kristen Anundsen, *Creating Community Anywhere* (New York: Putnam Publishing Group, 1993), 9.

9. Amaury deRiencourt, *Sex and Power in History* (New York: David McKay Company, Inc., 1974), 103–4.

10. Ibid.

11. Thomas Flaherty, Editor in Chief, *The Domestic World: The Invention of Home Life at the Medieval Hearth; The Family Domain; A Castle for Everyone.* (Alexandria, Va.: Time-Life Books, 1991), 31

Chapter 1 — Family Bonding

1. *The Gift of Friendship Calendar,* Mary Catherwood, June 10 (Marshalltown, La.: Thoughtful Books STA-KRIS, Inc., 1994).

2. Ibid., Maria Edgeworth, March 3.

3. Rodger Doyle, "House to House," *The Atlantic Monthly* 271–71 (March 1993), 95.

4. Wallace Stegner, *The Angle of Repose* (New York: Penguin Books, 1971), 17–18.

5. Ibid., 28–29.

6. Judith Viorst, *Necessary Losses* (New York: Ballantine Books, 1986), 250.

7. Marian Kinget, *On Being Human,* (New York: Harcourt Brace Jovanovich, 1975), 207–8.

8. New York Times News Service, "Family Change is World Wide: Working Mothers a Big Factor," appearing in the *Richmond Times-Dispatch* (1 June 1995), A4.

9. Helen Fisher, *Anatomy of Love* (New York: Fawcett Columbine, 1992), 305.

10. Anne Tyler, *Ladder of Years* (New York: Alfred A. Knopf, Inc., 1995), 68.

Chapter 2 — The Psychology of Kinship

1. Robin Fox, *Reproduction and Succession* (New Brunswick, N.J.: Transaction Publishers, 1993), x.

2. Christopher Ellison, "Family Ties, Friendship, and Subjective Well-being among Black Americans," *Journal of Marriage and Family* 52 (May, 1990), 298–310.

3. Ellen Bass, and Laura Davis, *The Courage to Heal* (New York: Harper & Row, Publishers, Inc., 1988), 306.

4. Kathy D. Schick and Nicholas Toth, *Making Silent Stones Speak: Human Evolution and the Dawn of Technology* (New York: Simon & Schuster, 1993), 15.

5. Karl Menninger, *The Vital Balance* (New York: Viking Press, 1963), 359, 365.

Chapter 3 — Ancient Roots of Kinship, Community, and Love

1. Sydney L. W. Mellen, *The Evolution of Love* (San Francisco: Freeman, 1981), 4.

2. John L. Bowlby "Attachment and Loss: Retrospect and Prospect." *American Journal of Orthopsychiatry* 52 (1982), 668.

3. Helen Fisher, *Anatomy of Love* (New York: Facwett Columbine, 1992), 233–34.

4. Sydney L. W. Mellen, *The Evolution of Love* (San Francisco: Freeman, 1981), 131.

5. Martin Daly and Margo Wilson, *Homicide* (New York: Aldine De Gruyter, 1988), 73.

6. Anastasia Toufexis, "The Right Chemistry," *Time* 141:7 (15 February 1993), 50.

7. Ibid., 51.

8. Alice S. Rossi, "Advice from the Pros: Life, It's Not for the Weak" *Psychology Today* 26:2, (March/April 1993), 48.

9. Howard Fineman, "Race and Rage," *Newsweek,* 125:13, (3 April 1995), 24.

10. Gerald Early, "Understanding Afrocentrism," *Civilization,* 1:3 (July/August 1995), 34.

11. Rochelle Sharpe, "Oliver's Twist: Affirmative Action Lifted Mr Lee, and He Has Never Forgotten." *Wall Street Journal* (27 December 1995), 1.

12. Frank Zappa, "Sunbeams," *The Sun: A Magazine of Ideas* 226 (October 1994), 40.

13. New York Times News Service, "Obsessed by a Trial: Simpson Case Permeates American Culture," appearing in the *Richmond Times-Dispatch* (12 June 1995), A1, A3.

Chapter 4 — Fish in Little Water: Solutions to the Modern Mismatch Dilemma

1. Thomas J. Bouchard, David T. Lykken, Matthew McGue, Nancy L. Segal, and Auke Tellegen, "Sources of Human Psychological Differences: The Minnesota Study of Twins Reared Apart," *Science* 250 (1990), 228.

2. Lori Lineberger, "Time is Worth More Than Money," Knight Ridder News Service, appearing in the *Richmond Times-Dispatch* (10 December 1995), G1, G6.

3. Ellen Graham, "Working Parents' Torment: Teens after School," *Wall Street Journal* (9 May 1995), B1.

4. Elizabeth Rapoport, "Eight Ways to Get Your Husband to Help," *Redbook* 186:1 (December, 1995), 53.

5. John Gray, *Men Are from Mars: Women Are from Venus* (New York: HarperCollins Publishers, 1992).

6. Marian G. Kinget, *On Being Human* (New York: Harcourt Brace Jovanovich, 1975), 129.

7. *American Demographics* statistic reported by Margot Adler in a new study on work trends in "All Things Considered," National Public Radio (May, 1995).

8. Barry Lopez, *Arctic Dreams: Imagination and Desire in a Northern Landscape* (New York: Charles Scribner's Sons, 1986), 38–40, 298.

9. William M. Carley, "Unabomber's Package Leaves Decades of Pain and Shattered Dreams," *Wall Street Journal* (17 October 1995), 1.

10. Daniel P. Moynihan, On Understanding Poverty (New York: Basic Books, 1969), 48.

11. Kent G. Bailey, "The Sociopath: Cheater or Warrior Hawk?" *Behavioral and Brain Sciences* 18 (1995), 542–43.

12. Ann Rule, *The Stranger Beside Me* (New York: Norton, 1980), 13.

13. Judith Viorst, *Necessary Losses* (New York: Ballantine Books, 1986), 11.

14. Ellen Bass and Laura Davis, *The Courage to Heal* (New York: Harper & Row, Publishers, Inc., 1988), 209–10.

15. Walt Whitman, "I Dream'd in A Dream." First published in 1867. Reprinted in *Whitman Poetry and Prose* (New York: The Library of America, 1982), 284.

16. Ibid., "To A Stranger," 280.

Chapter 5 — Alienation of Family

1. James Agee and Walker Evans, *Let us Now Praise Famous Men* (Boston: Houghton Mifflin, 1960), 55.

2. Cynthia Grant, *Kumquat May, I'll Always Love You* (New York: Atheneum, 1986), 5, 119.

3. Ellen Bass and Laura Davis, *The Courage to Heal* (New York: Harper & Row Publishers, Inc., 1988), 301.

4. Ibid.

5. Ellen Graham, "Childhood Circa 1995, Leah: Life Is All Sweetness and Insecurity, *Wall Street Journal* (9 February 1995), B1.

6. Judith Viorst, *Necessary Losses* (New York, Ballantine Books, 1986), 163–64.

7. Christopher O'Kennon, "Leave It To Butt-head: While We're All Trying to Earn a Living, No One Is Bringing Up Beaver," *Style Weekly* 13:14 (4 April 1995), back page.

8. Ibid.

9. Gloria Thomas, "Razor Wire and Families," *Shafer Court Connections* (VCU Almuni Magazine)2:2 (Winter 1996), 17.

10. Dr. Lee Salk. *Familyhood* (New York: Simon & Schuster, 1992), 25.

11. Christopher G. Ellison, "Family Ties, Friendship, and Subjective Well-Being among Black Americans," *Journal of Marriage and Family* 52 (May, 1990), 298–310.

12. Judith Stacey, *Brave New Families: Stories of Domestic Upheaval in the Late Twentieth Century America* (New York: Basic Books, 1991), 7.

13. William Manchester, *The Glory and The Dream* (New York: Bantam Books, 1975), 732–33.

14. Diana DuBois, *In Her Sister's Shadow: An Intimate Biography of Lee Radziwill* (Boston: Little, Brown & Company, 1995), 337, 380.

15. Mother Teresa, "Sunbeams," *The Sun: A Magazine of Ideas* 223 (July 1994), 40.

Chapter 6—Kinship in the Nineties

1. Nancy Schlossberg, "Till Death Do Us Part: The Growing Need for Family Care," *Cosmos: A Journal of Emerging Issues* 1:1 (1991), 86.

2. Deborah Laake, "A Family of Friends," *New Woman* 25:4 (April 1995), 88

3. Susan Kenney, "Ringing in the Net," in *Between Friends,* Edited by Mickey Pearlman (Boston: Houghton Mifflin, 1994), 238.

4. Dr. Lee Salk, *Familyhood* (New York: Simon & Schuster, 1992), 23.

5. Ibid.

6. Ibid., 24.

7. [Editors], "This Is What You Thought; Were the Courts Right to Send Jessica DeBoer Back to Her Biological Parents?, *Glamour* 92 (January, 1994), 77.

8. Leslie Bennetts, "The Baby Jessica Story: Why the Court Was Wrong," *Parents'* magazine 68 (September 1993), 198.

9. Nancy Gibbs, Andrea Sachs and Sophfronia Scott Gregory, "In Whose Best Interest?" *Time* 142 (July 19, 1993), 46.

10. [Editors], "This Is What You Thought; Were the Courts Right to Send Jessica DeBoer Back to Her Biological Parents?, *Glamour* 92 (January, 1994), 77.

Chapter 7—Cyberfamilies

1. Don Steinberg, "Inside the Noisy World of Online Chat," *Virtual City: Your Guide to Cyber Culture* 1:2 (Winter 1996), 35, 37.

2. Christopher O'Kennon, "Around the World in 30 Seconds, Cyberspace Communities Are almost as Close-knit as Real World Communities, Sometimes More So," *Style Weekly* 13:20 (16 May 1996), backpage.

3. Eric Marcus, in Nancy Andrews, *Family: A Portrait of Gay and Lesbian America* (San Francisco: HarperSanFrancisco, 1994), 1.

4. Charley Murphy, quoted in Peter Hawes, "Casting a Wider Net", *Common Boundary* 13:6 (November/December, 1995), 35.

5. Mark Bowes, "Computer 'Pen Pal' Is Charged in County," *Richmond Times-Dispatch* (28 March 1995), 1.

6. Carolyn R. Shaffer and Kristin Anundsen, *Creating Community Anywhere* (New York: The Putnam Publishing Group, 1993), 140.

7. Peter Hawes, "Casting a Wider Net," *Common Boundary* 13:6 (November/December, 1995), 35.

Chapter 8—Afrocentrism: Magical Kinship

1. Maya Angelou, in Sherry Ruth Anderson and Patricia Hopkins, *The Feminine Face of God* (New York: Bantam Books, 1992), 211, 212.

2. *Statistical Abstracts,* 1994, A projection for 1995, Table 18, Washington:

U.S. Bureau of the Census, "Current Populations Reports," P25–1095, P25–1104 and Population Paper Listing 21.

3. Harold, M, Rose "The Evolving Spacial Pattern of Black America: 1910–1980," *Ethnicity in Contemporary America: A Geographical Appraisal,* Editor, Jesse O. McKee (Dubuque, Iowa: Kendall/Hunt Publishing Co., Dubuque, 1985), 55.

4. Terry McMillan, *Waiting To Exhale* (New York: Viking, 1992), 326, 396.

5. Ibid.

6. Gerald Early, "Understanding Afrocentrism," *Civilization* 1:3 (July/August 1995), 39.

7. Theresa Funiciello, *Tyranny of Kindness: Dismantling the Welfare System To End Poverty in America* (New York: Atlantic Monthly Press, 1993), 290-91.

8. Ruth Shalit, "Family-Mongers, Washington's New Consensus," *The New Republic* 209:7 (16 August 1993), 12.

9. Christopher Ellison, "Family Ties, Friendship, and Subjective Well-Being among Black Americans," *Journal of Marriage and the Family* 52 (May 1990), 299.

10. Colin Turnbull, *Man in Africa* (Garden City, N.Y.: Anchor/Doubleday, 1976), 253–54.

11. Ibid.

12. Langston Hughes, an untitled poem in Dorothy and Thomas Hoobler, *The African American Family Album* (New York: Oxford University Press, 1995), 15.

13. Margaret Musgrove, *Ashanti to Zulu: African Traditions* (New York: The Dial Press, 1976), 3.

14. Erin Burnette, "Black Males Retrieve a Noble Heritage," American Psychological Association's *Monitor* 26:6, (June, 1995), 1, 32.

15. Rhoderick Watts, Ph.D., quoted in Ibid., 32.

Chapter 9 — The Genetics of Racism: Shattered Kinship

1. Gary W. Fenchuk, *Timeless Wisdom* (Midlothian, Va.: CakeEaters, Inc., 1994), 14.

2. Ibid., 14.

3. Toni Morrison, *Beloved* (New York: Penguin Books, 1987), 251.

4. Mark Twain, *The Adventures of Huckleberry Finn* (Franklin Center, Penn.: The Franklin Library, 1979). 121.

5. Ibid., 301, 302.

6. Albert R. Hunt, "A Flawed Verdict, but Tread Carefully," *Wall Street Journal* (5 October 1995), A15.

7. Constance Johnson, "More Black Lawyers Work for the Prosecution Team," *Wall Street Journal* (12 October 1995), B1.

8. Study by DeVos and Wagatsuma, in Philip G. Zimbardo and Floyd L. Ruch, *Psychology and Life* (Glenview, Ill.: Scott, Forseman and Company,1975), 602.

9. Editor, Jesse O. McKee, "America: 1910–1980," *Ethnicity In Contemporary America: A Geographical Appraisal* (Dubuque, Iowa: Kendall/Hunt Publishing Co., 1985), 55.

10. The Associated Press, "Environmental Injustice Cited," appearing in the *Richmond Times-Dispatch* (25 August 1994), 2.

11. Los Angeles Times/Washington Post News Service, "Poll Suggests White Race Views Distorted," appearing in the *Richmond Times-Dispatch* (8 October 1995), 1.

12. Headline, "Self-Employment Rates Differ Greatly among Racial and Ethnic Groups," *Wall Street Journal* (16 August 1994). Also consider these *USA Today* statistics: 54 percent of black-owned businesses are in the service category. Only 2 percent are in the more lucrative fields of manufacturing; only 7 percent in finance/insurance/real estate; and only 7 percent in construction. ("USA Snapshots," *USA Today* [11 April 1996], B1.)

13. David C. Korten, "Economies of Meaning," *Tikkun* 11:2 (March/April 1996), 17–19.

14. Sherry Ruth Anderson and Patricia Hopkins, *The Feminine Face of God* (New York: Bantam Books, 1992), 223.

Chapter 10—Making Family

1. The Dictionary of Literary Biography: American Novelists since World War II (New York: Gale Research Co., 1978), 2:506–7.

2. Dr. Nancy K. Schlossberg, "Till Death Do Us Part: The Growing Need for Family Care," *Cosmos: A Journal of Emerging Issues,* 1:1 (1991), 86.

3. Carolyn R. Shaffer and Kristin Anundsen, *Creating Community Anywhere* (New York: Jeremy P. Tarcher/Perigee, The Putnam Publishing Group, 1993), 171–72.

4. Margaret Harmon, quoted in Mary Lord, "Feathering a Shared Nest: How Three Groups of Seniors Created Their Own Alternative Lifestyles," *U.S. News & World Report* 118:23 (12 June 1995), 86.

5. Mihaly Czikszentmihalyi, quoted in Carolyn R. Shaffer and Kristin Anundsen, *Creating Community Anywhere* (New York: The Putnam Publishing Group, 1993), 173.

6. M. Scott Peck, *The Road Less Traveled* (New York: Simon & Schuster, 1978), 119.

Bibliography

Agee, James, and Walker Evans. *Let Us Now Praise Famous Men*. Boston: Houghton Mifflin, 1960.

Anderson, Sherry Ruth and Patricia Hopkins. *The Feminine Face of God*. New York: Bantam Books, 1991.

Andrews, Nancy. *Family: A Portrait of Gay and Lesbian America*. San Francisco: HarperSanFrancisco, 1994.

Bailey, Kent G. (1988). "Psychological Kinship: Implications for the Helping Professions." *Psychotherapy* 25 (1988): 132–42.

Bailey, Kent G. *Human Paleopsychology: Applications to Aggression and Pathological Progesses*. Hillsdale, N.J.: Erlbaum, 1987.

Bailey, Kent G. "The Sociopath: Cheater or Warrior Hawk." *Behavioral and Brain Sciences* 18, 1995, 542–43.

Bass, Ellen and Laura Davis. *The Courage to Heal*. New York: Harper & Row Publishers, Inc., 1988.

Bates, Carolyn M., and Annette M. Brodsky. *Sex in the Therapy Hour: A Case of Professional Incest*. New York: Guilford, 1989.

Bowlby, John. *A Secure base: Parent-Child Attachment and Healthy Human Development*. New York: Basic Books, 1988.

Burnette, Erin. "Black males retrieve a noble heritage," *Monitor* (American Psychological Association publication) 26:6 (June 1995).

Daly, Martin, and Margo Wilson. *Homicide*. New York: Aldine DeGruyter, 1988.

DeRiencourt, Amaury. *Sex and Power in History*. New York: David McKay Company, Inc., 1974.

Diamond, J. *The Third Chimpanzee: The Evolution and Future of the Human Animal*. New York: HarperCollins, 1992.

Early, Gerald. "Understanding Afrocentrism," *Civilization* (The Library of Congress) 1:3 (July/August 1995): 39.

Eaton, S.B., M. Shostak, and M. Konner. *The Paleolithic Prescription*. New York: Harper & Row, 1988.

Ellison, Christopher, G. "Family Ties, Friendship, and Subjective Well Being among Black Americans." *Journal of Marriage and the Family* 52 (1990): 298–310.

Erickson, M. T. Rethinking Oedipus: An Evolutionary Perspective on

Incest Avoidance. *American Journal of Psychiatry* 150:3 (1993), 411–16.

Fenchuk, Gary W. *Timeless Wisdom.* Midlothian, Va.: CakeEaters, Inc., 1994.

Fisher, Helen. *Anatomy of Love,* New York: Fawcett Columbine, 1992.

Fisher, Helen. *The Sex Contract.* New York: William Morrow, 1982.

Flaherty, Thomas, Editor in Chief. *The Domestic World.* Alexandria, Va.: Time-Life Books, 1991.

Freeman, Derek "Kinship, Attachment Behavior, and the Primary Bond." In J. Goody (ed.), *Character of Kinship.* Cambridge: Cambridge University Press, 1974.

Funiciello, Theresa. *Tyranny of Kindness: Dismantling the Welfare System to End Poverty in America.* New York: Atlantic Monthly Press, 1993.

Gaier, David, "Readers Write: The End of the Day." *The Sun: A Magazine of Ideas* 240 (December 1995): 28.

Gray, John. *Men Are from Mars: Women Are from Venus.* New York: HarperCollins Publishers, 1992.

Hawes, Peter. "Casting a Wider Net." *Common Boundary* 13:6 (November/December 1995).

Hrdy, Sarah. B., & C. S. Carter. "Hormonal Cocktails for Two." *Natural History* 104 (1995): 34.

Hughes, Langston, untitled poem in *The African American Family Album.* Dorothy and Thomas Hoobler, New York: Oxford University Press, 1995.

Johanson, Donald and James Shreeve. *Lucy's Child.* New York: William Morrow, 1989.

Kenney, Susan, "Ringing in the Net." *Between Friends.* Mickey Pearlman, ed. New York: Houghton Mifflin, 1994.

Kinget, G. Marian. *On Being Human.* New York: Harcourt Brace Jovanovich, 1975.

Lewis, Dawn K. *Psychological Kinship and Self-Concept: Differential Patterns in African-American and White Women.* Unpublished Master's Thesis, Virginia Commonwealth University, 1995.

Lopez, Barry. *Arctic Dreams: Imagination and Desire in a Northern Landscape.* New York: Charles Scribner's Sons, 1986.

Lord, Mary, "Feathering a Shared Nest: How Three Groups of Seniors Created Their Own Alternative Lifestyles," *U.S. News & World Report* 118:23 (June 12, 1995).

Lykken, David. T. *The Antisocial Personalities.* Hillsdale, NJ: Lawrence Erlbaum & Associates, 1995.

MacLean, Paul D. *The Triune Brain in Evolution.* New York: Plenum Press, 1990.

Masters, Roger. *The Nature of Politics*. New Haven: Yale University Press, 1989.

McMillan, Terry. *Waiting To Exhale*. New York: Viking, 1992.

Mellen, Sydney. *The Evolution of Love*. San Francisco: W. H. Freeman, 1981.

Menninger, Karl. *The Vital Balance*. New York: Viking Press, 1963.

Morris, Desmond. *The Human Zoo*. New York: Dell, 1969.

Moynihan, Daniel. P. *Understanding Poverty*. New York: Basic Books, 1969.

Musgrove, Margaret. *Ashanti to Zulu: African Traditions*. New York: Puffin Books, 1992.

Nava, Gustavo R. *Actual and Perceived Social Support, Love, Liking, and Family Love as Predictors of Perceived Obligation/Entitlement in Depression*. Unpublished Doctoral Dissertation, Virginia Commonwealth University, 1994.

Nava, Gustavo. R., and Kent. G. Bailey. "Measuring Psychological Kinship: Scale Refinement and Validation." *Psychological Reports* 68 (1991): 215–27.

Nesse, Randolph. M., and George, C. Williams. *Why We Get Sick: The New Science of Darwinian Medicine*. New York: Random House, 1995.

Outlaw, Frank, "Watch Your Thoughts." *Timeless Wisdom*. Midlothian, Va.: CakeEaters, Inc., 1994.

Rose, Harold, M. "The Evolving Spacial Pattern of Black America: 1910–1980," *Ethnicity In Contemporary America: A Geographical Appraisal*. Editor, Jesse O. McKee. Dubuque, Iowa: Kendall/Hunt Publishing Co. (1985): 55.

Rule, Ann. *The Stranger Beside Me*. New York: Norton, 1980.

Russell, Robert, J. *The Lemur's Legacy: The Evolution of Power, Sex, and Love*. New York: G. P. Putnam, 1993.

Salk, Lee. *Familyhood*. New York: Simon and Schuster, 1992.

Schick, Kathy D., and Nicholas Toth. *Making Silent Stones Speak: Human Evolution and the Dawn of Technology*. New York: Simon and Schuster, 1993.

Schlossberg, Nancy. "Till Death Do Us Part: The Growing Need for Family Care," *Cosmos: A Journal of Emerging Issues* 1:1 (1991): 85.

Shaffer, Carolyn R., and Kristin Anundsen. *Creating Community Anywhere: Finding Support in a Fragmented World*. New York: The Putnam Publishing Group, 1993.

Sharpe, Rochelle, "Affirmative Action Lifted Mr. Lee, and He Has Never Forgotten." *The Wall Street Journal* 226:124 (1995) 1–5.

Stacey, Judith. *Brave New Families*. New York: Basic Books, 1991.

Stegner, Wallace. *Angle of Repose*. New York: Doubleday & Company, Inc., 1971.

Steinberg, Don, "Inside the Noisy World of Online Chat," *Virtual City* 1:2 (Winter 1996).

Twain, Mark, *The Adventures of Huckleberry Finn*. Charles Neidor, ed., New York: Doubleday, 1985.

Van den Berghe, Pierre. *Human Family Systems: An Evolutionary View*. New York: Elsevier North Holland, 1979.

Viorst, Judith. *Necessary Losses*. New York: Fawcett Gold Medal, 1986.

Walsh, David. *Selling Out America's Children*. Minneapolis: Fairview Press, 1994.

Whitman, Walt, "I Dream'd in A Dream." First published in 1867. Reprinted in *Whitman Poetry and Prose*. New York, The Library of America, 1982.

Wood, Helen E. *The Construct of Psychological Kinship: Roles of Familial Love, Classification, and Support*. Unpublished master's thesis, Virginia Commonwealth University, Richmond, 1995.

Wright, Robert, "20th Century Blues," *Time* 146:9 (August 28, 1995).

Zimbardo, Philip G., and Floyd L. Ruch. *Psychology and Life*. Glenview Ill.: Scott, Foresman and Company, 1975.

Index